THE NO-EXCEPTIONS GUIDE TO CREATING MONEY, SUCCESS, & BLISS

BONI LONNSBURRY

Inner Art, Inc.
1750 30th Street, Suite 543
Boulder, CO 80301
www.InnerArtInc.com

Editor: Bryna René Haynes, TheHeartofWriting.com
Cover design: Bryna René Haynes, TheHeartofWriting.com
Cover Image: Adobe Stock #65241573 © Romolo Tavani
Interior graphics: Devon Gibbs/Dreamstime stock images
Interior layout and design: Bryna René Haynes, TheHeartofWriting.com

Ordering Information
Quantity sales. Special discounts are available on quantity purchases by corporations, associations, and others. For details, please contact the publisher at the address above.

Publisher's Cataloging-In-Publication Data
Lonnsbury, Boni
The Map to Abundance: The No-Exceptions Guide to Creating Money, Success, & Bliss / Boni Lonnsburry.
p. cm.

ISBN13: 978-1-941322-14-7

Library of Congress Control Number: 2017950757

1. Nonfiction > Self-Help > Personal Growth > Success
2. Nonfiction > Body, Mind & Spirit > New Thought

DEDICATION

This book is dedicated to Lazaris. My knowledge, ability to receive, and enjoyment of abundance are thanks to their love, healing, and grace.

TABLE OF CONTENTS

THE MAP PROCESS

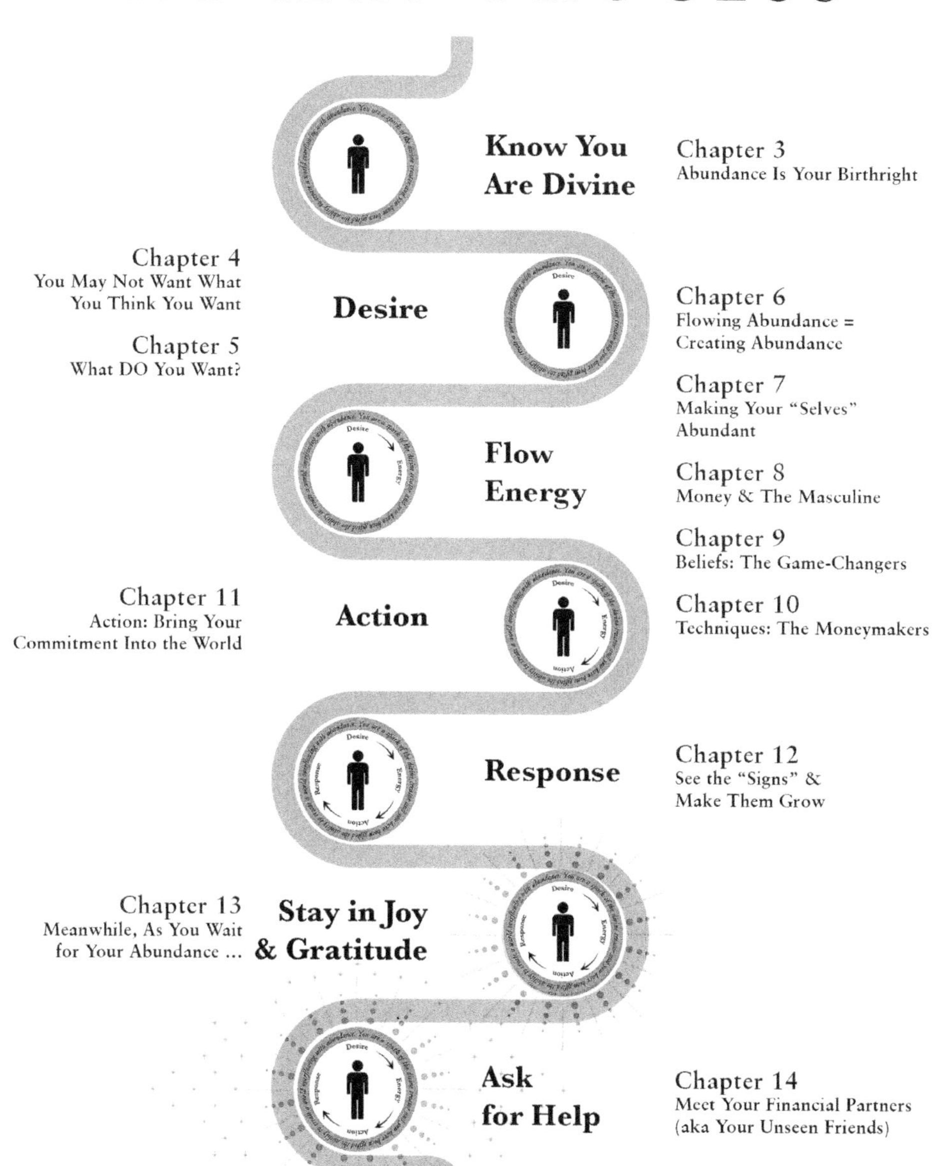

INTRODUCTION

How The Map Works

"Perhaps one of the most startling secrets about prosperity is the truth that the door lies right within yourself."

~ REBECCA CLARK

If you've picked up this book, you probably have one burning question: "Will this book help me create money?"

The answer is, yes it will—and so much more!

As I wrote in my award-winning book, *The Map—To Our Responsive Universe, Where Dreams Really Do Come True!* we are all more powerful than we know. We are literally creating our entire universe twenty-four hours a day, seven days a week—and yet, most of us *don't know that we are doing this.* Even those who think they know how to consciously create don't really know, own, or use the full scope of their power and ability. None of us do.

I hear from readers every day how their realities have changed after implementing what they learned in *The Map.* People are creating romantic partnerships, jobs, extra money coming in from places they never could have dreamed of ... You name it, they are creating it. More, they are realizing that they have power beyond what they could have ever imagined.

One man stunned himself with how quickly the universe

can respond when we focus our energy and intention. An engineer, he felt he had gone as far as he could in his current company. Not sure what his next move would be, he read *The Map* and did the One-Minute Manifestor Technique twice a day. Within one week, he received a call about a new position. A week after that, he accepted an offer for his dream job.

"From that minute on," he told me, "I absolutely knew that the power to create anything exists within me."

If you can think and feel, you can consciously create. It's as simple as that.

There's no special talent or skill needed to create your reality; existing on this planet is enough. It's not a matter of learning how to create your reality (in fact, you already do create your reality perfectly, albeit unconsciously); it's a matter of owning that ability and power *consciously*. Once you do, your creation skills will become more and more amazing.

The Map to Abundance will help you take your power and ability to the next level—the fully conscious, totally-at-your-fingertips level. This will allow your world to be not only financially sound, but fully abundant as well.

Yes, *fully* abundant. There's a reason I didn't name this book *The Map to Money.*

Let's take a look at the definitions of abundance (non-relevant definitions excluded):

abundance (n):
1. a copious supply; great amount;
2. affluence

Notice that "abundance" is defined as both affluence (money) *and* a copious supply. True abundance is when you have more than enough of everything you need to be happy, joyful, fulfilled, and powerful in your life.

MONEY ALONE ISN'T ENOUGH

If you desire an abundant life, you'll want to create money *and* unlimited abundance in every aspect of your life.

For far too long, making money has been synonymous with struggle and sacrifice. People have surrendered their families, their friendships, their health, their preferences, their time, their hobbies, and their peace of mind for even the hope of "getting ahead." "If I can just get there," they think, "maybe the struggle will ease a bit."

Unfortunately, that energy of struggle and sacrifice only attracts more struggle, and sadly, more sacrifice.

If we do create every part of our reality (and we do), why can't we create as much money as we want, as much time as we want, as much fun as we want, as much joy as we want, as much love as we want, and as much freedom as we want?

The answer is simple: *we can.*

This book will teach you how to consciously create abundance in every area of your life, including money—and how to have fun doing it. (Struggle=more struggle, remember?)

But unless abundance comes very naturally to you, you will need a "map" out of the money maze.

You see, we've all been sold a bill of goods about money.

Chances are, our false beliefs were planted when we were children. Those who told us how difficult it was to make money, and what we must sacrifice to have money, meant well (for the most part). Our parents, for instance, passed down their beliefs about money as a way to "prepare us for the cruel and unforgiving world." Others had less altruistic motivations, and used scare tactics as a way to manipulate and control us to do what they wanted us to do—like buy their insurance, watch their TV show, or support their war.

Most of our personal criticism about and around creating money stems from those same beliefs that keep money from us: that wanting money is selfish, bad, wrong, unspiritual, and/or greedy.

The bottom line is, our beliefs about money are just that: beliefs. They are true or false only in the context of how we relate to them. If we believe them, they will be true—and they will shape our reality. If we no longer believe them, they will cease to have power over us.

The bottom line is: money is *energy*, and it's no different than any other energy. Air is energy too—but do we worry about running out of air to breathe? Of course not. Air, as we all know, is abundant, and …

So. Is. Money.

And yet …

MONEY IS JUST THE BEGINNING

Being abundant is about far more than having money—although that is a splendid way to begin. Being abundant is about being able to receive *all* the gifts of this world, and the worlds beyond.

You see, the trick of being physical is to realize you are creating the physical. Reality is like a movie that you both write and star in—a blank canvas on which you create your life. It is your dream, your nightmare, or a little of both. The power to choose is always yours.

Chances are, you want many abundances. For example, wouldn't it be nice to have an abundance of love? And an abundance of ideas and creativity? How about an abundance of clean air and crystal-clear water? An abundance of peace? Joy? Connectedness? Chances are, you want these things as much as—or even more—than you want money.

Because of your divine origin, you've been given a priceless gift: the power to single-handedly create abundance in every area of your life. Learning to *receive* that gift is at the heart of abundance.

ABOUT THIS BOOK

If you have already read *The Map—To Our Responsive Universe, Where Dreams Really Do Come True!* you will already be familiar with many of the truths, concepts, and techniques in this book. Here, you'll learn how to apply these things specifically to money and abundance.

If you haven't read *The Map*, don't worry—this book stands on its own. In your hands, you hold everything you need to claim your gift of infinite creative power and start manifesting abundance in every area of your reality. This book will help you deactivate all of your unhelpful beliefs and internal saboteurs so you can look at money in the same way that you look at air: as a resource that's plentiful, easily accessible, and limitless.

If you're familiar with my work already, you may be asking, "Why did you choose to make your first narrowly-focused book about money? Why not relationships, health, happiness, or career?"

It's true that the principles that underpin the work begun in *The Map* can be applied to lots of other important categories. But I chose money first because most people need it first. Unless you are facing a health challenge, personal crisis, or living in an unsafe place, your primary need is likely financial stability.

Money is a paradox. It isn't the most important thing in the world, but it is critical to have enough money to survive. When you're afraid you won't have enough money to survive, money *becomes* the most important thing in your world.

In order to successfully focus your energy on other creations, you must be free of your preoccupation about having enough money. Once you have survival handled, you'll have the stable foundation and freedom you need to create other abundances in your life—like true love, great relationships, work you adore, happiness, joy, and greater health and vitality! (Bonus: "Map" books on all of these topics will follow *The Map to Abundance*!)

Money is the easiest thing to create on our planet—and yet, we've made it so very difficult. There is a reason for that, and once that reason is understood and changed, money can flow like water. That's what you'll learn in this book—and I promise, if you implement what I will teach you here, you will be able to use your powers of creation to bring to life all the abundances you dream of.

So, let's get started, and create even more of the life you came here to live!

In joyous creation,

Two More Things Before You Go On ...

First, if you're reading this book in a desperate attempt to keep from drowning financially right at this moment, please go directly to Appendix A and read *In Case of Financial Emergency—Read This!* It will help you calm down and get centered enough to read and apply this book thoroughly, and institute permanent change.

Second, I discuss a lot about negative beliefs in this book—because I'd bet anything that your beliefs are a big factor in what stops your abundance. For your convenience in testing for and changing those beliefs, I have added the corresponding positive beliefs for each chapter in Appendix C, an explanation of how to test for negative beliefs in Appendix B, and a short description on how to change beliefs in Appendix D.

CHAPTER ONE

You Never Need to Worry About Money Again

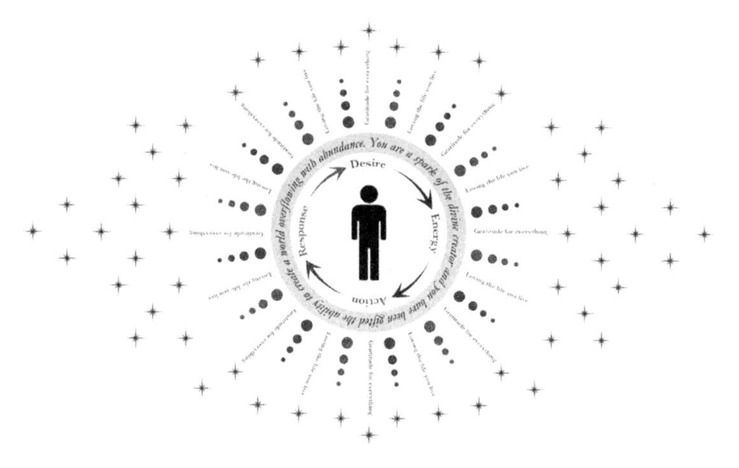

"When you are in touch with the essence of what you desire, you can have it in many ways. If you do not focus on a specific thing to bring you what you want, the universe can truly begin bringing you abundance in many ways."

~ SANAYA ROMAN

Yes, I know: this chapter's title is a pretty bold statement. I wouldn't have believed it myself, unless I had experienced it firsthand.

I manifested money out of thin air at a time when I was flat broke, scared out of my mind, and so deeply in debt I didn't think I'd ever consider myself abundant. Now, I have more money than I ever dreamed of, and I no longer worry about money. Ever.

I've consciously created enough money, and for long enough, to know that even if I lost all of my money by somehow going unconscious and mis-creating my reality, *I could create all of that money again.*

Thousands, if not millions, of people have had experiences with consciously creating abundance. But even people who have magically made money appear are oftentimes hard-pressed to repeat the process at will. Money will seem to magically appear in times of great need or struggle, when the only choice is to surrender—but once things are back to the status quo, that ability to magically allow money seems to go back into hiding.

That cycle of stress and desperation needn't be your reality. It is possible for you to become so good at creating money (and other abundances) that you never have to worry again.

I Wasn't Born with a Silver Spoon

I didn't come from a wealthy family. In fact, my father grew up during the Great Depression. His father was out of work during those years, and their family of seven farmed their tiny piece of land to stay alive.

My mother grew up on a street that was nicknamed Garbage Alley. You can imagine how charming that neighborhood must have been. The daughter of an alcoholic single mom, my mother was given up as a teen and lived in an orphanage with three of her siblings until she graduated from high school.

My parents did manage to do a bit better financially than their parents did (which wasn't saying much), but struggle was still a constant. My father worked two jobs and grabbed overtime as often as he could. My mother taught and sold ceramics out of our home to make ends meet.

With four kids in the family, we couldn't afford many of the things my friends were able to enjoy—like ski lessons and summer camps. But we had the basics, and unlike my parents, we never went hungry.

Of course, my parents gifted their "lack consciousness" to me—and unknowingly, I took it. Despite brains, ability, and some decent education, as a young adult I could never manage to get ahead financially.

I got married in my early twenties to someone who shared the "struggle" mindset. We did more of what our parents did: living from paycheck to paycheck, never getting ahead, and never questioning why.

But then, when I was about thirty, I learned about ...

THE LAW OF ATTRACTION

I have to tell you, the idea that we "attract" what shows up in our lives simply blew me away. I mean, come on—why didn't we learn about this in school? Why didn't everyone know about this? This was *huge.* I was ecstatic to think that my days of struggle and scarcity could change without me having to sell my soul or work a job I hated.

For my whole life, I'd been under the impression that, if you wanted to work like a dog, you could (just maybe) get ahead—but you'd have to sacrifice your time, health, and oftentimes your relationships to do it. The only other option seemed to be to go to school for years and years and get a job doing something you didn't really like, but that paid you lots of money.

But to think I could just change *myself* and get ahead? That caught my attention. I was all in from the start.

However, as I soon discovered, *knowing the Law of Attraction* and *consciously creating an abundant reality* are two totally different things.

I did have some astounding, if sporadic, success with

consciously creating money, but it took an entire decade before I *really* understood what it takes to create true abundance. It took another decade after that before I began to allow unlimited abundance into my life. In between those quantum leaps, I slid to some pretty desperate low points.

I didn't go from poverty to total abundance overnight. It took time for me to get clear about everything I believed, and to become conscious of my thoughts and emotions around money, deserving, prosperity, and abundance. But every step I took toward consciousness created a discernable change in my reality.

I now live a life that seems like a fairy tale. I live on a gorgeous lake in total privacy outside of Boulder, Colorado, I am surrounded by loving friends and family. I am healthier than I've ever been. I do creative work I adore. I have a spiritual life that feeds my soul, I have absolute control over my time, my creativity, my lifestyle—it's *all* my choice.

That is *my* abundance. I am overflowing with gratitude for it each and every day.

And if I did it, you can too.

Everything you will learn in this book is based on one simple premise:

You Create It All

You create your own reality. Yes, you really do. *All of it*—the good parts and the bad.

And because you create everything, there is absolutely no reason that you can't be as abundant as you desire.

None. Zip. Zilch. Nada.

If you aren't jumping up and down in joy (at least inside your head) right now, you, my friend, do not understand what I'm saying.

In a very real (and simultaneously metaphorical) way, money *does* grow on trees. Everyone—including you—can create an abundance of money, resources, opportunities, and everything else under the sun. You just need to be willing to plant that money tree seed, and tend it as it grows.

How can that *not* excite you?

If you're skeptical, I fully understand. If you haven't watched money materialize before your very eyes, you probably *should* be skeptical; there are plenty of snake oil salesmen and "get rich quick" schemes preying on hopeful, scared, and lack-filled minds to make anyone skeptical.

But this isn't snake oil. It requires nothing of you monetarily (let's face it, you could've borrowed this book). What it *does* require is your time, patience, emotional honesty, and your willingness to irrevocably change some of your dearly-held beliefs, patterns, thoughts, and feelings around money.

How Money Shows Up

I remember the very first time I attempted to "create" money. I was brand new to the concept of the Law of Attraction, and just barely opening up to my spirituality.

There was a spiritual seminar I really wanted to attend. Unfortunately, it was far enough away to require a plane ticket and a hotel on top of the admission costs.

At that point in my life, I'd never even been out of New York State. Money was extremely tight in our little family. I wasn't working at the time, and my husband and I had two preschoolers to care for, plus a hefty mortgage. I couldn't, in good conscience, spend money we didn't have to go to a weekend-long seminar hundreds of miles away.

"But," I thought, "if I *created* the money, that would be

different." If I created it, I would feel good about using that extra money in whatever way I desired.

And so, I stole some time early one morning, before my boys woke up, to do a technique to manifest the $1,000 I needed to attend the seminar. I did a quick visualization, imagining myself on the plane with my suitcase in hand, excited for the upcoming event, ecstatic that all expenses had been paid.

It felt good. I felt empowered. I *expected* that money to show up.

Then, I got up and made my kids breakfast. It felt a little incongruous that life could be so magical in one moment, and so mundane in the next.

Later that day, as my sons settled down for their naps, I straightened up the house, did the lunch dishes, put on a coat, and prepared to brave the chilly Buffalo afternoon to retrieve the mail.

On the way to the mailbox, I thought excitedly about that seminar and how it might change my life. I opened the box and lifted out a pile of envelopes. As I wandered back to the house, I sifted through the mail. Of course, it was mostly bills. But then, I came upon something that wasn't a bill. Showing clearly through that waxed paper window was a check.

The check was not made out to me. It wasn't even *addressed* to me. In fact, it was addressed to a company in a state four hundred miles away.

How had a check become that diverted? I suspected that it had been caught inside a magazine and then dislodged just before being placed in my mailbox, but there was no real way to know.

But I *did* know one thing: this was a sign that my visualization was working! I was *changing my reality* around finances by changing my thoughts and feelings around money—specifically around having extra money to attend that seminar.

I intended and expected more money to come to me. Even though I couldn't take it to the bank, that check was an indication that I was headed in the right direction.

I was so elated and excited that I did another technique before my boys got up from their naps.

I committed to doing one technique a day for the next thirty days, and was largely successful. I missed a day here and there, but I stayed focused on that thousand dollars coming to me effortlessly, and envisioned myself attending that seminar.

The following week, I received a check in the mail that *was* made out to me. It was for an insurance claim that had been previously denied.

Wow! Honestly, I was flabbergasted that this stuff was actually working. I was also excited and hopeful, and that kept me motivated to do more techniques.

A week and a half after that, I received a card in the mail from a relative. Inside, it read, "I just want you to have this—use it for something you really want." Enclosed was a $100 bill. I nearly wept with joy.

Eventually the entire $1,000 (and then some) manifested through avenues I never would have thought possible. I did attend the seminar, more certain than ever before that I have the power to create my reality.

Since that first attempt at consciously creating money, I've had some amazing successes—and some dismal failures.

Sometimes, I was able to manifest money out of thin air, like I did for that seminar. Other times, I hit my own ceiling of disbelief, and couldn't create a dime. And sometimes, I would manifest abundance only to have my reality snap back to my former level of "just scraping by." When that happened, everything I had previously created would disappear.

But every single time I mis-created, there was a *reason*. Ultimately I determined what each of those reasons were, and my finances settled into a lovely state of abundance. Now, I trust myself and my ability to consciously create. The gut-clenching worry that used to accompany practically every thought I had about money is a thing of the past. I've created a beautiful life for myself—a life overflowing with abundance. I have a gorgeous home, work I love, and a lifestyle of travel, luxury, and freedom.

More important than the *things* I enjoy, though, are the *feelings* I've created. I've created a sense of safety, trust, and a *knowing* that I am abundant—in money, in resources, in creativity, in health and vitality, and in love. And that feels wonderful indeed.

Are you ready to start creating *your* abundance? I thought so! But first, let's ...

GET CLEAR ON THE PROCESS OF CREATION

You are vastly more powerful than you know.

But, chances are, your parents didn't teach you this. Nor did your teachers, your friends, or the television. In fact, the knowledge that you create your own reality may be a revelation to you.

Our power to consciously create our reality is quite possibly the world's best-kept secret. I mean, this is *epic*, right? And yet, few people know about it, and fewer yet manage to actually change their lives with that knowledge.

Why?

Because most people don't really know how it works. Even those who have read the books and attended the seminars struggle with exactly how to create a reality.

The truth is, creating your reality is not hard at all. Actually it's easier than breathing. You already create your reality whether you know it or not, and you do it *all of the time.* We all do. We can't help but create our reality.

It's the way our universe works.

Most people aren't conscious of how they create. They aren't aware of the thoughts, feelings, beliefs, and patterns playing out in the background of their lives. And so, they end up with realities that seem totally unrelated to what they say they want. They're creating *unconsciously.*

As it pertains to abundance, your unconscious creations usually look like what your parents (or other authority figures) created, or what your parents (or authority figures) expected you to create. Why? Because you unconsciously learn to create unconsciously from other unconscious creators.

Boy, that's a mouthful.

Let me put it another way: you take on the thoughts, feelings, and beliefs of those around you. Most particularly, you take on the thoughts, feelings, and beliefs of those you deemed powerful when you were growing up. And, since your thoughts, feelings, and beliefs create your world, if you're not fully aware of what you took on without knowing it, you can end up creating your life in the image of others' lives. It's sort of like watching a remake of an old movie: the actors, scenes, and special effects are different, but the plot is exactly the same.

How do you get off the replay loop? First, you need to change the way you *feel* about your reality—both the one you have, and the one you want.

Emotions Generate Realities

Your emotions are the most important component of your ability to create. In our responsive universe, your emotions draw your physical experiences into your world.

And, because every thought creates an emotion, thoughts are pretty important as well. The most powerful thoughts are those with strong emotions attached to them. Less powerful thoughts are those with little or no emotion attached to them—but any thought will become more powerful the more often you think it.

Beyond your conscious thoughts and feelings lie your subconscious thoughts and feelings—aka your *beliefs*. Beliefs are thoughts and feelings that are so ever-present you've accepted them as absolutes. They are your take on how the world works.

Beliefs never sleep. They never take a break. They are the background music in your personal movie; they create your reality all day, every day.

Beliefs are the hidden key to conscious creation. That's why a major portion of this book is dedicated to helping you discover and change your subconscious beliefs around money and abundance. Until your thoughts, feelings, and beliefs are aligned and can work in concert, you will not be able to create with the ease and power that is your birthright.

So, my thoughts, feelings, and beliefs are creating my money, work, opportunities, ideas, etc.?

Exactly.

Okay, then tell me what thoughts to think, what feelings to feel, and what beliefs to hold in order to be a billionaire!

Well, it doesn't exactly work that way.

Why not? Because …

You Can't Control the Way Abundance Shows Up

This is probably the toughest concept to understand in creating abundance. So, I'll say it again:

You can't control the way abundance shows up.

This one concept thwarts so many creations. If you're trying to make abundance show up in a certain way—through a certain job, from a certain person, or in a certain dollar amount—it generally won't work.

You see, you can control the *essence* of your abundance, but you can't control the *form*.

So I can't create being a billionaire?

I didn't say that. You may or may not create a billion dollars. But what you absolutely *can* create is a reality that feels abundant to you—and that means plenty of the money, opportunities, jobs, and creative ideas that *make you feel abundant.*

I'm going to come back to this concept over and over again throughout this book. Money alone doesn't equal abundance. It isn't the goal.

Having a life that is perfect for you: *that* is the goal.

It would have been easier for you if you were taught about this as a child, but you weren't. Maybe you weren't ready for it then, or maybe you chose to experience some struggle first. But you are ready for the knowledge now. You *are* ready to take the concepts of conscious creation and apply them to creating all of the abundance you want in your life.

It's not too late to radically shift your reality. But before you begin, you need to realize ...

WHY MONEY IS DIFFERENT

I remember sitting in my dentist's office years ago. After we stopped talking about my horrible teeth, we got sidetracked with a conversation about the Law of Attraction.

"Money is the easiest thing to create!" my dentist said with a smile. "Just wait. When you 'get it,' you'll be amazed at how easy it is!"

At the time, I was a single mom with an ex-husband who was haggling with me about paying child support. I had no job, and no prospects for a job. I was about to lose my home to a foreclosure. I was late on *every* bill I owed—and, on top of all that, I had lousy teeth and a mouth full of mercury amalgam that my dentist was warning me should be removed.

"Most people with teeth like yours come to see me in a wheelchair," he said threateningly.

I appreciated the warning, but quite honestly, I had bigger fish to fry. I had to figure out how I would *survive*. First I needed to create enough money to keep a roof over our heads and food in our bellies; *then* I could figure out how to stay healthy.

My dentist, on the other hand, seemed to have it all figured out. And although I had read my share of books about creating your own reality and manifesting money, for the life of me I could not figure out how this guy could say that money is easy to create. It was a mystery to me.

Back then, I thought money was hard to create, and even harder to *earn*. I wanted desperately to be free of my financial dependence on my ex-husband, but I didn't want to sell out and take a job I hated. I *wanted* to believe I could create my reality, but it just wasn't working.

I tried my hand at self-improvement coaching and speaking, but I never made enough money to cover expenses let alone support myself.

Then, I tried multi-level marketing. I knew *some people* made money in that business—but not me. The little bit I managed to earn went right back out the door for phone bills and to buy leads. Obviously this wasn't my "path to freedom."

I even tried doing some catering for a friend of a friend—and while it wasn't a dismal failure like the marketing venture, it felt like one. One night, I was in charge of preparing and serving a dinner party. Halfway through the event, I took the bottom off the blender instead of the top, and dumped the extra-large pitcher of margaritas all over the floor. Do you have any idea how *sticky* margaritas are? It was horrifying.

I was out of ideas. I didn't know what to try next, and I was running out of time. My ex was about to take our boys to live with him—and, when that happened, the child support payments that had kept me afloat for the two years since our divorce would end for good.

What was I going to *do*? I was panicked, scared, totally out of ideas—and, apparently, about to die from a mouth full of mercury.

Visions of homelessness danced in my head. I had three brothers, and I knew any one of them would take me in—but I didn't *want* to move away from Colorado. I also didn't want to live in my car (assuming it wouldn't be repossessed). I imagined ending up as a street person, rolling my cheap knockoff designer luggage behind me everywhere I went, still caught in the fantasy of making my dreams come true.

My books, and my dentist, made creating money sound so easy. But I was living proof that it was *hard*. Maybe I just wasn't cut out for this whole reality-creation thing.

It was a rock-bottom moment. And there I might have stayed for the rest of my life.

But I didn't. Instead, I finally figured out what it takes to create financial abundance. Here's what I learned ...

Money Is Different Because It's *Survival*

We believe we will die without money as surely as we'll die without food, water, or air. Money is the reason most wars are fought, and the reason most violence happens. Money is the key to power in most people's minds. We believe that money is *real*, money is *necessary*, and money is *in limited supply*.

That's why money is different.

Above all else, we believe that we *need* money. Money will buy us health care and medicine when we're sick. Money will buy us food when we're hungry. Money will ensure that we have clothes to wear, and clean water to drink. Money will educate us. Money will allow us the freedom to travel and create. Money may not buy happiness—but it sure can make unhappiness more comfortable.

Even more than that, money has been made "weighty" in our world.

We Have Vilified Money

Although the famous quote actually reads, "The love of money is the root of all evil," many of us have been conditioned to believe that *money itself* is the root of all evil. Somewhere, deep inside, some part of us believes that *having* money, *wanting* money, and *creating* money is somehow not okay.

Check out some various quotes on the subject:

"Money often costs too much." – Ralph Waldo Emerson

"Goddam money. It always ends up making you blue as hell."
– J. D. Salinger, *The Catcher in the Rye*

"No one can earn a million dollars honestly." - William Jennings Bryan

"If you want to know what God thinks of money, just look at the people he gave it to." - Dorothy Parker

"The rich are the scum of the earth in every country." - G. K. Chesterton, *Flying Inn*

"Money has never made man happy, nor will it; there is nothing in its nature to produce happiness. The more of it one has, the more one wants." - Benjamin Franklin

"Wealth and want equally harden the human heart." - Theodore Parker

Want them or not, own them or not, believe them consciously or not, those statements are part of your reality—and unless you have deliberately changed them, they're part of your subconscious belief system about money.

What's more, not only have we vilified money ...

We Have "Deified" Money

We have revered money (and those who have it), given it power, and made it bigger than life. Just look at these quotes:

"Money makes the world go round." - John Kander, *Fred Ebb*

"Money is power, and you ought to be reasonably ambitious to have it." - Russell H. Conwell

"You can be young without money, but you can't be old without it." - Tennessee Williams, *Cat On a Hot Tin Roof*

> *"In this country, you gotta make the money first. Then when you get the money, you get the power. Then when you get the power, then you get the women."* – Tony Montana (from the movie *Scarface)*

> *"Money isn't everything ... but it ranks right up there with oxygen."* – Rita Davenport

> *"When I was young I used to think that money was the most important thing in life. Now that I am old, I know it is."* – Oscar Wilde

Somewhere inside, you've taken on beliefs about the god-like power of money as well. You've given it status and supremacy unlike anything on the planet.

Along with the survival factor, the weight of those two worldwide beliefs about money—that it is evil, and that it is all-powerful—make money different from any other energy on the planet.

But also ...

Money Is Always Top-of-Mind

While you're working on creating other things—such as a romantic partnership, a child coming into your life, a new job, or greater health—you can usually put energy into your creation, and then forget about it for a little bit while you focus on other things. You're giving your new creation the time and space it needs to facilitate change in your world without the opposition of worry, fear, and other constricting energies.

But most of us can't do that with money. The bills don't stop coming. You can't stop eating, or sleeping, or driving, or needing money to exist.

The lack of money is *always in your face*—which makes it doubly difficult to shift your thoughts, feelings, and beliefs around it.

Yes, most people on the planet have been assigned a unique challenge when it comes to consciously creating money. Our worldwide adherence to the concept of the "realness" of money only cements those weighty and contradictory beliefs in our subconscious minds.

But if money isn't "real," what is it?

Money is simply *energy*—like a chair, or a flower, or air. Everything that is physical is essentially energy, and no energy is better or worse than any other energy.

You think of money differently than air because you *believe* what people have said about money. I mean, if you'd been told from birth that all chairs were dangerous and would swallow you whole if you sat on them, you might have some funny ideas about them, too!

Wait, no! I don't believe money is bad!

You may not believe money is "bad" per se. However, our society has collectively expended a lot of energy in order to make money, keep money, steal money, hide money, manage money, understand money, and judge money.

Unless you were brought up in a cave, or under the sea, and had no social interactions during your formative years, this attention to money in our world *has* affected you. And (unless you've already changed them) it *has* left you with beliefs[1] such as those on the next page:

(1) I have included the corresponding positive beliefs to all the negative beliefs below and in subsequent chapters in Appendix C.

- MONEY MAKES THE WORLD GO ROUND.
- MONEY IS DIFFICULT TO COME BY.
- MONEY IS IN LIMITED SUPPLY.
- A VERY SMALL PERCENTAGE OF PEOPLE HAVE MORE THAN ENOUGH MONEY.
- THE RICH GET RICHER AND THE POOR GET POORER.

And even ...

- MONEY IS NECESSARY TO SURVIVE.

Wait—money is *necessary to survive!*

Actually, it's not. But boy, is that belief deeply imbedded in our subconscious minds! And so, we engage with money *as though it is necessary to survival*. But the truth is, thinking you need money to survive is simply a belief.

You need air for survival, you may need shelter for survival, and you need food and water for survival (technically, needing food is a belief too, since Breatharians *do* survive without food), but you don't need money to survive. It does bring up a lot of fear, though, if you *believe* you do.

These beliefs put you in a place (energetically) where you subconsciously believe that you have an *absolute need* of money—and, at the same time, have a snowball's chance in hell of ever having an *abundance* of money.

Yikes! No wonder so many people struggle their entire lives to get ahead. With beliefs like that, it would be impossible not to struggle—and also impossible to get ahead.

Yes, my friend ...

Money Is the Weightiest Thing on Our Planet

Money is not difficult to manifest—but *weighty things* are.

If you make something weighty, it means that you've placed too much importance on it. You've made it too "real." You've made it bigger than life, and in doing so, you have made it nearly impossible to manifest with ease.

In other words, you're telling your subconscious (and thus the universe):

- I CREATE MY OWN REALITY, BUT MONEY IS THE EXCEPTION.

Guess what you'll create with that belief?

Scarcity. Lack. Struggle. Loss.

Money is different from any other energy on our planet, but only because of our *perception* of it. If you want to consciously create more money, this difference needs to be understood and addressed.

CREATING MONEY IS EASY!

My dentist was actually right: money is one of the easiest things (if not *the* easiest thing) to manifest.

Now that I've gotten the hang of it and look back on it, I agree: it's pretty easy. There are so many possible places from which money can manifest! It exists outside of our bodies and independently of other people (as long as you let it be), so compared to other things, it *is* easy. Just replace the word "money" with "wind" or "electricity" in your mind, and you'll see what I mean.

It's okay if you're not there yet—in fact, it's just fine.

Let's face it: you weren't *taught* to be abundant. You were taught that money was a tricky, difficult, challenging, and laborious thing to come by. It's going to take some time to unlearn what you've learned about money. But once you do, *you'll never have to worry about money again.*

Money can be hard—but it can also be a joy. It can be easy. It can be elegant. It can even be fun!

The Map to Abundance is more than just a map to money. It's a map to an abundant life—a life filled with the joys of being mentally, physically, emotionally, and spiritually alive. It is a map to allowing the rewards and riches of being a god-being on this planet.

This reality is all an illusion anyway—so why not have as much illusion as you want?

IT'S OKAY TO DOUBT

When I say that you can create money (and other forms of abundance) out of thin air, it probably sounds too good to be true. So many of us have been disappointed when our hopes of getting out of debt, scarcity, and lack have been dashed. We've leapt into the unknown with only the *hope* of our ability to manifest as effortlessly as we've been told is possible—only to feel the pain of failure.

Now, here I come, telling you that money *does* grow on trees (sort of). It makes sense if you feel like this has as much chance of being real as Cinderella's gold-plated pumpkin coach.

But even as you indulge your skepticism about this book—yet another abundance book that will get your hopes up, only for them to be dashed against the rocks of "real life"—you hope that *this* book, *this* system, will be different. You feel the call of a brighter future.

It doesn't matter how doubtful you are. I was doubtful, too. What matters is that, despite the doubt, you keep your mind open. If you do that, I'll help you melt that doubt little by little—not with my words, but with your own successes. They might be small successes at first, but they will grow.

Just please, especially in the beginning ...

Be Gentle With Yourself

There are reasons why money has been problematic in your life. No matter the monetary heartache you've endured—the fear, the terror even, the sadness, and the pain—there is a reason. And in conscious creation, where there's a reason, there's a remedy.

Your money issues may be deep. They may stem from childhood or early adulthood. They may be wrapped up in other painful and unhelpful beliefs and emotions related to worthiness, competence, and the spiritual merit of struggle. But wherever they came from, they can be healed. *Everything* can be healed. And, once healed, your reality will change.

Because you are literally healing your reality from the inside out, it is important to allow yourself the time and space to do this work. You didn't get here overnight, and you likely won't create your new financial reality overnight. This work isn't a Band-Aid for your money problems. It's a whole new way of living with, and relating to, money and abundance.

Part of you is probably longing for that "quick fix." Even when you start to see your reality change, you'll likely be impatient at times, and frustrated that the answers, and the money, aren't coming more quickly. But impatience won't speed things up. In fact, it will slow things down. You wouldn't rush a brain surgeon or an airline pilot through their training, would you? No, you'd want them to learn what they needed to know thoroughly and methodically, because if they didn't, lots of things could go dangerously wrong.

Just like brain surgery or the ability to land an airplane skillfully in a snowstorm, your ability to manifest abundance can take a dire situation and turn it into a victory—but only if you have the training to think, feel, act, and react appropriately when the situation arises.

Remember that any skill worth learning takes time to develop. There is a cadence and flow to inner growth, too. Try to make self-love a priority on this journey—and above all else, enjoy the process.

A TRUE STORY OF CONSCIOUSLY CREATING ABUNDANCE

Two years ago, I was an absolute wreck. I was a depressed alcoholic in a volatile marriage. I was also carrying so much debt that I never thought I could dig out from under the mountain. After hitting bottom (hard) and going through rehab, I began searching for ways to transform my life of hopeless desperation into something worth living.

After separating from my husband of twenty years, I spent six months without a home, living with coworkers and in a motel. During that time, I purchased The Map *and began a gradual but consistent shift in how I was creating my life.*

I developed a new mantra, "I am a brilliant, powerful spark of the Divine!" and I repeated it over and over. I even painted the phrase on a board that I intended to hang over the bed in the new home I hoped to create.

I started with the intention of creating a beautiful sanctuary in which to live. I found a foreclosure home and began mentally renovating it. I picked up little treasures here and there, waiting for the day when I would be able to move in. I bought that home, and it's absolutely darling!

I began affirming my abundance. I made a good living, but I'd had my head in the sand about finances during my entire marriage, and our spending habits had left us with almost an insurmountable amount of debt. I took a long, hard look at my list of debts, and came up with a plan to become debt-free.

I began paying off my bills with ease and pleasure. Since I started this process, I have gone from about twenty revolving credit accounts to none. Even while paying off all this debt, I have put away tens of thousands in savings, and that amount increases every month.

Once my money situation was under control, I made a list of what I wanted in a love relationship, and began to become the best version of myself in order to attract my life partner. I affirmed my value and worth every day. I made room in my new home for him before he was even in my life; there was a closet, drawers, and a night stand just waiting for my mate.

Within a year, I met an incredible man who treasures and adores me. He proposed to me at Christmas, and we are building a truly high-quality relationship together. I have transformed myself from a righteous and resentful wife to a warm, generous partner who constantly strives to "fill my own tank" so I can give my highest and best to others. I am even finally at my perfect weight (eighty pounds lighter than my heaviest weight). My man tells me that I have inspired true and meaningful changes for him, too.

My prosperity is overflowing! I now own two homes. I have traveled to four countries in the last year, and am saving thousands of dollars every month. Even though I am only in my forties, I am already planning my retirement vacation! My fiancé is equally financially secure, and our prospects seem bright.

Although I don't always see how much I am growing every day, and it oftentimes feels like I'm taking two steps forward and then a step back, when I look back on the last two years, I am barely recognizable.

Two years ago, I was at rock bottom. Today, I am absolutely rich beyond measure. I am truly living a life I love—and I created it all!

- Angela S.

ABUNDANCE-ALTERING TAKEAWAYS

- It is possible to become so good at creating money and other abundances that you no longer have to worry, ever.

- Ultimately, it's your feelings that create. Your thoughts are important because emotions flow from thoughts. And your beliefs are important because they are thoughts and feelings that are always with you.

- Money is simply energy—like a chair, or a flower, or air. You think of money differently than air because you believe what people have said about money—not because it's inherently different.

- Thoughts with strong emotions accompanying them are powerful. Those with weak or no emotion accompanying them are less powerful. The number of times you think a thought increases its power.

- You live in a society where a lot of energy has been expended to make money, keep money, steal money, hide money, manage money, understand money, and judge money. Unless you've been brought up without societal interaction, our world's attitude toward money has affected you.

- Money is different from other things in life because our perception of it is different. When you're seeking to consciously create more money, that difference needs to be understood and addressed.

- We've been particularly challenged when it comes to consciously creating money because of the weight of it. We hold subconscious beliefs that it's evil, that it's uber-powerful, and that we require it to survive. That last belief leaves us with a "time is of the essence" feeling that makes the concept of money more weighty than ever.

- There are reasons money has been problematic in your life. No matter the monetary heartache you've endured—the anxiety, the terror, the sadness, and the pain—there is a reason. And in conscious creation, if there is a reason, there is a remedy.

- Impatience won't speed things up. It will slow things down.

- Like any skill, conscious creation takes time and practice. There is a cadence and flow to inner growth, too. Try to make self-love a priority on this journey, and be patient with yourself.

- Above all else, enjoy the process!

YOUR NEXT STEPS

- In a notebook, journal, or a page in your word processor, write your answers to the following questions. (If you don't like to write, you can speak them into a voice recorder.)
    - What was your childhood like regarding money? What did your parents or other authority figures say and do when it came to money?
    - What are your earliest memories of money (or lack of it)?
    - How easy has it been for you to create money and other abundances in your life as an adult?
    - What is the pattern of money flowing in (and out) of your life?
    - Have you ever felt you had to sacrifice anything for money? What was it?
    - How easy is it for you to accept the fact that you are creating 100% of your wealth and other abundances (or lack thereof)?

- Use the applied kinesiology techniques in Appendix B to test for constricting beliefs. Document the beliefs that need to be changed, and set them aside. (You'll learn more about beliefs and how to change them later in this book.)

CHAPTER TWO

The Map to Abundance

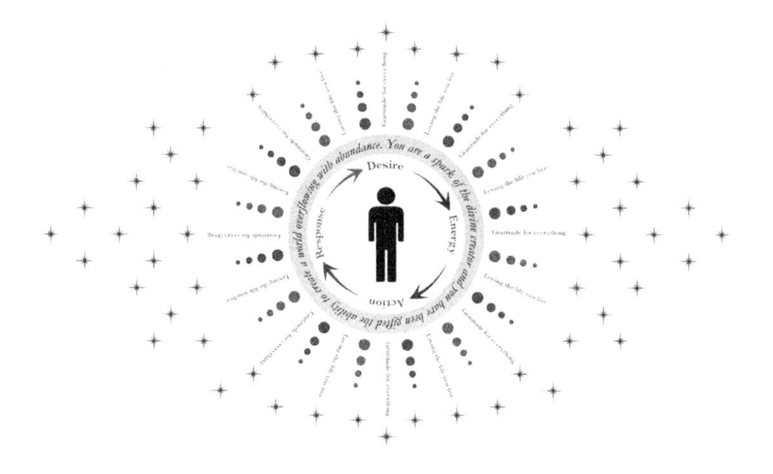

"Your prosperity consciousness is not dependent on money; Your flow of money is dependent on your prosperity consciousness."

~ LOUISE HAY

Creating an abundant life—a life filled with money, resources, opportunities, freedom, time, joy, health, love, and anything else you want in abundance—is available to you, and to every other sentient being on the planet.

At first, I'll admit, it can be a little tricky to navigate abundance. But—like my dentist told me that day in the chair—once you get it, you'll wonder why it took you so long.

Some things are just like that.

When I began taking scuba lessons, I couldn't manage to clear my mask. It didn't make sense to me that my mask could fill with water while I was submerged in the water and that I could get the water *out* of the mask without surfacing.

My son came over to my house. We got into the pool, and he slowly repeated the same instructions I'd read and heard from my instructor, patiently demonstrating how it worked. "Mom," he said, "you're going to get this."

Again and again, he showed me how to blow out quickly through my nose, lifting the mask slightly away from my lower face. We did it over and over until, finally, I managed to pull it off.

Grinning sheepishly, I said, "This was so easy! How on Earth did it take me this long?"

Conscious creation of money (or anything else) is like that too. Before you do it, it feels like it just won't work. But it *does* work—and it *can* work for you.

I know, I know. You're afraid that you might be the exception—the *one person on the planet* for whom the Law of Attraction doesn't work. So let me ask you this: Are you exempt from the law of gravity? Do you need to be tethered to your house to keep from floating away? Of course not!

The Law of Attraction is a Universal Law. The Universal Laws govern our energetic universe with as much certainty as the laws of science govern our physical reality on Planet Earth. So, as silly as it is to think that you could be immune to gravity, or Newton's Third Law of action and reaction, it is equally as silly to think that you could be immune to the Law of Attraction.

By the time we are done with our work together in this book, you'll know how to put the Law of Attraction to work for you. Starting right now, we are going to go through all of the reality-changing steps in my award-winning book, *The Map—To Our Responsive Universe, Where Dreams Really Do Come True!* and apply them directly to your personal abundance with greater detail and clarity than ever before.

But first, I want to share with you how I finally became skilled at creating abundance in my own life.

HOW I BECAME SKILLED AT CREATING ABUNDANCE

I learned how to consciously create abundance the hard way: by first creating sickening, petrifying, mind-blowing scarcity.

When I was divorced from my first husband, I thought I had it under control. I was getting alimony and child support, and although it wasn't a lot of money, it was comfortable, and I felt secure.

Then, the very same month my alimony ended, my sons unexpectedly decided to move in with their father. As I shared in Chapter One, I attempted to start several "work from home" businesses, but nothing was sticking. The bills began to mount. I maxed out all of my credit cards. Before long, my house was in foreclosure.

I've never felt so powerless in my life, before or since. The frustrating thing was, I knew about the Law of Attraction. I *believed* that I could create my own reality.

And yet, I couldn't seem to corral my emotions. I panicked. I wallowed in self-pity. I despaired that my life was over. I was destined to be homeless and penniless, and I was totally helpless to change my situation.

It was truly my lowest of lows.

Looking back on those weeks and months, I can see that I had a hidden agenda: I was hoping to be "rescued" by the man I was dating. He owned a townhome that could have easily housed us both—but I never spoke to him about it. At the time, I wasn't even able to be honest with myself, much less with him.

My damsel in distress strategy didn't work. (Imagine that?) He stood by, being supportive, but not in the way I'd hoped.

The ball was back in my court.

That was when I decided that feeling lousy sucked. So did wishing and hoping that my life would miraculously change (read: that someone would swoop in to rescue me).

Then and there, I chose to stop feeling scared, stop trying to manipulate my guy, and just *enjoy* life. After all, they hadn't yet taken my home. I was still in good health. My boys were safe and happy, even though they didn't live with me.

I had a lot to be thankful for, and so I made feeling happy a priority, and refused to pay attention to what I didn't like.

I wasn't in denial; I knew the score. But I was tired of feeling sad and scared. I took a break from "creating my dream" (which, in reality, was focusing day in and day out on the part of my dream I *didn't* have), and instead focused on the "now" moment, and on feeling as much gratitude, happiness, and joy as I could.

Sure enough, that tiny shift in my emotions worked. I got a job offer: working as a temp two days a week for $10 an hour. It wasn't enough to save my house (I did end up losing that house, and declaring bankruptcy), but it still felt like a huge step forward.

Giving up my fear, victimization, and martyrdom made everything feel so much *lighter.* And, despite the house thing, my life was looking better. I thought, "Why not see if I can create even more?"

With that new perspective, I tiptoed back into the realm of "creating my reality."

I spent ten minutes each morning doing a visualization to direct my day. I'd imagine myself sitting at an outdoor bistro table at a riverside café in the south of France, sipping tea and nibbling croissants. At the table with me were my higher self, my future self (the one who lived the phenomenal life I dreamed of), and my subconscious mind personified.

These three entities shared tea with me, and listened as I told them how I wanted to feel each day: passionate, excited, prosperous, happy, loved, loving, like I was making a difference in the world. Then, I would *feel* those feelings for them, so they'd know what I meant.

Sure enough, it worked! I started having days that felt *exactly* like the days I'd requested. Just a few weeks later, my temp job took me to the marketing department of a mortgage company. Within two weeks they offered me a full-time position which paid more than double my temp rate. I'd be writing copy and articles, doing a little graphic design, and planning marketing strategies—all work I loved.

The downside was it was a long commute—over an hour with traffic. I didn't do well for long stretches in a car, and two hours a day was too much time to spend shuttling back and forth. I turned the job down, holding the thought that this was a sign that a job as good, or better, was on its way.

And it was! The company came back with an offer for me to work at home three days a week, and enjoy flexible hours on my two commuting days. I was thrilled, and took the job! But I also explained it was my dream to work for myself, and asked them not to think of me as a permanent employee. "Understood," my new boss said.

The job was even more fun than I'd imagined. I adored what I did, and even loved spending those two days in the office, talking and brainstorming together with my colleagues. The balance was perfect for me.

My new strategy for creating was working well. The evidence was right there in front of me. I started to believe, deep down, that creating my own reality according to my dreams was not only possible, it was *easy*. So, even as I enjoyed my new job, I continued flowing energy toward my ideal life of owning my own company and enjoying unlimited abundance.

Two years later, the president of that $10 billion mortgage

company approached me and the entire staff of the marketing department. "I'm opening my own mortgage company," he told us. "And I'd like you all to join me in opening a marketing services company."

He offered to make me the vice president and give me a percentage of ownership. My dream was coming true!

I had so much fun with that startup. Unfortunately it was short-lived. Just six months later, the founder pulled the plug.

I was jobless and moneyless again. I could have panicked. I could have fallen back into victimhood.

But *I had changed.* I decided that this was simply the next step on my great adventure. Maybe it didn't look like I'd expected, but that didn't mean I wasn't getting my dream. It only meant I didn't know exactly how my dream was going to manifest.

Two days before the doors closed on the startup, my boss, the president of that startup, approached me. "How would you like to open a similar marketing company together? You could run it from your home, and I'd be the silent partner."

What did I have to lose? We each put in $50 for the filing fees, and I took a field trip to downtown Denver to incorporate In Touch Today.

At first, I worked three other jobs to keep food on the table. But within six months, I was able to borrow enough to buy my partner out. Within the year, we were profitable, and had outgrown my spare bedroom.

I continued to flow energy toward my dream. More, I worked relentlessly on the beliefs that stood in the way of my success (and there were a lot of them). The company grew steadily, and within five years, our annual sales were in excess of $5 million.

Other than that original $50, and a loan to buy a commercial building and a digital printer, I never invested a single cent of my own money into that business. (After my bankruptcy, I was pretty gun-shy about loans!) The company grew entirely from its own profits.

I truly enjoyed everything I did with In Touch Today. When I encountered tasks I didn't enjoy, I created other people to do them better than I could do them myself! I also continued to work on myself and my "stuff" around money and abundance; I changed any beliefs that were holding me back, and expanded my concepts about how easy and elegant life could be.

During that period, my growth was my top priority. (Okay, who am I kidding—my growth is still my top priority.) I sought to be impeccable with my thoughts. I attended spiritual workshops a few times a year. I discovered that, although my creations didn't always work the way I'd planned, my energy *always* created my reality, without exception.

When I met my second husband, my concept of abundance was suddenly stretched one thousand fold. He had achieved levels of financial and personal success I hadn't even imagined. That brought up more "stuff" for me—like old, dirty stories about worthiness, hard work, and earning money (as opposed to receiving abundance).

But I worked through it. I expanded my beliefs about what was possible. Now, although that marriage is over, I've created the life I'd always dreamed of—a life filled with an abundance of health and vitality, love and being loved, work I adore, successes abound, beauty, elegance, ease—and yes, plenty of money.

I wasn't "lucky," or "special." I didn't end up here by accident. I created this incredible life, my friend—just like you can create your incredible life, if you follow the seven key steps in *The Map to Abundance.*

The Seven Key Steps in *The Map to Abundance*

- **Step 1:** Own Your Power & Divinity
- **Step 2**: Get Clear on What You *Really* Want
- **Step 3**: Flow Energy Toward the Abundance You Seek
- **Step 4**: Take Action to Accelerate Your Creation
- **Step 5**: See the "Signs" & Make them Grow
- **Step 6:** Stay Happy, Grateful, & Feeling "As If"
- **Step 7:** Ask for Help

Seven simple steps. Are you ready?
Great! Let's begin!

STEP 1: OWN YOUR POWER & DIVINITY

It begins with *you*.

If life is an illusion and you are creating it all ... Well then, it always comes back to you, doesn't it?

You are the star in your life movie. You're also the director, screenwriter, and casting director. Everyone else who shows up on your movie set is in a supporting role—meaning, they can't call any of the shots unless you give them permission.

Why have you been given this powerful job as creator of your world? It's because you, too, are divine. You achieved your divinity the minute you were created by God and Goddess.

When you decided to come to Earth and play in physical form, you knew before you came that the entire "game" was pretend. It is a very real illusion, and one you felt was important to experience for your soul's growth—but an illusion nonetheless.

What's more, you thought it would be fun to forget everything you knew about your divinity, your indestructible connection to the Divine, and your ability to create your world, just so you could have the experience of *remembering*.

That's why, in order to create the abundant life, which is your birthright, you begin by remembering who you are and what you are capable of—which, of course, is literally creating your reality.

Once you've accepted that you are a divine creator, you can move on to …

STEP 2: GET CLEAR ON WHAT YOU *REALLY* WANT

You probably think you want to be rich. And maybe you do. But there's more to creating abundance than stacking up piles and piles of money.

Piles of money, in and of themselves, are nothing more than stacks of intricately-printed paper—so unless you plan to pile them up to climb out of a deep well, or use them to start your wood stove, or something else like that, they are as useless as any other stacks of paper.

The value of money lies, not in what it is, but what it can *give* you. And what you think money will give you will clue you in as to the real reasons you want to be rich.

Maybe you want more freedom. Maybe you want to work less, or have more fun. Maybe you want to travel. Maybe you want to create greater beauty, peace, health, or education in your life. These things are what money represents to you.

Ultimately, it doesn't matter why you want what you want. But in order to create what you want in your reality, you need to *know* what you want, and you need to be at peace with it. If you're not, you will sabotage your dream.

Way back when I was first trying to create an abundant life, I thought I wanted money. What I *really* wanted was someone to step in and give me the security I was missing. So, not only was what I was asking for different from what I really wanted, I was placing the power to create it in someone else's hands! No wonder I kept falling flat on my face!

Step 2 of *The Map to Abundance*—understanding exactly what you want—will help you to get clear on what your real dreams are, and start manifesting them.

Then, once you're clear on the dream ...

STEP 3: FLOW ENERGY TOWARD THE ABUNDANCE YOU SEEK

Remember, *emotion* creates your reality. The more you can feel the emotions that are in alignment with what you want, the more abundance you'll receive.

Easy-peasy, right?

Well, not always.

Human beings are complex creatures. You say you want one thing—but there are aspects of you that very clearly want another. Why? Because those aspects fear the very thing you want.

For instance, let's say that you want to double your income so you can start your own company. Part of you—the "adult you"—may be totally on board with that. But at the same time, the "seven-year-old you" may be scared to death. That fear will sabotage your dream. That child self is flowing the energy of fear and overwhelm—and you probably know nothing about it. The only evidence that it's happening is that your dream isn't manifesting.

So Step 3 is not only about flowing positive energy, it's about seeking out negative energy like a bloodhound on a scent, and doing what's necessary to transform it into dream-creating energy.

Hallelujah, right?

We have so freakin' many negative beliefs about money that, for most of us, this is the longest step in *The Map* process—but oh, is it valuable! Once those bad boys have been changed, they'll stay changed for good, and you'll be free to create endless abundance ... forever!

And once we've shifted the beliefs that are stopping you, you can flow energy toward your dreams of abundance so that they have no choice but to manifest.

Then, once those negative beliefs are out of your way and you've begun to flow energy toward what you *do* want ...

STEP 4: TAKE ACTION TO ACCELERATE YOUR CREATION

In order to create abundance in your physical reality, you've got to bring *energetic abundance* into this three-dimensional world. How do you do that? You begin to take *action* on your dream.

Taking action in the world *as if your abundance is imminent* is proof—to you, your subconscious mind, and the universe—that you believe this will happen, and that you're ready to receive the abundance.

For example, when I was offered that first marketing job as a temp, I told my bosses that I was planning for something bigger—as in, owning my own business. It didn't stop me from doing a great job for that company for two years, but I planted that seed right from the get-go. I *acted* as though my dream was imminent.

If you are feeling resistance, fear, or doubt around taking action, all that means is that you have more work to do with your beliefs, or that you don't really want what you think you want. Those are fabulous things to know, because once you know them, you can go back to the drawing board, figure things out, and start really making things happen. And don't worry—I'll help you through this and every step down to the tiniest details.

Once you've taken action, it gets really exciting ...

STEP 5: SEE THE "SIGNS" & MAKE THEM GROW

After you've changed your abundance energy in the first four steps, it's time to get curious and notice what the universe is sending you. It's like you've placed an order for what you want, and now you're waiting for that mysterious box to show up on your doorstep.

Soon after you've flowed some positive energy, and started taking action, you should start to see "signs" that your energy around abundance is shifting. They may be little signs, and you may be tempted to let yourself fall into disappointment. But they're not the main course of your reality creation; they're simply the *amuse-bouche.*

Remember when I told you in Chapter One how I created $1,000 for that retreat when I had no money? Remember the check that showed up in my mailbox—the one that wasn't for me? I could have easily thrown up my hands when I saw that, and taken it as a sign that money was meant for other people. Thankfully, I didn't—and, eventually, I ended up receiving what I had asked for, and more.

Many people fall into the trap of thinking that the signs they receive are the end of the road for their creation process. They see a sign or two, get excited that things are showing up, then slip back into their old scarcity-riddled resonance once more. Doing that is like cancelling your meal order after the appetizer, then saying the restaurant has no food for you. Silly, right? (And what about dessert? Who wants to give up before dessert?)

Don't worry if you've cancelled your universal orders in the past. It happens to everyone in the beginning. In this book, I'll teach you how to sustain your resonance and bring your abundance to full fruition.

Meanwhile …

STEP 6: STAY HAPPY, GRATEFUL, & FEELING "AS IF"

It's not just the moments during which you're focused on your dream that matter in conscious creation. You're flowing energy toward *something*, all day, every day—so pay attention and make sure that you don't un-create your dream.

If you can stay happy for at least most of each day, it will go a long way toward supporting the manifestations of your abundance.

If you add gratitude for the abundances you already have to that happiness, you'll double the impact.

And if you can manage to feel as if the abundance you seek is already yours, you'll triple it.

Positivity is that powerful. *You* are that powerful.

But you don't have to do it all alone, because there are some beings out there who are even more powerful than you are!

STEP 7: ASK FOR HELP

You didn't come to this planet by accident. And you didn't come without a tether to the more "real" world you came from. There are those in that "real" world who wait for you, who love you, and who will support you any way they possibly can. These beings are your *unseen friends.*

They are the best friends and allies you'll ever have. They believe in you more than you have ever believed in yourself—and they're standing by, ready and waiting to assist you in creating abundance in every area of your life.

But there are two caveats, two little rules that *everyone*, on every plane of existence, must abide by in this Earth-game:

Rule #1: If You Want Your Unseen Friends' Help, You Have to Ask

If you ask, they can lend a hand (or several hands, or a whole entire universe full of hands). They will do everything in their power to make sure that your desires manifest in the best possible way for you, your happiness, and your soul's purpose here on Earth.

Rule #2: No One Else—Not Even God—Will Do Your Work For You

Not one of your unseen friends will hand you your abundance on a silver platter. They love you too much for that. You came to

Earth to learn how to consciously create, and they won't take that away from you, no matter how hard your human self begs them.

But if you ask for their help, they will come, and they will help. Every now and then, they'll even offer a miracle or two.

A FEW MORE THINGS TO REMEMBER ALONG THE WAY

Conscious creation is not difficult. Anyone can do it; we're born with the ability to create, and nothing can take that away from us. But conscious creation is complex. There are nuances that are not readily apparent—and it's those nuances that trip people up again and again. However, if you follow this Map, and stay awake and aware, you *can* create your life to be abundant.

Before we dive in, though, I want to give you a little extra leg up. This entire process will be easier if you remember the following:

Be Impeccable

As we progress through this work, you'll be required to answer questions about yourself, your past, and your feelings. Finding the answers to these questions will require both time and reflection. I urge you not to settle for the easy, top-of-mind answers, or throw out some superficial fluff to get the question out of the way. Instead, challenge yourself to gain as much clarity as you can about your thoughts, feelings, and motivations.

I'm not asking this of you because I need you to answer to me. I'm simply speaking from personal experience. If you don't put your all into this, your creations will never reach their full potential—and the only person that will hurt is you.

Be Intimate

If you're serious about this work and creating your abundance, you're going to have to get to know yourself a lot better. You'll be required to become intimate with not only yourself, your feelings, and your desires around abundance, but with money itself. Getting close to something allows you to see it with different eyes, and from different angles. Knowledge is power: the more you know, the more you will be able to create.

Be Honest

It's not easy to be honest, especially when it comes to your life and how you've created it thus far. You'll be reluctant to admit where you've fallen into victimhood, self-pity, martyrdom, or apathy—and even more reluctant to take ownership of what those feelings have created in your current reality. But you'll only be able to change your world when you're willing to see, acknowledge, and deal with what your world actually looks like.

In other words, you can fool yourself till the cows come home, but it won't change your reality one tiny bit.

Be Patient

Ah, that terrible "P" word! No one wants to be patient when it comes to money (or growth, or anything else we want). You want to know the "secret" to abundance, and you want it to manifest in your life right now!

Well, I have some news for you: *there is no secret*. There is only information for you to understand, and a process for you to complete. During that process (and even after you've finished), patience is critical. Because we live in a physical reality, it takes time for the changes you've created to manifest in your world. Paradoxically, the more patient you are, the quicker you'll experience abundance.

Be Relentless

The phrase, "Never, ever, *ever* give up" has never more appropriate than it is for you right now. As you go through this work, you'll be tempted to throw in the towel. You'll be tempted to put your inner work on the back burner. You'll be tempted to throw it all out the window when you don't get the signs you wanted, or when you mis-create something in your reality.

By all means, feel those feelings. Throw those miniature temper tantrums. Wallow in your frustration for an hour, or even two.

But then, get up, dust yourself off, and get back to work. Remember who you are, and what you're capable of.

The reason my life is so spectacular right now isn't because I'm special, or uniquely talented. It's because I'm stubborn as hell, and once I've got something in my sight, I refuse to give it up. Sometimes, that bullishness is not a useful trait—but for this work, it's a huge asset.

Be Open to Receiving Help

Remember, you don't have to do this alone. It doesn't have to be a struggle.

Ask your unseen friends to help you understand these concepts, discover your beliefs, and "see" where you give up your power. Ask them to help you learn patience. Ask that *anything* that stands in the way of your total, joyous abundance be brought to your attention, gently but fully—and then, ask for help in healing and releasing those obstacles.

You can ask for help from your physical friends, family, and community, too. If you need professional help with healing something in your past, get it. If you need help discovering your subconscious beliefs, ask your friends to share what they observe. Be willing to let others into your life, and let them help you with your creation process.

Get Ready to Change

I am not the same woman who, nearly twenty years ago, lost her house, filed for bankruptcy, and blamed herself for not being "able" to create the reality she wanted. I'm simply not that person anymore.

I'm not even the same woman who, ten years ago, had her notions of abundance blown out of the water when she met her second husband, and needed to reassess her entire concept of wealth and how one lives with it.

I am more "myself" today than I have ever been before. But I am no longer the "me" I used to know. I had to let that woman go to make room for the woman who had the strength, power, and tenacity to create what she really wanted, and live with it every day.

This process will *change* you. You will ultimately begin to love, accept, and honor yourself more than you ever have. And you'll discover, in that change, how unequivocally deserving of abundance you are.

A TRUE STORY OF CONSCIOUSLY CREATING ABUNDANCE

Not too long ago, I was at an all-time low. I had been divorced for a while, and was living on my own for the first time (I had to stay with my mom for a few years after my separation). My self-esteem and confidence had vanished, and I felt completely out of control of my life. I felt like the proverbial bit of flotsam on the stormy sea.

Very negative things began to happen. I was evicted from my house because a developer wanted to build a parking lot. My new rental was a mess, complete with a leaking roof and defunct appliances. My windows were shot out with a BB gun, and my house was broken into. I lost my beloved horse to a broken leg. My best friend—a man I was very much in love with—started dating someone else. And (as if all of those things weren't enough), I was suffering from terrible stress and exhaustion in my toxic work environment, and my health was taking a hit.

I was living in a nightmare.

The last straw came when I was evicted from my rental house because the owner wanted to sell it. That was it. That was the turning point. I was so far down that I decided the only way was up.

That was when I came upon Boni's www.LiveALifeYouLove.com website and subscribed to the daily e-mails (365 Days of The Map*). Bingo! My mind and spirit sat up and took notice immediately. I very carefully pondered what I was reading. It went against everything we are taught as humans—and yet, I knew it was truth.*

I began by focusing on a new home. I decided to buy a home for the first time ever, so I called the Realtor who was selling my rental house. It turned out that he was a musician like me, and was friends with some of my friends. I had an amazing feeling in my gut—a feeling that, from that day forward, good things were going to start happening.

I was scared to death and had a hell of a lot of healing to do, but I was on the "up" elevator, and I was going to ride it all the way to the top!

I had a copy of the book, The Map, *too, so I was well equipped. I bought a wonderful home—a 1920s bungalow in a sought-after community in downtown Indianapolis. From there, everything else started to fall into place. My life did a complete turnaround. All I did was keep feeling the way I wanted to feel, and acting as if I already had what I wanted.*

Now, I am happy, safe, healthy, and abundant. More, I am able to send good energy out into the world, and feel it come back to me. My friend—the man I have always loved—is now deeply in love with me. He lives a few blocks away, in the same neighborhood. We have started exploring our passion for music together as a duo performing folk rock and Native American-style flute. We're writing songs, learning new instruments, and taking our creativity to new levels. I can see a path to make music a means of making a living, as I wanted to do many years ago!

I'm still hard at work on my intentions, and more dreams are coming true every day. My life has turned completely around since I began reading The Map.

- Carol H.

ABUNDANCE-ALTERING TAKEAWAYS

- Creating an abundant life—a life filled with money, resources, opportunities, freedom, time, joy, health, love, and anything else you want in abundance—is available to you, and to every awake and thinking being on the planet.

- Chances are, you don't want money; what you're truly seeking is what money can give you. That might be freedom, security, time, beauty, peace, or health.

- It's not easy being honest with yourself, but it is absolutely required if you want your life to change. Only when you are willing to honestly look at yourself will you be able to take responsibility for your world—and then change it.

- Be relentless. The phrase, "Never, ever, ever give up" was never more appropriate than as applied to conscious creation! You'll be tempted to throw in the towel or back-burner this work when it doesn't happen the way you envisioned. By all means, have those feelings and those mini-temper tantrums. Then, get back to work.

- You don't have to do this alone. You simply don't. It doesn't have to be a struggle. Ask for help whenever you need it, from your friends both seen and unseen.

YOUR NEXT STEPS

Ask yourself, "Am I ready to commit to being ..."

- **Impeccable.** Are you ready to tackle this journey with everything you have, without excuses, leaving no stone unturned and bringing as much of your full self to the table as possible?

- **Intimate.** Are you willing to let yourself see your dark side, your weak side, and your fearful side? Are you willing to be totally transparent—at least with yourself?

- **Honest.** Are you willing to see yourself clearly and accept that you may not be (entirely) who you think you are?

- **Patient.** Are you willing to give yourself all the time you need to heal the past, change your beliefs, and create your abundance?

- **Relentless.** Are you ready to accept this as your mantra? "No matter what I create, there is always, always a reason for it—and if there is a reason for it, that reason can be found and changed. I will never give up learning how to create my reality."

- **Open to receive.** Are you willing to give up control and to let your unseen friends lift you, guide you, and assist you in creating your dream of abundance and the dream of abundance that they hold for you?

- **Ready to change**. You won't be the same person you were before you began this journey. Are you willing to let go of the old "you" and embrace the new?

CHAPTER THREE

Abundance is Your Birthright

"True abundance is not about gathering more things, it's about touching the place in us that is connected to the divine source of abundance, so that we know what we need in the moment will be provided."

~ MARY MANIN MORRISSEY

I recently offered gifts to two friends of mine. The gifts were slightly different—one was about creating money, the other about creating love. I asked them which of the two gifts they preferred.

One of the young women said, "You decide what we deserve."

"You both deserve love, money, success, joy, and everything good you can possibly imagine," I declared.

And it's true. They do. You do too. We *all* do. Because no matter who you are or how you lead your life, you still deserve.

You can't *not* deserve.

And you can't *not* be divine.

You are both divine and deserving by your very nature—by the very fact that you exist. Why?

Because God and Goddess created you out of themselves, that's why.

If you were created out of divinity, you must be divine. And if you're divine, of course, you must deserve all good things.

Yet, as it did for my friends, the feeling of deserving eludes many of us. We want someone else to be the judge—but even when someone else does declare us deserving (as I did for them), we still don't believe it.

That feeling of "I don't deserve" will stop abundance in its tracks. And the irony is ...

RECEIVING ABUNDANCE HAS NOTHING TO DO WITH "DESERVING"

I remember the day it dawned on me that success and wealth weren't caused by deservability.

I was twenty-one years old, and it was the first day of my new job. I worked for a small advertising firm and I was calling on the owner of a wildly successful new car dealership.

The moment I walked into his office, I was awestruck by how "unsuccessful" this man appeared. He was unshaven, unkempt, and dressed in rumpled clothes. More, he was crass and rude. After a thirty-minute conversation, I realized that he wasn't even very smart—and he was more than a little lecherous.

How could this be? How could this man have opened a new car showroom and guided it to stellar success, and yet be such a jerk? Weren't successful people smart, educated, and kind, and somehow *better* than other people?

It was a rude awakening, but an important one. That day, I learned that:

You don't create success and abundance because you deserve it. You create success and abundance because you *believe* you deserve it.

Since many of us weren't taught as children that we're divine, and that we deserve every good thing under the sun, we have to change our beliefs around deservability in order to let those good things in.

Feeling "undeserving" isn't the only thing that will stop abundance. So will ...

- Feeling guilty for having abundance.
- Feeling as if there is only so much to go around, and if you have it others won't.
- Feeling as if you don't "do" enough to earn the abundance you desire.
- Feeling like you have to work *really hard* for abundance.
- Feeling powerless to make money "just happen" in your life.

Truly, the list could go on and on, but you get the picture. Many things will stop you from being abundant, and from allowing money, opportunities, and wealth in all forms to become a permanent part of your reality. These things have stopped you for years; there's nothing new here.

But there is something new in your reality, and it's happening right now.

WHAT *IS* NEW?

What's new is that now, the tables have turned, and you are in the driver's seat. You *know* you have a choice, and that your abundance is not outside of your control.

You see, when you believe there's no choice about how you experience your reality, there really is no choice. But when that curtain of possibility has been raised even a sliver, you, my friend, can never go back.

You can never un-know what you now know. And if you're reading this, you're ready to acknowledge that some part of you, the deepest part of you, knows that *you create it all.*

Oh, you may push the knowing aside for days, weeks, months, or years. You may, if you want to, even push it away to work with in another lifetime—but you'll never forget again. The knowledge you now carry will bring you back, again and again, to the ultimate choice: Do I take my power back *now*, or keep making excuses?

In truth, it doesn't really matter when you make the choice. In some lifetime, sooner or later, you'll decide enough is enough, and say to yourself, "It's ridiculous to continue to suffer when it's been in my power to be abundant all along." Then, you'll create your way into abundance.

But, I have to ask: Why wait? Why suffer? Why struggle? Why live in poverty, or lack, or scarcity for *one single second more* than you have to? *Why?*

There's no reason for it—unless you think it's what you deserve. Maybe you were told as a child that you didn't deserve to be happy. Maybe you believe that, somewhere along the way, you've done something so wrong that you should be punished for all eternity. But even when the reasons for your struggle go that deep, sooner or later, in this lifetime or another, you'll forgive yourself, and finally allow yourself to be abundant.

Then, you'll ask yourself, "Why did I wait so damn long?" (You may even be asking yourself this question right now!)

It doesn't matter why you haven't created abundance until now. For whatever reason, you simply weren't ready. But you *are* ready now.

So, choose. Right here, right now, say these words, in your head or aloud:

> *I choose to claim my divine right to be abundant. I ask my unseen friends to accompany me on this journey of growth and empowerment and to help me along the way. I ask that you gently point out where I get stuck, show me the beliefs I need to change, and help me to change them. Assist me please, to the greatest extent possible. Thank you in advance for your support, love, guidance, and grace.*

Great. You've made the choice. Now, I have to ask: how fully did you choose?

Yes, it's a simple question, but a profound one. *How fully did you choose?*

Was it an, "Okay, sure, what the heck?" kind of choice? Or was it an I-feel-this-in-the-pit-of-my-stomach, iron-willed, absolutely positive "*YES, I choose THIS!*" kind of choice?

Because, my friend, it *matters.*

If you honestly desire abundance, you're going to have to work at it. (Now don't get me wrong, I didn't say work *for* it. They're two different things.)

Because money is so weighty, and so twisted in our society, this work won't always be easy. You'll have to divest yourself of your old energies around money, and take on entirely new energies that will result in an entirely new resonance (and reality) around money.

It *can* be done. I'm living proof of that. Every abundant

person on the planet is living proof of that. Abundance *never* happens by accident—and that is the best news you could ever receive, because if abundance is caused by *essence and energy,* you need only change your essence and energy to create abundance.

MAKING THE COMMITMENT TO A LIFE OF ABUNDANCE

For some reason, many of us want to shun our birthright of abundance. I've seen it in myself, and I'm sure you see it in yourself. You'll get so far, and then, suddenly, you'll just quit. You'll get too busy, put this book down, and forget to do your techniques for days, weeks, or months at a time. Then you'll remember that you have the power and ability to create abundance—and you'll begin again.

It's okay. It's your journey, and you should take it at the pace that is right for you.

There's more to this passive resistance than internal cadence. Honestly, I think our human selves simply can't let it all in at once. I think we have trouble accepting just how wonderful the universe is. I think we have doubts about just how magical we are. I think we have trouble believing how loved we are by God, Goddess, and our other unseen friends.

We simply cannot believe (not at first, anyway) that we deserve to live an unlimitedly abundant life. And so we push it away, until we can handle the next little piece.

This is why I prompted you to be very, *very* clear about your commitment to abundance. Your commitment to invite abundance into your life is that first critical piece of the whole picture.

What Commitments Have You Made?

I find it interesting that there are two definitions for "commitment" in the dictionary:

commitment (n):
1. The state or quality of being dedicated to a cause, activity, etc.
2. An engagement or obligation that restricts freedom of action.

Committing to a life of abundance is not as straightforward as it might seem. You have current "commitments" that are in opposition to a life of abundance. You are committed to struggle, lack, scarcity, victimhood, martyrdom, mediocrity, and being asleep.

Wait a minute, I'm not committed to those things!

Yes, actually, you are. We all are—until we deliberately cancel those commitments. Your identity is tied up in your thoughts, your beliefs, your actions, and your expectations of what can and will happen in your world. These are the commitments that restrict your access to abundance.

When you make a commitment to abundance, you're making a commitment to live a different life than the life you are currently living. You're committing to change your thoughts, beliefs, actions, expectations, and feelings about the world and how you show up in it.

Whether you have allowed a little or a lot of abundance thus far, you'll want more. You'll always want more. You won't stop wanting more, ever. Each level of abundance requires another commitment to the next level of abundance, and the next and the next ... *ad infinitum*.

So what is a "commitment to abundance"?

I thought you'd never ask!

A commitment to abundance is simply acknowledging, in advance, that although it may not be fast or easy, you will do what needs to be done in order to attain a life of real abundance. This is a promise you make to yourself and your unseen friends.

I suggest printing out and signing the Commitment to Abundance below.(1) Post it someplace where you can see it often. Read it whenever you can, both in your head and aloud.

If that sounds like a lot of work, remember: this is your *life* we're talking about. What could be more important than transforming it into one of unlimited love, health, freedom, resources, opportunities, elegance, and ease—and of course, financial abundance?

The Commitment

Out of my love for myself and the love I have for my higher self, soul, God, and Goddess, I make these commitments with the intention to live a life of abundance:

I commit to remembering the truth: that I am divine by my very nature. I am a part of God and Goddess.

I commit to remembering that my unseen friends love me unconditionally.

(1) You can download a printable version of the Commitment to Abundance at www.LiveALifeYouLove.com/commitment-abundance.

I commit to remembering that I live in a reality of my own making—a reality that has the potential to be limitlessly abundant.

I commit to doing the work necessary to free myself to live that unlimitedly abundant life, no matter how difficult and uncomfortable the process may be.

I commit to being totally honest with myself about my limitations, agendas, beliefs, rationalizations, and payoffs.

I commit to forgiving myself for all the times I settled for struggle and hardship, when, looking back, I could have created abundance.

I commit to remembering that abundance is more than money, more than things, more than what "I have." Abundance is who I am becoming: a spiritual being in a physical body who knows beyond a doubt that ease, elegance, resources, magic, synchronicity, love, and guidance are not only my choice, but my birthright.

I commit to asking for and receiving help from my unseen friends, so that they can help me make the journey to a life of abundance as easy, elegant, rich, and fun as possible.

Sign and date your commitment to seal your contract with yourself before you post it on your wall. Treat it with the same reverence and respect that you would any other binding contract.

I'm not expecting you to be "perfect" at this, nor should you expect that of yourself. However, I will ask that you remember one thing:

> **If abundance isn't showing up in your life, there's *always* a reason.**

If you keep coming back to that truth (provided you actually believe it), you'll begin to discipline yourself. You'll keep digging for the "key" to unlock the next door to abundance for yourself. That digging—that internal excavation—is really what the Commitment to Abundance is all about. You aren't just committing to receive abundance; you're committing to doing whatever it takes to open that next door to receive.

That said …

Go With the Flow

This work doesn't have to be hard, or long, or frustrating—but sometimes, it just is.

This isn't because you're doing something wrong, but because money is weighty. It sometimes takes longer to undo all of the habits, beliefs, and patterns that you've accumulated around weighty things, because, well, they're entrenched.

But, in the end, so what? What matters is that you're doing the work, not how long the process takes. And, if you keep your eyes open, you'll receive lots of signs along the way. Your reality will keep changing incrementally. That alone should keep you pumped up and moving forward.

Let's face it. It's time. This change is long overdue—for you, for others, and for the planet. So let's get started!

A TRUE STORY OF CONSCIOUSLY CREATING ABUNDANCE

I never stop reading your book, The Map. *Every time I go back and pick it up, it always tells me something I need to hear in that moment.*

After reading The Map, *I visualized my daughter's acceptance to the college of her dreams. It happened just as I pictured, but we were still a little short on funds, even with all the scholarships (yes, she deserved them, but I helped manifest them!), so I started envisioning the rest of the costs being covered easily and effortlessly.*

We soon received a call from her guidance counselor that she might be eligible for additional assistance because she is dyslexic. Guess what? New York State came through and paid the exact amount we needed! They even sent a voucher to her bookstore to cover all of her course materials!

I am now working on my dream of owning a shop. I intend to see that take shape this year!

- Donna G.

ABUNDANCE-ALTERING TAKEAWAYS

- You don't receive success and abundance because you deserve it. You receive success and abundance because you *believe* you deserve it.

- When you believe there's no choice, there really is no choice. But when that curtain of possibility has been raised even a sliver, you can never go back.

- It doesn't matter why you haven't created abundance until now. You can do it now. You are ready now. Choose *now*.

- When you make a commitment to abundance, you are making a commitment to live a different life than the life you're currently living.

- If abundance isn't showing up in your life, there is always a reason. You can find that reason and change it.

- Creating abundance can sometimes be difficult, take longer than you'd like and/or become frustrating. This is not because you're doing anything wrong, but because money is weighty. Because of this weightiness, it can take longer to undo all of the habits, beliefs, and patterns that you've been working with around money. Be patient with yourself!

YOUR NEXT STEPS

- Take a few moments each morning just after waking, and each evening just before sleep, to remind yourself that you are a divine being—a piece of God and Goddess—and that you have been given the ability to create your reality.

  Sit with that truth. Let it in. Ask God and Goddess to help you own that fact more deeply than ever before. Then, go about your day as if you were divine.

- Download a printable version of the Commitment to Abundance at www.LiveALifeYouLove.com/commitment-abundance, or type out your own Commitment. Sign it to seal your commitment to yourself. Then, post it in a place where you can see and read it often. While you're doing this work, read it daily. Re-commit mentally—and, every so often, aloud.

- Make notes about any resistance that came up for you when you read this chapter. Ask yourself, "Why do I feel resistance to this?" Write down whatever comes up for you.

CHAPTER FOUR

You May Not Want What You Think You Want

"It is not inconceivable, in fact it is completely conceivable, that when you hang around in the vortex and you're feeling tuned in, tapped in, turned on, you could be inspired to stop at the 7-Eleven and inspired to the timing of the ticket and inspired to buying the ticket that is the winning of the lottery—but you've got to be in the vortex to do that. And you don't do that all of a sudden."

~ ABRAHAM

You probably think you know exactly what you desire when it comes to abundance. In fact, you were probably tempted to skip right over this chapter.

Well, that would be a big mistake.

Why? I know *what I want—I want money—lots and lots of money.*

Of course you want money! I know that. So do I. But you and I both want more than just money—and, ironically, it's the "more" that brings you the money.

Huh?

Yes, I know: it's a convoluted concept. But it is an important one. In fact, it's critical to creating abundance in all its forms—including those piles of money you've been dreaming about.

Let's start by clarifying a basic fact ...

MONEY, IN AND OF ITSELF, IS USELESS

What? What do you mean money is useless?
I have plenty of uses for money!

I said money, "in and of itself," is useless. It's just paper printed with fancy images and a series of numbers.

Don't believe me? Imagine these scenarios:

- You have a suitcase filled with millions of dollars. But you (and it) are stuck in the bottom of a dry well, and no one is around for miles.
- You have several million dollars in the bank, but you're contractually obligated to work a job you hate for the rest of your life. If you quit, you'll lose the money.

- You're a billionaire, but the money is technically your spouse's. Your marriage is miserable, but you signed a prenup that says that, if you leave, you don't get a dime.
- You have enough money to keep you living in style for the rest of your life, but you're constantly filled with fear and anxiety that something will happen to your money.
- You have limitless wealth, but you also have agoraphobia and cannot leave the tiny house you were born in.
- You have all the money you've ever wanted, but you aren't healthy enough to enjoy it.

In each of the above situations, money itself isn't useful. Instead, it's worthless, unhelpful, or even a trap.

The point is, you desire *more* than an abundance of money. You also want an abundance of freedom, health, love, happiness, peace, safety, security, and fun. Without these additional abundances, any money you had would be nearly, if not completely, useless.

I don't bring this up to play some sort of guilt trip, or remind you that there is more than money in this world. Wanting money is nothing to feel guilty about, and you already know that there's more to life than dollars and cents. No, I bring this up so that when you create your intentions around abundance, you'll remember that an abundant life is a life overflowing with abundances of *all* kinds.

I also bring it up because, unlike many of the other things you consciously create …

Your Desires Around Money May Be Loaded with Booby Traps

Remember how, in Chapter One, I told you that money is different? That's why we need to take this part of *The Map* very slowly.

Your negative beliefs around money, abundance, deservingness, worth, and possibility are like land mines hidden under the surface of your mind. We need to deactivate them so they don't keep blowing up your dreams of abundance.

The first thing we need to dismantle are your booby-trapped money dreams, like ...

WINNING THE LOTTERY

When people learn about the Law of Attraction, the first thing many of them try to do is win the lottery. But this is (in my humble opinion) a really bad idea.

Oh, I get why you love the concept. It's a juicy fantasy. It requires little to no work on your part. You don't have to start a business, or write a book, or invest in real estate. It won't take you years to work your way to the top. All you have to do is walk into a store, buy your golden ticket, and wait for the amazing payouts.

The record (at the time of this writing) for Powerball payouts was $590.5 million. With that kind of cash at stake, even if you had to share your win, you'd still be rolling in dough.

So if there are no limits as to what you can create, why not take this simple route to Easy Street? Seems like a no-brainer, right?

Wrong.

Theoretically, it is *possible* to consciously create winning the lottery. But for most people, especially when they're just learning how to create abundance in their realities, trying to create winning the lottery hurts more than it helps—and here's why:

Deciding How Your Abundance Will Appear Reduces the Ways Your Abundance Can Manifest

The first rule of conscious creation is: *you can't control how your dream manifests.*

The more you honor that rule, the more you'll be able to create. Every time you try to control how something manifests, you cut down on the number of possible ways it could come to you.

For instance, if you want to create abundance, that abundance could come to you in thousands, maybe millions of ways.

No way.

Way. For instance, here are thirty ways abundance could come to you (and I haven't even begun to exhaust the list):

1. You get a raise at work.
2. You receive a new job offer.
3. You get a check from someone who hired you and stiffed you years ago.
4. You find a wallet with $1,000 cash, and no ID in it, on the street.
5. Someone offers to pay you to house sit while you rent out your own home at the same time.

6. You win an award.
7. You are given stock or ownership in the company where you work.
8. Your partner gifts you with seed money for a new company.
9. You're offered a really fun part-time gig.
10. A family member spontaneously gifts you with money.
11. Your insurance company surprises you with an unexpected check.
12. You realize you have far more money in your account (checking, savings, stock, etc.) than you thought you did.
13. You score the deal of a lifetime on a major purchase.
14. Much to your amazement, your five-year-old son finds real gold coins in a tree you told him was magical.
15. You're given a gift card to a restaurant for a free meal.
16. You win a $100 Visa card.
17. Your neighbor gives you $50 for shoveling snow—even though you did it as a gift, not for money.
18. You move money around in your current accounts to reduce your mortgage debt by three years.
19. You immerse yourself in gratitude for a car expense that a friend was able to fix for less—and then your parents pick up the whole tab.
20. Your business inexplicably picks up.
21. The company you work for is sold—and instead of getting laid off, you get a raise.

22. You receive a check from an anonymous source for a dollar amount that was exactly what you need.
23. You receive a bigger paycheck due to a bonus that you were not expecting.
24. You get a postcard in the mail offering a free set of pearl earrings (or whatever else you've been dreaming of purchasing).
25. Your bank miraculously forgives the debt on your home loan.
26. You win free food at McDonalds.
27. You receive an extra paycheck at work.
28. You choose to sell your company by a certain date, and magically the buyer appears.
29. You decide every day what your tips will be, and allow the universe to comply.
30. A friend treats you to dinner.

By the way, this list is not imaginary. Every single item on the list really happened to someone I know—and whatever happens for others can also happen for you.

Deciding your abundance will show up by winning the lottery is trying to control the way abundance manifests. And it cuts down on all the possible ways for money and abundance to come to you.

But I don't want those little abundances—I want to win the big lottery!

Ah, yes, I thought so. There is nothing wrong with dreaming of being wealthy. However …

Going From Broke to Millionaire Is Too Big a Jump

As I mentioned earlier, you need to start where you are. Learning to consciously create an abundant life—a life where money is no longer an issue—is a gradual process. If you try to skip steps and jump to "instant-millionaire-lottery-winner," you are probably going to be disappointed.

Why?

Well first of all it's not likely to happen. Statistically your chances of winning the lottery are 175,200,000 to one. Yes, you read that right: *175 million to one.*

When you hang your hat on winning the lottery as a quick fix to your abundance issues, part of you knows it is not likely to happen. Yet you do it anyway. Why?

One reason is because you believe it's the only way you're going to get really rich, really fast. And I'd rather see you change those beliefs so that you don't sabotage yourself, and so that you build a strong foundation in order to create and receive abundance *forever.*

The second reason you hang on to lottery dreams is that you have a self-sabotaging aspect, which I call the *negative self.* Your negative self encourages you to bypass the work of conscious creation. It whispers in your ear, "Skip the hard work and go straight for the big lottery win!" It's tempting, and so you believe it.

Meanwhile, your negative self knows that you'll never get that win (at least, not without doing the work). It *wants* to disempower you, so it encourages you to keep buying those tickets week after week, hoping against hope that someday Fate, or the universe, or God will take pity on you and let you win.

Your negative self wants you to fail. And it knows ...

Trying to Win The Lottery Can Hurt Your Ability to Consciously Create

Did you get that? Attempting to win the lottery can handicap your ability to create abundance.

Why?

Because by setting your sights on winning the lottery as the only means to your abundance, you are effectively telling the universe:

- I AM NOT POWERFUL ENOUGH TO CREATE ABUNDANCE ANY OTHER WAY, SO I WANT MY MONEY TO COME TO ME THE ONLY WAY I CAN IMAGINE IT COMING, EVEN THOUGH IT'S THE LEAST LIKELY WAY POSSIBLE.

You want to win the lottery because you don't (really) trust your ability to create unlimited abundance, and you are impatient about the idea of building wealth more slowly.

You don't really believe you can manifest money out of thin air—but you hope you can get lucky so why not use this book to create getting lucky and winning the lottery?

You cannot imagine creating big abundance other than winning the lottery.

And, my friend, if you can't trust your ability to create it ...

If you don't believe it is possible to create it ...

If you can't imagine it ...

It *won't happen*—with or without the lottery.

And while you keep fooling yourself by trying to manifest a lottery win, you effectively ignore what will truly bring you abundance—a commitment to doing the work.

What makes the lottery even more of a losing proposition is that on a deeper level you know that ...

Even Big Winners Seldom Create Lasting Wealth

Do you know there are $800 million in unclaimed lottery winnings? Even when people win, and the money is waiting for them, they can't receive it.

Yes, they created being that winner, but they don't allow themselves to receive the wealth. Doesn't this tell you something about how our reality works?

And, what about the winners who go on to lose it all? Many of them suffer so many negative repercussions that they wished they'd never won in the first place.

Have you ever asked yourself why this happens?

It happens because our reality is created by our thoughts, feelings, and beliefs. Someone who doesn't think of themselves as wealthy, who doesn't *feel* wealthy, and who doesn't *believe* they are worthy of being wealthy, is going to have a really hard time *being* wealthy, no matter how much money they have in the bank.

So ...

What Is Your "Lottery Love Affair" Telling You?

If, despite everything I've shared, a lottery win still seems like the answer to your money woes, it's telling you:

- You don't (really) believe you create your own reality. If you did, you would know money could come to you in a million easy and fun ways.
- You have forgotten how reality is created. You can't choose "how" your wealth arrives. If you try, you will block all other avenues of wealth from showing up at your door.

- You don't think you're powerful enough to create abundance in any other way. If you did, you'd be too busy feeling wealthy, and watching the signs (and money) roll in, to worry about playing the lottery.

Focusing on a lottery win keeps you sidetracked by a fantasy. It's easier to hang on to a pipe dream than to do the real work of becoming abundant. But, as I'm sure you've guessed, avoiding the real work won't get you anywhere other than where you are now.

However …

If You Still Love the Idea of the Lottery

Instead of betting it all on Powerball, use your local lottery as a fun game to win small amounts. This technique is a fun tool to measure your ability to receive, because it shows you whether you are allowing abundance.

But, here's the key: don't imagine *all* your money coming from the lottery. That mindset is a trap that will keep you wishing instead of creating. Instead, think of it as a "bonus" from the universe.

Here's what I mean:

A few years ago, I went to Las Vegas to participate in a marketing trade show. This was after I had become rather proficient at creating abundance (although I wasn't nearly as abundant as I am today).

After the show, I headed for the airport for my flight back to Denver. As usual, I was early. I had thirty minutes until the flight boarded, so I decided to play "Let's Manifest" with the nearest slot machine.

I visualized a win, put in a quarter … and won!

Let's see if I can win again, I thought. And of course, I did. I kept imagining I would win—and it worked, over and over again.

But after several minutes, I got bored. *Who wants to stand around a casino to make money,* I thought, *when it's so much more fun to create money coming to me through my companies?*

I never gambled again.

When you really understand how easily money can flow into your life, and you allow it to do so, gambling is simply not necessary. To me, it's not even enjoyable. But hey, if it floats your boat, go for it. Just don't use it as a tool to build your wealth. Instead, treat it like a game to measure your ability to manifest quickly, and have fun with it.

There's a big difference between having fun with a game and depending on it to make your dreams come true. If you find yourself falling into that trap, stop, reassess, and get down to work. Change your thoughts, feelings, and beliefs so you can allow abundance to come to you in a myriad of ways.

Then, once you've proven to yourself that you don't need the lottery to create abundance, and it still feels fun, then you can play with it to create bigger wins—but not before.

And here's another sabotage-laden dream to watch out for …

MAKING LOTS OF MONEY TO RETIRE EARLY

Early retirement is another dream common amongst beginning creators, and it loves to sabotage real abundance.

In and of itself, no dream is better or worse than any other, nor is it more or less difficult to create. But if any part of you is uncomfortable with a dream, that emotional discomfort will incapacitate the dream. According to the Law of Attraction, it has to.

Sometimes, that's not a bad thing.

Wait … What?

If you want to create lots of money to watch TV and play amateur golf forevermore—or even if you want to spend your years traveling the world in style—you're not likely to allow yourself to succeed.

Why? Because meaningful work is a part of a meaningful life for every human being on the planet. As my friend Lazaris says, "Everyone *needs* meaningful work."

If your dream is to never work again, a deeper part of you (such as your higher self and soul) may have a problem with that—and maybe you should, too.

You see, you came here for a reason. Part of that reason is to learn how to consciously create one hundred percent of your reality. But as big as that reason seems, it's not the only reason you're here. You also have talents, strengths, abilities, and gifts that are meant to be expressed in the world.

Some part of you wants to have a positive, uplifting impact on others, and to find meaning in your existence and interaction with the world.

This purpose could play out on the world stage, or quietly amongst your family and friends. "Meaningful work" doesn't necessarily mean writing the next best-selling spiritual book, or solving the world's pollution problems. It *does* mean finding what you're good at and what you love to do, and bringing your brilliance into the world.

But I don't want to work!

Why would you think that? Why wouldn't you want to do something in which you could find deep satisfaction, joy, pride, and a sense of fulfillment? Most likely, it's because …

You Have Misconceptions About What Work Is

What if "work" were the most exciting thing possible? What if finding your genius, and expressing it, was the best feeling on the planet? What if you could name your own hours and work only the days you wanted? What if you could design the optimum workplace, and collaborate with people whom you like and respect?

What if your work was your dream?

But it's not!

And why do you think that is? It's because you hold beliefs that stand in the way of creating that reality!

For example, you might be carrying beliefs like:

- I DON'T KNOW WHAT MY MEANINGFUL WORK WOULD BE.
- I DON'T HAVE A GENIUS TO BE EXPRESSED.
- I CAN'T FIND MY GIFTS, TALENTS, AND STRENGTHS.
- I CAN'T MAKE ENOUGH MONEY DOING WHAT I TRULY LOVE.
- I CAN'T CREATE WORK THAT IS IN ALIGNMENT WITH MY TEMPERAMENT.
- I CAN'T CREATE WORKING WITH PEOPLE I LOVE.
- I CAN'T CREATE MY WORK BEING MY DREAM.
- IT'S A DOG-EAT-DOG WORLD OUT THERE.
- MOST ENTREPRENEURS FAIL, THEREFORE THE ODDS ARE STACKED AGAINST ME.
- SUCCESS IS DIFFICULT.

- IN ORDER TO HAVE THE WORK I DESIRE I HAVE TO GIVE UP SOME THINGS I VALUE.
- WORK IS HARD, BORING, AND THANKLESS.
- I DON'T HAVE THE MONEY TO START MY OWN BUSINESS.

These are just a few of the beliefs that many of us hold around work. Once you change them, your work life will change. It's as simple as that.

Also, remember that "meaningful work" doesn't have to look like any work you've previously created. You may need to create ...

A New Vision for Meaningful Work

The idea of meaningful work doesn't necessarily mean work that feeds the hungry or builds shelter for the homeless. It simply means work that is significant to you. The work that fills you with purpose may have meaning for other people, your community, or even the world—but then again, it may not.

For example, for some people, meaningful work could be raising a family. But for others, raising a family, while important, doesn't utilize their talents, gifts, and strengths in the way that other work does. Same goes for volunteer work: it's a wonderful thing to do, but if it doesn't use your talents, gifts, and strengths, it's not meaningful work *for you*.

What makes work meaningful is that *you* feel it matters, and that, in doing it, you express your greatest gifts (or take a step toward expressing those gifts). It engages your curiosity. It asks you to stretch beyond your limits and become more.

In this way, a new high school graduate might find meaningful work in an internship because it presents new challenges. A woman who always depended on her husband for income might find meaningful work in a coffee shop because it increases her self-esteem and gives her a new level of independence.

Meaningful work always involves working in a job you love. You may not love it every day, but overall, you do. Meaningful work also feels *satisfying*—again, not every single minute, but overall.

It may take you a while to find your meaningful work. And then, once you've found it …

Your Meaningful Work Could Change

Oh, I know that adolescent part of you who just wants to "get this done and over with" is appalled by the fact that your meaningful work could shift and change.

But, you see, life isn't about "getting it over with." It's about growth, change, and enjoying the process. The work that felt meaningful in your twenties may burn you out in your forties. What filled you with purpose when your family was young may be boring to you when you're an empty-nester.

If this happens, it's okay. Each and every work experience you have will build on itself to bring you to the next level of your meaningful work—and that next level will offer you an even greater opportunity to share your gifts with the world in a deep and impactful way.

No matter what stage you're at, the most important thing to remember is to …

Follow Your Passion & Trust The Process

If you follow what excites you, at every stage of your life, and change the beliefs that say you can't be both abundant and follow your passion, you will absolutely be led to your meaningful work (not to mention your destiny). Suddenly, the idea of a work-free retirement won't feel so wonderful after all.

Oftentimes the ultimate "work we love" isn't a straight line. Although that adolescent part of us wants to "just get there", the wiser part of us knows it is a process that will reveal itself each step along the way.

And, if you like a lot of things about your current job, but it's not totally right or meaningful, you can always recreate it to be the work you love!

Let's face it: there is no right or wrong when it comes to work. The only right or wrong is what is right or wrong for you. And hey, if you create it all, why not create "meaningful work" that fits you absolutely perfectly, and that offers you opportunities to rock your best assets in ways you totally love? Why not create work that fills you with happiness and joy—and do it every day, knowing, beyond a shadow of a doubt, that abundance will find its way to you—either through this work or via another avenue—because abundance is your choice?

If you created work like this, you wouldn't have to wait until retirement to start enjoying your abundant life. In fact, you'd probably never want to stop working, because you'd consistently be creating joy and abundance every day!

And that brings us to the last unsupportive abundance dream ...

GETTING RICH AND GIVING IT ALL AWAY

Dearest heart, I hear your unselfish wish to create abundance in order to donate it to your friends, family, and the neediest charities, and make the world a better place. All that money could make so many people's lives better, easier, and more joyful.

I bless you for your benevolence. But it just won't work.

Excuse me? I thought it was all about using what I have to make the world a better place!

You're right, it is—especially when it comes to your talents, gifts, strengths, passion, purpose, and meaningful work. But if you want to create abundance only to give it all away, there are some problems in your logic and belief systems that will keep the abundance you seek from entering your life (at least, in a prolific and super-elegant way).

First, I have to share an absolute truth: *Throwing money at a problem doesn't help!*

We've been conditioned to believe that, if we can just figure out what's causing the problems in the world, and bring enough attention to those causes, we can make the problems go away. But that isn't true.

Problems exist in the world because those same problems exist inside each and every one of us. We let these problems happen, not because we want them, but because we don't know (yet) how to eradicate them from the inside out.

So if the real cause of the world's problems is our consciousness (and it is), all the money in the world won't solve those problems.

Of course there are diseases you would love to see eradicated, and causes you feel passionate about. But "warring against" what you hate only brings more to hate. Instead, I suggest you love the opposite of what you thought you hated: health, humanity, wholeness, and compassion.

If you want to use the abundance you create to make the world a better place, don't dream of creating money to "fight" the problem. Instead, dream of a solution to the problem. Dream of a world where the problem no longer exists.

The same philosophy applies, on a smaller scale, to family and friends.

Why Helping Family and Friends Isn't Always a Great Idea

We love our family. We love our friends. We want to help them. But *it isn't always a good idea*, and the guilt, resentment, anger and martyrdom that come up around this issue can stop your abundance from manifesting!

This is something *everyone* needs to get clear on. Whether you want to create wealth to give away to your loved ones who are struggling, or you are frightened that if you create tons of wealth your loved ones will expect you to be their fairy godmother, the issue of gifting money to those you love is filled with confusion.

Financial handouts are a muddy, messy area. And you have to have clean energy (i.e. energy with no hesitation) to create abundance.

So here's the bottom line: you've been taught to believe money solves problems, and that if you love someone, you should *always* fix his or her problems if you can.

But by seeking to "fix" their problems, we may be robbing our loved ones of *the very thing they created their problem to obtain*—the empowerment to heal it themselves.

You see, the minute you say to your loved one, "Don't

worry, I'll solve your problem," you essentially say to them, "You are unable to solve your problems for yourself. You are not powerful, smart, or savvy enough to do this on your own. And, because you are so [less than/lame/undeniably lacking/choose your derogatory term], I have to solve your problem for you."

Come on, now. Is that the message you want to send to those you love?

Of course not! You would never say that to someone you care about. But in order to be able to disconnect from the codependent part of you, you may have to change some negative beliefs, like:

- I AM RESPONSIBLE FOR [NAME] IN EVERY WAY.
- IF [NAME] CHOOSES TO SUFFER, I MUST SUFFER ALONG WITH THEM.
- [NAME] CANNOT SURVIVE UNLESS I TAKE RESPONSIBILITY FOR THEM.
- [NAME] IS YOUNG, INNOCENT, AND VULNERABLE.
- [NAME] IS UNABLE TO BE SUCCESSFUL IN THE WORLD WITHOUT HELP.
- [NAME] HAS DEBILITATING ISSUES THAT PREVENT THEIR SUCCESS.
- I CAN'T LOVE [NAME] WITHOUT BEING PULLED INTO NEGATIVE EMOTIONS SUCH AS GUILT, SHAME, AND FAILURE.
- IF I DON'T GIVE [NAME] WHAT THEY WANT, THEN I OWE THEM.

- IF I DON'T HELP [NAME], THEY WON'T LOVE ME ANYMORE.
- IT IS EMPOWERING TO THOSE I LOVE FOR ME TO FIX THEIR PROBLEMS.
- BY FIXING OTHERS' PROBLEMS, I PROVE MY OWN WORTH.

Of course, I'm referring to adults here. If your children are under eighteen, of course they can (and should) depend upon you. But once they, and others, are adults, there is no reason why they cannot create abundance, just as you're doing. To rob them of that opportunity is to rob them of their power.

Don't enable those you love to stay helpless. Be the example. Show them how it's done, while compassionately detaching from their dramas. Allow them to create whatever realities will help them learn and grow.

However …

Please Don't Misunderstand

I'm not saying that it's bad or wrong to support charities, or to give your loved ones a helping hand. There are all kinds of charities that provide great services, and which merit your support, time, and money. And, sometimes, family and friends really *do* need temporary assistance. I've received gifts from friends and relatives that totally rocked my world and gave me the boost I needed to take the next step on my journey.

All I'm saying is, don't let bailing others out become your sole motivation to create abundance in your life. There is a fine line between "fixing" and supporting a new future.

How can you tell what your motivation is?

Ask yourself, "If I give money to solve this problem, do I truly expect this situation to be fully healed and resolved? Do I think the people involved will be empowered?"

If the answer is no, change the beliefs that are keeping you in this place of conflict.

Always solve the problems *inside* of you before trying to solve the problems *outside* of you. If you don't accept abundance within, and for, yourself first, you are unlikely to create it for anyone else.

But there's one more facet to this money dream that undermines your successful creation of abundance, and that is ...

Your Wish To Give It All Away Tells You the Reason Why You Won't Create It

The fact that you want to create abundance only to give it all away tells me you have some beliefs about abundance, money, the world, and yourself that will not allow you to create wealth.

You wouldn't declare, "Don't give me an abundance of air. Save it for others who need it more. I would prefer to struggle for every breath I take, as long as others can breathe deeply and fully." That would be silly. What do you gain by struggling for every breath while others enjoy limitless oxygen? Nothing! Yet that is precisely what you're declaring when you say that you're okay with creating money, as long as it's not for yourself.

Yes, your desire to create wealth to give it away tells you that your beliefs need to change.

In order to get at those tricky beliefs that make you think it is a good thing to give all of your (as yet un-manifested) money away, begin by examining why you don't want to keep at least some of this money you seek.

Ask yourself these questions:

Do I believe money is as plentiful as air? Or do I believe that there is a limited supply, and if I keep "more than my fair share" I will deprive others who need it more than me?

Then, consider whether you hold these beliefs:

- I LIVE IN A UNIVERSE WITH A LIMITED AMOUNT OF ABUNDANCE.
- THERE IS A LIMITED AMOUNT OF MONEY ON THIS PLANET.
- THERE ISN'T ENOUGH MONEY TO GO AROUND.
- IF I TAKE MORE THAN JUST ENOUGH MONEY, OTHERS WILL SUFFER.

Do I believe it is somehow wrong to want an abundance of money for myself?

Consider whether you hold these beliefs:

- IT IS GREEDY TO WANT AN ABUNDANCE OF MONEY.
- IT IS UNSPIRITUAL TO WANT AN ABUNDANCE OF MONEY.
- A GOOD PERSON GIVES AWAY HIS/HER MONEY.
- IT IS SELFISH TO WANT LOTS OF MONEY FOR MYSELF.

Do I think that giving money to charities or my family will solve their problems?

Consider whether you hold these beliefs:

- IF I DON'T HELP THE NEEDY, THEY WON'T BE HELPED.
- THE BEST WAY TO CREATE CHANGE IS THROUGH FINANCIAL SUPPORT.
- I AM POWERLESS TO CHANGE THE WORLD AROUND ME EXCEPT THROUGH MONEY.
- THOSE I LOVE AND CARE ABOUT ARE POWERLESS TO CHANGE THEIR CIRCUMSTANCES WITHOUT ADDITIONAL RESOURCES.

Do I think I'm worthy or deserving of the gifts of abundance—such as freedom, ease, security, and wealth?

Consider these core beliefs:

- I DON'T DESERVE ABUNDANCE.
- I DON'T DESERVE A LIFE I LOVE.
- I AM NOT WORTHY OF UNLIMITED ABUNDANCE.
- I AM NOT WORTHY OF A LIFE I LOVE.

The above are beliefs, not facts. If you don't change these (and similar) beliefs, you won't allow abundance to enter your life for any reason.

But here's a hopeful truth for big-hearted, loving, compassionate people the world over …

REAL PROSPERITY & ABUNDANCE BENEFIT ALL MANKIND

You are always impacting the world around you by your resonance. Whenever you raise your resonance to create an increase in abundance (or any other good thing) in your life, you're impacting others positively.

It can be no other way; this is the way our universe works. What is good for you is good for the world. So be abundant—for yourself, and for others!

A TRUE STORY OF CONSCIOUSLY CREATING ABUNDANCE

In 2008, my partner was in and out of the hospital with life-threatening health issues. At the same time, my income dropped significantly. Almost overnight, we could no longer afford to live in San Francisco. Our house had lost its value. We managed to sell it just before foreclosure.

It was a terrifying time. We had invested our life savings in our (now devalued) house, and owed the real estate agent $2,000 to close the sale. Money was scarce—and now, we, our four dogs, and our cat were without a place to live.

My credit was still good, thankfully, and I was able to get a job transfer. We chose Austin, Texas for our next home. We had to move not only our animals but also a large collection of valuables and everything else we owned. I worried about pulling it all off.

I made a wish board to keep myself positive. This project was a light for me in a very dark tunnel. I was very specific about what I added to my board. I printed a photo of a house I wanted to buy in Austin, and one of a new truck for my partner. I also added a photo of myself with Bobbi Brown, the makeup artist whose company I had worked for and wanted to work for again.

While the movers packed our belongings, I tearfully said goodbye to our gorgeous home. I almost forgot my wish board, but at the last minute grabbed it to pack in my car. In a fit of anger over my circumstances, I ripped off the photo of Bobbi Brown and me and tore it into pieces.

Miraculously, we were able to buy a dream home in Austin. The house was even better than the one on my board! We also bought my partner the truck she wanted. The visualizing I did through my wish board made our dreams come true!

However, I never got the position working with Bobbi Brown, despite the fact that I had very strong connections, had worked with the company for years, and knew her assistant personally.

It just goes to show that we really do get everything we ask for!

- Deborah S.

ABUNDANCE-ALTERING TAKEAWAYS

- You desire more than an abundance of money. You also want an abundance of freedom, health, love, happiness, peace, safety, security, and fun, because without these additional abundances, money itself can be nearly (if not completely) useless.

- If you set your sights on winning the lottery (or being "rescued" by some other lump sum of cash) as your only path to abundance, you're effectively telling the universe: "I want my money to come to me the only way I can imagine it coming, even though it's the least likely way possible, because I am not powerful enough to create abundance any other way."

- If you want to create lots of money to retire early and travel the world (or just sit at home and watch TV forevermore), you're not likely to allow yourself to succeed. Meaningful work is a part of a meaningful life for every human being on the planet.

- By seeking to "fix" their problems, we may not be empowering our loved ones to heal their problems, but instead robbing them of the very thing they created the problem to obtain.

- Whenever you raise your resonance to create abundance (or any other good thing in your life), you're benefitting all mankind.

YOUR NEXT STEPS

- Have you been waiting for your abundance to appear through the lottery or some other "lucky break"? If so, what beliefs can you change to enable broader possibilities for your wealth?

- Have you dreamt that you'd get rich, retire, and never have to work again? Which beliefs about work and your personal gifts, talents, and strengths need to be changed to shift that vision?

- Is your motivation for creating abundance to give it all away? Why do you think you've held that dream? What beliefs might you want to change to expand it?

- If you're not sure which (if any) negative beliefs you're carrying, use the applied kinesiology techniques in Appendix B to test for constricting beliefs. Document the beliefs that need to be changed, and then change them as soon as possible using one of the techniques in Appendix D.

CHAPTER FIVE

What *Do* You Want?

"Abundance is the ability to do what you need to do, when you need to do it. It's not a checkbook balance."

~ BASHAR

Now we get to the exciting part—dreaming your juicy, fulfilling, succulent future of abundance!

As I've mentioned before, no dream about abundance is inherently wrong. No matter what you want, you *can* have it. The universe always says "yes."

But, here's the catch: just because it's possible to create something doesn't mean you will create it.

The universe always says "yes"—but if you're sending out mixed messages through subconscious negative beliefs, the universe is saying "yes" to *all* of your contradictory desires, many of which will sabotage each other, cancel each other out, or place conditional restrictions on each other.

It's my intention to help you *create* what you desire. But because the concept of money is twisted and weighty in most people's subconscious minds, we need to untangle all of your conscious, subconscious, and unconscious beliefs and desires so that you can send a clear message to the universe and get exactly what you ask for, and more, with no strings attached.

I want to make you aware of what is going on beneath the surface of your dreams in order to heal and change any energy that may be sabotaging them. I also intend to help you get clear on what it is you truly desire—because *true desires are always creatable.*

That's why, in this chapter, we're going to take a close look at the details of what you say you want, and see if we can figure out the rest of the (subconscious) story.

Because ...

THE "WHAT" TELLS A STORY

When people first learn about conscious creation, many have a tendency to put limits on their dreams, especially when it comes to money. I encourage folks to dream big, yet when I ask them what kind of financial abundance they want to create, many respond with, "Not a lot."

If your answer to that question is something like, "I only want a little bit of money," "I don't need much to be happy," or, "I just want enough to be comfortable," you may hold some beliefs that can sabotage your abundance.

Now, please don't misunderstand me: there is nothing wrong with embracing a simple life with simple needs, *if* that's truly what makes you happy.

But if the underlying reason for such statements is that you don't feel you deserve a lot of money, that it's somehow wrong to want money, that if you "take" a lot of money it leaves less for others, or that eschewing money makes you a better or more spiritual person, chances are you have some beliefs you'll want to change, such as:

- I DON'T DESERVE TO BE RICH.
- I DON'T DESERVE TO BE ABUNDANT.
- I AM NOT GOOD ENOUGH TO BE WEALTHY.
- MONEY IN THIS WORLD IS LIMITED.
- IF I CREATE MORE MONEY FOR MYSELF, SOMEONE WILL GO WITHOUT.
- IT IS WRONG TO DESIRE MONEY.
- MONEY IS BAD.
- SPIRITUAL PEOPLE DO NOT DESIRE MONEY.
- GOOD PEOPLE DO NOT SEEK TO BE WEALTHY.

If you don't change those beliefs, you won't allow yourself even the little bit of money you say you want.

Did you get that? Being "nice" can work against you, because your "niceness" may be based in guilt, self-sacrifice, martyrdom, and other beliefs that will *deny* you abundance.

In order to get rich, you have to get real—whatever that looks like for you. If you're constantly judging what you want, and how much you want, you will keep sabotaging your creations and blocking your manifestations.

God doesn't care how much money you have. Why would He? Does He judge how much dirt you have in your backyard, or how many hairs you have on your head? Of course not. Why would He judge one illusion and not another? When you think about it, the concept is ridiculous.

Those outdated, archaic concepts about money and abundance weren't put there by God—they were put there by people. And you accepted them, without question, from authority figures, religions, society, the media, and your prior experience with this illusion we call Earth. Now, those sabotaging beliefs are solidly entrenched in your subconscious mind.

You can change these beliefs. But first, you need to discover them.

It's not just "too little" that can indicate problems—"too much" also sets off an alarm. If your dream is to create ten billion dollars, you might want to ask yourself why you might need so much money.

But you just said I could create anything I want!

Yes, and I meant it. But why would you want $10,000,000,000? Could it be that you're afraid of running out of money, and you think that if you create an absurdly huge amount you'll never have to worry about running out? Because if that's the reason, your dream shows me that you really don't trust the universe, or you don't trust yourself to manifest abundance whenever you need or want it.

If you think you need to create a large amount of money in case of some calamity, or in case you can't manifest money in the future, you may hold beliefs such as:

- I CAN'T TRUST MONEY TO COME IN EXACTLY WHEN I NEED OR WANT IT.
- I CAN'T TRUST MYSELF TO CREATE MONEY WHEN I NEED OR WANT IT.

- I HAVE TO BE UBER-PREPARED IN CASE OF EMERGENCY.
- JUST WHEN SOME THINGS GO RIGHT, THE OTHER SHOE WILL DROP.
- I MAY BE ABLE TO MANIFEST MONEY SOMETIMES, BUT NOT ALL THE TIME.

Or, you may want the huge amount of money to show other people that you're not a loser, or that you're better than them. Both reasons demonstrate beliefs that *you* are not valuable—beliefs such as:

- I AM NOT WORTHY.
- MY WORTH IS BASED ON WHAT I HAVE, NOT WHO I AM.
- I AM NOT VALUABLE.
- I AM A FAILURE.
- I AM A DISAPPOINTMENT.

If anything here rings a bell for you, make a note of it. Later in this book, you'll learn how to change beliefs like these—beliefs that have messed with your abundance and conscious creation for your entire life.

It's not just the "what" that bears paying attention to. In addition …

THE "WHY" TELLS A STORY

When I ask people about their dreams and desires, many begin by saying, "I want to have a lot of money." It's only when I ask them why they want the money that they reveal the real truth of their dreams, and the sabotaging beliefs that are getting in the way of creating those dreams.

We addressed some of these "whys," such as wanting money so you can quit your job and retire early, and wanting money in order to give it away. If either of these have been your motivations I strongly urge you to discover your specific beliefs underlying your reasoning and change them.

But there is another common "why" that isn't easy to look at ...

Wanting Money to Prove Something to Someone (or to Yourself)

Many of us feel inadequate in one way or another—like we will never measure up to others or their expectations for us (not to mention our expectations for ourselves). We feel, sometimes subconsciously, that if we became rich and successful it will prove something about us—maybe that we're not a loser, maybe that our parents, siblings, ex, etc., were indeed wrong about us, or that we were wrong about ourselves.

In my late twenties, I decided to go back to school to complete my Bachelor's degree. I was hoping the degree would make me feel valuable, but it didn't. I then applied to an MBA program, and then decided to add a JD to the MBA and also started attending law school. These choices weren't motivated by a love of business or the law, but rather by my desire to be thought of as smart, interesting, and successful. I very specifically remembered thinking, "I need something impressive to talk about at cocktail parties."

Back then I used wealth and status as a measure of success—which, given the reality I had created at that point in my life, always left me feeling "not quite good enough."

Today my gauge for success is happiness, staying present, and following my passion. Ironically, I find it takes more courage, consciousness, and wisdom to stick to my current definition than to my previous one.

If your secret motivation for money is to prove you are not flawed, that you are enough, that you are better than others, or that you are as worthy as others, it will undermine your dreams for abundance. Try as you might, you will never, ever create the security, confidence, and certainty you're looking for, because *money cannot provide those things.* The more you make money responsible for creating your self-worth, the more money will elude you.

Your worth, your value, your divinity, is inherent within you. Nothing can prove it—but nothing can disprove it, either. It simply *is.* Any "evidence" you have to the contrary is tied to a sabotaging belief, such as:

- I NEED MONEY AND SUCCESS TO PROVE I AM WORTHY.
- I AM INHERENTLY FLAWED, AND THEREFORE UNABLE TO CREATE ABUNDANCE.
- I MUST BE SUCCESSFUL IN ORDER TO PROVE I AM AS GOOD AS [NAME].
- I AM NOT GOOD ENOUGH.

Beliefs can be changed, but not by money.

And, while we're looking at the stories our dreams can tell, we must also remember that …

THE "HOW" TELLS A STORY

When I ask people to think about how money might come to them, they generally have a short list of possibilities.

What tops the list? The lottery.

I've already outlined the reasons you'll want to steer clear of trying to create winning the lottery. But if this was your dream (and I burst your bubble—sorry!), you may hold beliefs such as:

- THE UNIVERSE IS NOT ABUNDANT.
- MONEY CAN COME TO ME ONLY IN VERY LIMITED WAYS.
- THE ONLY WAY I CAN BECOME EXTREMELY WEALTHY IS BY WINNING THE LOTTERY.
- MONEY IS DIFFICULT TO CREATE.
- I AM NOT CAPABLE OF CREATING MONEY OUT OF THIN AIR.
- I AM NOT SMART ENOUGH TO CREATE MONEY OTHER THAN BY WINNING IT.
- YOU HAVE TO BE SMART OR LUCKY TO CREATE MONEY.
- I NEED TO RECEIVE MONEY FROM SOMEONE OR SOMETHING OUTSIDE MYSELF, BECAUSE I CAN'T CREATE IT ON MY OWN.

The lottery dream isn't the only limiting idea out there. Here are some other ways people think money must show up for them:

- Their current job (they must get a raise or promotion).
- A new job (they must leave their current job).
- Moving away from their current city/state/country.
- Their spouse's (or future spouse's) income.
- An inheritance or court settlement.

If you find yourself thinking along these lines, realize that your belief system has you locked in a box—and it's not a box of abundance. If this is the case, don't worry. You have the key. It's called *changing your beliefs*!

Right now, we are discovering the beliefs you may hold around abundance and how they can show up in your reality, so make note of any beliefs you think you have (even if you're not totally sure). The changing part will come later.

Before we move on, there's one more aspect of your dreams for abundance that can clue you in about your beliefs, and that is ...

THE "WHEN" TELLS A STORY

A friend once asked me how long it would take me to create abundance and start living the life I longed to live. I thought for a moment and said, "Ten years."

She looked at me and said, "That's when your children will be graduating and leaving home. Do you think there is a link there?"

She was right. I had a belief that I couldn't earn a good income while my boys were still living with me. You'd better believe I changed *that* belief right away.

You might have similar stipulations and excuses about when you will be able to create your abundance, such as:

- When I'm older.
- When I'm wiser.
- When I lose weight.
- When I'm divorced.
- When I'm married.
- When I finish my education.
- When my parents don't need me as much.
- When my spouse _________.
- When my kids _________.
- When my parents _________.

These are not real limitations, unless you create them as such. Again, make note of any of these excuses that are showing up in your reality. At first glance, they may seem like obstacles, but they are really nuggets of gold. You can call them "gold futures," because each and every one you change means more money in your pocket.

Once you've noted these beliefs, but before you move on to decide exactly what abundance you want to create, ask yourself …

WHERE ARE YOU NOW?

One of the most important considerations in creating abundance is to be honest about where you are right now. It may be hard to admit that your reality isn't what you want it to be, but honesty at this point will make the difference between the survival and the death of your "abundant self."

Imagine, for a moment, that one of your dreams is to climb K2, the second highest mountain in the world. You know that *one in five* climbers die trying to summit its peak. So what do you need to do in order to live through the experience?

You need time, preparation, and patience. Your to-do list might look something like this:

- Begin your training at least a year in advance, to gradually build muscle.
- Slowly increase your aerobic stamina.
- Climb lower hills with heavy packs.
- Gain weight (because you'll lose up to 20% of your body weight in the climb).
- Take a mountaineering course.
- Climb a lower mountain in preparation.
- Travel to other similar altitudes to learn to acclimate.
- Prepare mentally for the challenges.
- Schedule the time needed.
- Commit and plan for the finances necessary.
- Know what you'll be expected to bring, and purchase it.

It's a lot to take on, but this is serious stuff. You don't want to die in the pursuit of this dream.

So, my friend, if you would go through all that to climb a mountain—an activity which, while super-cool and amazing, isn't necessary to everyday life—why would you give any less attention to your abundance, which *is* part of your everyday life? Why shouldn't your pursuit of financial abundance and independence warrant the same level of preparation, time, and patience?

The difference, in most people's minds, is that climbing K2 is a matter of life or death. Creating abundance (beyond basic survival needs) feels less pressing because life itself isn't at stake.

But what if an aspect of your life *was* at stake? What if your abundant self could actually *die* as a result of neglect, poor preparation, or uninformed decisions?

It can happen. I've seen it. People just lie down and give up. They deny what's really happening in their world, and instead accept that the reality of struggle and lack that they've created is the *only* reality they can have. When that happens, their abundant selves die slow, lingering, painful deaths, and never come back in this lifetime.

I was perusing a website about climbing K2 and a man had posed this question online:

> *Can I climb K2 with no experience, and no training or lessons? I have no mountaineering experience, I have no rock climbing experience, and I have never even put on a crampon. I have a fear of heights, and have no interest in training, or being taught any of these things, but am thinking of climbing K2. I have a sturdy pair of walking boots, an overcoat, a scarf, a hat, Levi's, gloves, and a rope: what's the bet I conquer it?*

As you might imagine, he was laughed off the message board.

If you say you want to be a millionaire, and yet you haven't created enough money to move out of your parent's attic, you're being just as silly.

The lesson here: If you fool yourself about where you are right now, you may sabotage your ability to reach your own personal financial summit. And if you treat the information in this book as woo-woo, airy-fairy stuff that may or may not work, your chances of realizing your dreams are about as high as that dude's chances of climbing K2: not even slim to none. Just none.

You can create an abundant reality, just like you can climb K2—but *only if you do the work.*

I, for one, do not want to see your "abundant self" die. I want your hopes and dreams to live, and I want you to grow into the person I know you can be: a self-empowered, totally abundant human being who loves every second of life.

So, where do you begin?

Begin Where You Are

Your dream should be a stretch, but not a stretch out of the ballpark.

If you're currently unemployed and running out of credit, your "starter" dream might be finding a job and catching up on your bills, and putting aside a little nest egg.

If you're just meeting your bills, you might dream about some extra money for a vacation or a remodel.

If you want to quit your job and start your own company, dream about a bank account with a nice cushion which will sustain you while you create a job you love.

If you want to move to another state, see yourself happily in that state without a worry in the world.

Dream big, but be honest with yourself about the *believability* of that dream (to you). You can always dream a bigger dream tomorrow, or next week, or next year. After all, you need to be sure you can handle a two-mile hike before you plan for the K2!

Another important point as you begin dreaming your dream is to …

SEPARATE MONEY FROM WORK

Most people see work and money as closely intertwined. They have difficulty even thinking of them separately.

Of course they're intertwined. How do you think I'm going to create money if not from my job?

Well, there are a million ways to create money. But I'm not going to tell you about them right now, because if I did, you'd be too busy trying them all on for size (and considering whether to implement one or two). You'd go about it exactly the way most people do, by trying to figure out what to do to make extra cash. That's backwards thinking.

In order to consciously create money, you need to take on the essence of money by thinking about, feeling, and believing in abundance. From that essence-inspired place, you will be guided to take action to create abundance. You'll make that phone call, e-mail that friend, pick up that paper, or buy a book on that new idea you've been mulling over. When you do this, opportunities will present themselves, first in little ways and then in bigger and bigger ways. Then, finally, the money will roll in.

Living an abundant life will require that you trust the universe to deliver it without trying to figure out how it will look. This detachment from the "outcome" of your creations will be much easier if you separate abundance from work when it comes to creating them both. Otherwise, you risk falling into the trap of thinking that your work is the only way to create abundance.

Try to think about money coming to you not from your job, but from the universe. Your job might be where the money ends up coming from—and it might not. It's not really up to you. Ideally, you don't even care, or think about it much at all. You've chosen to be wealthy; it's up to the universe to figure out how to make that happen.

Also, begin to think about work as something you do because you love it, not because it pays you. Abundance will find its way to you no matter what job you take, because the universe—not your employer—provides it for you.

But I don't believe that!

Then *change* those beliefs! They may be something like:

- I CAN ONLY CREATE WEALTH THROUGH MY JOB.
- I CAN'T LOVE WHAT I DO AND BE WELL-PAID AT THE SAME TIME.
- IT IS DIFFICULT TO FIND A JOB I ADORE.
- I CAN'T LEAVE A PROFESSION IN WHICH I'VE INVESTED SO MUCH TIME AND/OR EDUCATION.
- I DON'T KNOW WHAT MY PASSION IS.
- I DON'T KNOW HOW TO CREATE A JOB I LOVE AND ABUNDANCE TOO.

There are no shortcuts to belief work. Your reality will not shift unless you change your subconscious mind along with your conscious mind.

If you don't separate work and money in your creation process, you'll risk selling out. You might get stuck in a job you don't like because it provides "security." When you do that, you tell the universe, "Money is difficult to create. I must sacrifice my dreams and myself to have enough money." You end up working for money rather than allowing the universe to work for you. And then you begin to resent your job and hate your life—which is not fun. And of course, that situation will create more to hate, and the cycle will continue.

When you make work you love a part of your dream, along with an abundance of money, you'll be rich *and* fulfilled—not to mention excited to wake up every day.

However ...

If You Can't Be With The Job You Love, Love The Job You're With

Moving from a life of struggle and scarcity to a life of ease and abundance won't happen overnight—but it won't happen at all if you're broadcasting dissatisfaction and resentment to the universe.

Even though you may still be at a job you aren't crazy about, you can shift your resonance around the job you're in and create more change, sooner.

Can I really change my situation by pretending to love my job?

No, not by *pretending* to love your job. If you do that, you'll still be flowing dissatisfaction every day (underneath the pretending). Instead, remember why you took the job in the first place, and focus on all the things that are good about it.

What if there's nothing good about it?

Impossible. There is something good about *everything.*

Maybe it's the tree outside your office window. Maybe it's the menial tasks that give your mind freedom to dream. Maybe it's working with people you like and respect. Maybe it's seeing a co-worker who has become a friend.

There *are* things you like about your job. You just need to uncover them.

From this moment on, think only about the good things about your job. First and foremost: you are getting a paycheck, right? Be grateful for everything you possibly can. Ignore the bad.

But if I ignore the bad, I'll become complacent and never find a new job!

That is a myth. And maybe even a belief like:

- IF I'M GRATEFUL FOR SOMETHING I CLOSE THE DOOR TO RECEIVING MORE.

Remember, your feelings create. When you feel happy, grateful, and abundant, you will get more things in your life that make you feel happy, grateful, and abundant.

But it must be genuine. Saying something is good when underneath you hate it won't fool the universe.

And while you love whatever you can find to love about the job you have …

Dream a Job You Love Even More

Imagine yourself in a job you adore. Imagine that your new motto is, "Thank God it's Monday!" You don't need to know what the job will be, or how much it will pay. You don't even need to know the industry it might be in. Just know that you'll discover it, and love it—and let the universe handle the rest.

This is a tough one for a lot of people. It's hard for me, too, at times. But it is a *critical* concept in conscious creation. You will be far more effective at both creating abundance *and* creating professional success if you keep the two separate in your mind and in your intentions.

Keeping work and money separate allows you to see the beliefs associated with each more easily. It also forces you to open up possibilities for abundance beyond your job, giving the universe many more avenues to fill your pockets.

Most importantly, it allows your professional success to be more fulfilling. When you think of work being the only avenue to create money, you begin to value your work according to how much it nets you financially, instead of how much fulfillment and joy it brings.

Also, it's important to remember ...

YOUR ABUNDANCE WON'T LOOK LIKE YOUR NEIGHBOR'S ABUNDANCE

I've said it before, and I'll say it again: you can't control what your dream will look like when it manifests.

People look at the lifestyle I created for more than a decade and ask, "Can I create private jets, sailboats, and homes in two countries like you did?"

Of course! Anything is possible. But when you're creating money and other forms of abundance, it's more elegant to *let go of the form*. It gives the universe many more possibilities to make you happy.

If you have a passion for sailing, creating a sailboat makes sense. But creating the trappings just to say you have them won't serve you.

Interestingly enough, I never set out to create the kind of lifestyle I created. I also never intended to create a multi-million-dollar marketing company. Why did it manifest that way?

I don't really know why our creations come in one form rather than another. I just know the universe mirrors the emotion you put out with more "realities" that bring you the same emotion.

And I also know what I did. I focused on *having fun*. I focused on *loving what I did*. I felt *gratitude for each and every dime* that came my way, as well as for the beauty, elegance, and ease of my life.

The universe gives you more of what you pay attention to. And so, I received more fun, love, money, ease, and elegance—some of which happened to show up in the form of homes, boats, and private planes.

I didn't know how that "more" would show up; I just trusted that the "more" would be right for me, no matter what it looked like. You don't know how your "more" will show up, either. If you let it be open-ended, your whole life can be one delightful surprise after another, and full of abundant realities you never even thought of.

But if you try to control what shows up, and when, and how, you are likely to struggle all along the way.

You can feel the difference in the two energies, can't you?

One says, "I trust the universe to deliver wonderful, abundant realities that will delight me in every way."

The other says, "I want this because I don't really trust the universe or my ability to create. Therefore, I must control each and every step."

What Will Be the Same?

What *will* be the same, for every person under the sun, is that the essence of the reality will match the essence you put out.

If you are focused on creating financial security, you might feel secure once you've set up a $1,000 emergency fund. Your neighbor, on the other hand, might feel secure once his mortgage is paid off. These realities can both bring feelings of security, even though they are different "forms" (and require vastly different amounts of money). In both cases, the result will match exactly the essence the dreamer puts out.

Projecting an overall essence (through your thoughts, feelings, and beliefs) of needing a *little* abundance will prompt the universe to respond with a reality that makes you *feel a little abundant*. That might mean a slight pay raise, or finding $20 on the street.

And, you know what? That's okay. Start where you are, remember? As you build your abundance, you will also build your belief in your power and ability to consciously create abundance. Ideally, as your belief grows stronger, you'll build on it, bit by bit, increasing your essence of abundance and allowing your reality to become more and more fruitful.

The essence you put forth is up to you, but the universe *must* respond to it exactly as you put it out. How you feel will result in more realities that make you feel the same way.

But I want to live the lifestyle of the rich and famous!

No, you don't. You don't want to live someone else's life, no matter how much you think you do. Why would you? It wouldn't make you happy. (Honestly, that life may not even be making them happy!)

What *will* make you happy is creating your version of rich and abundant. You'll want to be financially secure, financially free to do what you want to do, and enjoying a reality that feels prosperous and abundant *to you*.

Create what makes you happy. Live your happy life. Be open to the fact that it will probably look different than anyone else's, and your abundance will come more quickly and elegantly than you ever dreamed possible.

Let the universe show you what your "lifestyle of the abundant and magical" looks like. The form may surprise you, but the feelings you get when you receive it won't.

WHERE DO YOU BEGIN YOUR DREAM OF ABUNDANCE?

So—what do you want?

I want to be rich.

Yes—we all do. But what does being "rich" mean to you? What does it give you? What will you receive by becoming rich?

I'd like you to think about what it *feels* like to be fully abundant. What if you really did have a magic lamp, complete with a genie? What if you absolutely knew that your lamp would grant unlimited wishes, forever? What if, whenever you wanted something, you could just rub the lamp and your genie would pop out to grant your wish?

Your first thought might be about the things you desire. Let those go for now, and think about the emotional states you would enjoy—the freedom, security, peace, excitement, ease, elegance, beauty, expansiveness, creativity, and fun you could have—if you had instant access to all the money, abundance, and magic in the world.

And then ...

WRITE OUT YOUR INTENTIONS

The strongest way to begin to bring any reality into being is to write an *intention*.

Intentions are more than statements of desire. They are a *commitment to create*. They also acknowledge you may already have some (or all) of what you are intending, but that you will continue to create more of it. They are a strong plan and expectation for something to manifest.

Well, that feels really good, but what if I want a new house or car or pedigreed poodle? Is that not okay?

That is absolutely okay. But you see, there are different kinds of intentions. We'll get to your specific dreams (like cars and poodles) when we write your *immediate intentions*. But for now, let's create your ...

Overall Intention

This will be your main intention for living your life. Your overall intention might read something like this:

I INTEND TO LIVE A LIFE FILLED WITH JOY, CREATIVITY, LOVE, PASSION, EXCITEMENT, SPIRITUAL CONNECTION, FUN, ENERGY, HEALTH, HEALING, LEARNING, GROWING, HAPPINESS, AND ABUNDANCE!

Next, add intentions for all the different categories of your life (health, love, money, work, relationships, etc.). These are your ...

Core Intentions

These intentions should be as nonspecific as possible. So instead of this money intention—

I INTEND TO CREATE A BILLION DOLLARS BY INHERITING IT FROM AN UNKNOWN RELATIVE.

—consider this instead:

I INTEND TO CREATE A LIFE OF UNLIMITED ABUNDANCE IN WHICH MONEY, OPPORTUNITIES, IDEAS, CONNECTIONS, AND ALL FORMS OF WEALTH COME TO ME EFFORTLESSLY, WITH HARM TO NONE.

Write separate core intentions for every area of your life.(1)

When you're done, we'll move on to those specific things you want to create—the things you're focused on right now. I call these your ...

(1) You can find sample intentions beyond the abundance intentions covered in this book at www.LiveALifeYouLove.com/sample-intentions.

Immediate Intentions

Your immediate intentions are where you list the specific things you desire right now. They might read something like this:

I INTEND TO TRAVEL TO EUROPE NEXT YEAR.

I INTEND TO BUY A BEAUTIFUL HOUSE WITH AT LEAST 4 BEDROOMS AND 2.5 BATHS.

I INTEND TO CREATE A JOB I LOVE BY THE END OF THE YEAR.

I INTEND TO CREATE A NEW AUDI S5 CONVERTIBLE, WHITE WITH RED LEATHER INTERIOR.

I INTEND TO DOUBLE MY INCOME WITHIN THE NEXT YEAR.

But in order to give the above intentions even more of a boost, I suggest adding the emotional states as well as intentions about how the dream comes to you, like this:

I INTEND TO TRAVEL TO EUROPE NEXT YEAR. I intend that the financing, the trip itself, and everything surrounding this vacation will manifest in an easy, elegant, and magical way. I intend that this trip fills me with awe, wonder, expansion, creativity, excitement, connectedness, love, and gratitude.

I INTEND TO BUY A HOUSE WITH AT LEAST 4 BEDROOMS AND 2.5 BATHS that is rich with beauty, serenity, peace, joy, elegance, and openness. I intend that this home makes me feel secure, rich, safe, loved, happy, connected, warm, and grateful. I intend that the financing and purchasing of this house unfold in elegant, easy, and synchronistic ways, with harm to none.

> I INTEND TO CREATE A JOB I LOVE BY THE END OF THE YEAR that pays me more money than I currently make, holds opportunities for growth within the company, and allows me to travel to exciting places. In this job I will feel excited, passionate, creative, joyous, abundant, prosperous, grateful, fulfilled, and supported.
>
> I INTEND TO CREATE A NEW CAR—AN AUDI S5 CONVERTIBLE, WHITE WITH RED LEATHER INTERIOR. I intend that this car will be great, reliable transportation, and also provide me with the energies of fun, beauty, success, joy, freedom, dependability, and elegance.
>
> I INTEND TO DOUBLE MY INCOME WITHIN THE NEXT YEAR. I intend that this added prosperity comes to me easily, elegantly, and in fun and freeing ways. I intend that it provides me with a great deal of inner peace, safety, freedom, fun, and support. I ask that this additional income is created with benefit to all and harm to none.

Specific vs. Non-Specific Intentions

Both specific and non-specific intentions can be extremely beneficial to your creating, but it can be less than effective to include just one or the other.

For example, non-specific intentions may not excite you enough. Remember, emotions are the fuel in your manifestation machine. It's critical to be excited and joyous about creating your dreams. Having a picture in your mind is a great way to get your emotions engaged in creating the dream.

On the other hand, specific intentions may shut down many possibilities that you haven't even thought of—possibilities that you may like much better than the one you chose. Therefore, it's always wise to add: "this or better," if only in your mind.

Also specific intentions alone may ignore the deeper reasons you desire the dream in the first place, and you may forget to get in touch with the less-tangible emotional results of having that dream (such as security, safety, freedom, etc.).

A Note on "With Harm To None"

Some people who have been taught never to utter a word that is not "positive" have a problem with adding "with harm to none" to their intentions. But this is the exception that proves the rule.

When you are less than proficient at conscious creating, you don't fully know what might be lurking in your subconscious mind. The opportunity for self-sabotage is a real concern with any creation—but it's especially prevalent when it comes to money and abundance.

Money has been tagged with labels like "greed," "dirty," and "evil," among other things. An unconscious belief that associates money with evil and greed could result in money manifesting at the expense of your health, your family, or other things dear to your heart.

Adding "with harm to none" to your intentions means that your intention will not manifest at *anyone's* expense—not even your own. I add this statement to all of my intentions in my mind and heart, whether I write it out or not. I believe that this language is stronger and more inclusive than more "positive" versions (such as "with benefit to all").

If it really feels wrong to you to add that phrase to your intentions, don't do it—but be scrupulous with your beliefs. If you see any "harmful" ramifications to your abundance, reconsider adding the phrase.

SAMPLES OF ABUNDANCE-RELATED INTENTIONS

Intentions for Creating Your Reality

I INTEND TO LEARN TO CONSCIOUSLY CREATE 100% OF MY REALITY.

I INTEND TO ALLOW MY GROWTH IN THE AREA OF CONSCIOUS CREATION TO BE FUN, FREEING, JOYOUS, EXCITING, AND ENLIGHTENING.

I INTEND TO DRAW TO ME ALL THE SUPPORT I COULD POSSIBLY NEED FROM MY PHYSICAL WORLD (IN BOOKS, TEACHINGS, PEOPLE, ETC.) AND BEYOND THIS WORLD (FROM MY UNSEEN FRIENDS).

I INTEND TO BECOME PROFICIENT AT CONSCIOUSLY CREATING ABUNDANCE.

Intentions for Healing What Stops You

I INTEND TO FORGIVE MYSELF FOR CHOOSING LACK, STRUGGLE, SCARCITY, AND VICTIMHOOD, WHETHER CHOSEN CONSCIOUSLY OR UNCONSCIOUSLY.

I INTEND TO STAY AWAKE AND AWARE OF THE ENERGY I AM FLOWING INTO MY WORLD. I INTEND TO BE A CURIOUS OBSERVER AND GATHER INFORMATION TO DECIDE WHAT TO CHANGE.

I INTEND TO EASILY RECOGNIZE AND CHANGE ALL BELIEFS THAT ARE KEEPING ME FROM LIVING THE LIFE I WAS BORN TO LIVE. I INTEND THAT THESE BELIEFS ARE EFFORTLESS TO DISCOVER, UNCOVER, AND CHANGE.

I INTEND TO BE PATIENT AND LOVING WITH MYSELF ON THIS JOURNEY OF DISCOVERY, HEALING, AND RE-CREATION.

I INTEND TO ALLOW MY INTENTIONS TO UNFOLD IN PERFECT TIMING, AND TO KNOW, WITHOUT A DOUBT THAT THEY WILL INDEED MANIFEST.

I INTEND TO DISCOVER AND CHANGE AS MANY LIMITING BELIEFS AS POSSIBLE IN MY QUEST TO BE ABUNDANT. I INTEND THAT THIS PROCESS OF DISCOVERY AND CHANGE BE EASY, GENTLE, FUN, AND EFFECTIVE.

Intentions for Creating An Abundant Life

I INTEND TO BECOME PROFICIENT AT CONSCIOUSLY CREATING ABUNDANCE.

I INTEND TO BE OPEN TO AND ALLOWING OF THE MANY ABUNDANCES OFFERED TO ME.

I INTEND TO BE AWARE OF, AND EXQUISITELY GRATEFUL FOR, THE ABUNDANCE THAT FLOWS TO ME IN EVERY AREA OF MY LIFE.

I INTEND THAT THE RIGHT RESOURCES, CONTACTS, AND CONNECTIONS APPEAR AS I REQUIRE THEM, WITH EASE, ELEGANCE, AND JOY.

I INTEND TO CREATE A DELICIOUS LIFE FILLED WITH SENSUALITY, RICHNESS, FULLNESS, CONNECTEDNESS, AND JOY.

I INTEND TO CREATE EXACTLY WHAT I WANT AND NEED, EXACTLY WHEN I WANT AND NEED IT.

I INTEND TO REALIZE AT A CONTINUALLY DEEPENING LEVEL THAT I AM PROTECTED, CARED FOR, LOVED, AND PROVIDED FOR—AND THAT THERE IS NOTHING WHATSOEVER I NEED TO DO TO EARN THIS.

I INTEND TO MAKE MY FIRST PRIORITY THE ENJOYMENT OF THIS WONDERFUL LIFE, IN EVERY AND ANY WAY I CAN—NOW, AND AS GREATER ABUNDANCE MANIFESTS.

Financial Intentions

I INTEND THAT UNLIMITED CASH AND RESOURCES FLOW INTO MY LIFE EASILY, ABUNDANTLY, AND ENDLESSLY.

I INTEND TO BE OPEN TO THE MYRIAD WAYS THAT ABUNDANCE CAN SHOW UP IN MY LIFE.

I INTEND TO FEEL DEEP GRATITUDE FOR THE RESOURCES THAT FLOW TO ME WITH SUCH ELEGANCE, EFFORTLESSNESS, AND GRACE.

I INTEND TO BE GUIDED TO THE RIGHT PEOPLE AND INSTITUTIONS TO MANAGE, KEEP, AND GROW MY MONEY AND RESOURCES.

I INTEND FOR MY FINANCIAL ABUNDANCE TO PROVIDE GREATER AND GREATER LEVELS OF FUN, SATISFACTION, JOY, SAFETY, SECURITY, FREEDOM, EASE, ELEGANCE, AND GRATITUDE.

I INTEND TO BECOME 100 PERCENT DEBT FREE, WITH ELEGANCE, EASE, JOY, AND HARM TO NONE.

I INTEND TO BE GUIDED TO THE INSTITUTIONS, INDIVIDUALS, AND PROJECTS THAT CAN BE TRULY AIDED BY MY FINANCIAL AND ENERGETIC CONTRIBUTIONS, AND TO KNOW DEEPLY AND SURELY WHEN, WHAT, AND WHOM TO SUPPORT FOR THE GOOD OF ALL.

Work Intentions to Discover Work You Love

I INTEND TO DISCOVER AND UNCOVER MY TALENTS, GIFTS, AND STRENGTHS.

I INTEND TO CREATE WORK THAT IS MEANINGFUL TO ME.

I INTEND TO BECOME CLEAR ABOUT WHAT TYPE OF WORK WOULD FILL ME WITH PASSION, EXCITEMENT, AND JOY.

I INTEND TO CREATE A JOB OR BUSINESS WHERE I FEEL FREE, JOYOUS, EXCITED, AND PROSPEROUS, AND WHERE I'M MAKING A DIFFERENCE.

I INTEND TO CREATE A JOB OR BUSINESS WITH UNLIMITED OPPORTUNITIES FOR EXPANSION, GROWTH, AND ADVANCEMENT.

I INTEND TO CREATE WORK THAT HAS THE FLEXIBILITY FOR ME TO TAKE TIME OFF WHEN I FEEL LIKE IT.

I INTEND TO CREATE WORK WHERE I CHOOSE MY OWN HOURS AND TIME OF DAY TO WORK.

I INTEND TO CREATE WORK THAT I CAN DO AT HOME.

I INTEND TO OWN MY OWN COMPANY, ON MY OWN TERMS, THAT HONORS MY DESIRES AND TEMPERAMENT.

I INTEND TO CREATE WORK IN A PLACE WHERE I CAN FULLY BE MYSELF AND EXPRESS MY TALENTS, GIFTS, AND STRENGTHS, ALL IN AN ENVIRONMENT THAT SUITS MY TEMPERAMENT AND WITH PEOPLE WHOM I FULLY ENJOY.

I INTEND EVERY MINUTE I WORK TO BE FILLED WITH FUN, CREATIVITY, EXCITEMENT, ABUNDANCE, PROSPERITY, JOY, SERVICE, AND POSITIVE SURPRISES.

I INTEND THAT MY WORK COMES EASILY AND IS JOYFULLY INSPIRED.

I INTEND TO HAVE MORE FUN THAN I BELIEVED POSSIBLE IN MY WORK.

I INTEND FOR THE RESULTS OF MY SUCCESS TO AFFECT ME, AND THOSE I CARE ABOUT, IN ONLY POSITIVE AND UPLIFTING WAYS.

I INTEND TO BE DIVINELY GUIDED WITH MY WORK, AND REQUEST THOSE WHO SHARE THESE (AND EVEN HIGHER) INTENTIONS TO ASSIST ME IN WHATEVER FORM POSSIBLE, WITH HARM TO NONE.

I INTEND THAT THE CHANNELS TO THIS GUIDANCE AND MY ABILITY TO LISTEN ARE STRONG, CLEAR, AND WITHOUT INTERFERENCE.

Intentions on Receiving Help from Your Unseen Friends

I INTEND TO BE GUIDED, AIDED, SUPPORTED, AND ASSISTED BY ALL OF MY UNSEEN FRIENDS TO MANIFEST THESE INTENTIONS, AS WELL AS ANY INTENTIONS THAT MY UNSEEN FRIENDS MAY HOLD FOR ME THAT ARE EVEN GREATER THAN THOSE I HAVE STATED.

Examples of Immediate Intentions

I INTEND TO CREATE AN EXTRA $1,000 IN THE NEXT TWO MONTHS TO TAKE A WEEKEND GETAWAY IN THE MOUNTAINS.

I INTEND TO PAY BACK THE LOAN FROM MY BROTHER BY THE END OF THE YEAR.

I INTEND TO CREATE A PART-TIME BUSINESS ON THE SIDE FOR FUN, AND SO THAT I CAN PRACTICE MY ABUNDANCE-CREATING SKILLS.

I INTEND TO BE TOTALLY DEBT-FREE BY THE END OF NEXT YEAR.

I INTEND TO ALLOW MONEY TO MANIFEST IN SURPRISING AND DELIGHTFUL WAYS, BEYOND ANYTHING I COULD IMAGINE.

I INTEND TO CREATE A JOB I LOVE—A JOB THAT I'M PASSIONATE ABOUT, THAT I CAN HAVE FUN WITH, AND THAT MAKES ME FEEL CREATIVE, VALUED, INSPIRED, PROSPEROUS, EXCITED, JOYFUL, STRETCHED (IN A GOOD WAY), AND WHICH SUITS ME TO A T.

I INTEND TO CALL UPON MY UNSEEN FRIENDS EVERY NIGHT BEFORE BED TO HELP ME TO ALLOW GREATER AND GREATER LEVELS OF ABUNDANCE.

I INTEND TO WORK WITH PEOPLE WHO MAKE ME "MORE": PEOPLE WITH WHOM I LOVE WORKING, HAVE GREAT RESPECT FOR, AND LEARN FROM IN EVERY REGARD.

I INTEND TO RECOGNIZE AND FEEL GRATEFUL FOR THE ABUNDANCE I CURRENTLY ALLOW EVERY SINGLE DAY—ALL WHILE I ALLOW MORE AND MORE IN ALL THE TIME.

I INTEND TO FULLY APPRECIATE THE INCREDIBLE LIFE I HAVE IN THIS AMAZING UNIVERSE, AND MAKE THE ABSOLUTE MOST OUT OF EVERY SINGLE DAY.

Feel free to adopt any of the above intentions, write your own, or use a combination of the two. What's important isn't that they are original; it's that they represent your true heart's desire and feel emotionally positive to you.

If the expansiveness of these intentions brings up fear or incredulity, you have some beliefs that need to be changed. Every time you feel a constricting emotion such as doubt, cynicism, fear, hopelessness, etc., look inside yourself for why it is there. Find the belief it stems from, and change that belief. (We'll talk much more about beliefs in the chapters to follow.)

Let Your Intentions Morph

Your intentions are a snapshot of your destination. But like everything else in life, destinations can change.

I used to have a dream of living on a lake. I loved lakes. But once I got a look at the clear turquoise blue waters of the Bahamas, the idea of living on a lake lost its shine for me. I couldn't imagine settling for a lake when I could have a tropical ocean.

When the doors closed on my second marriage and I chose to make Colorado my permanent home, my love affair with lakes sprang to life again. I "found" a magical body of water, and created a home there. Now, surrounded by the placid lake, mountain views, and tranquil birds, I remember the ocean fondly but with no regrets.

Similarly, your dream is not set in stone.

Trust the process of your own evolution. Allow your dreams to shift and change as you do. You may head in one direction, and then suddenly see another direction that looks more enticing. When this happens, you may be tempted to judge yourself for heading in the "wrong" direction initially. But since it was that initial direction that opened the door to your new path, there was nothing wrong with it at all!

Your initial direction—even if it's not exactly where you're ultimately headed—is less important than taking the steps toward *something*. Your action, however "imperfect," tells the universe, "I am serious about creating this." Over time, the feedback you receive from the universe will bring you more clarity.

Trust the process. Follow your heart. Don't let anyone tell you that you can't create your dreams, and don't sell yourself short for anyone. It's your life and you are (hopefully) living it for yourself.

Once You've Written Your Intentions ...

Treat your intentions as living, breathing things. Dreams will come alive if you feed them.

Your intentions will keep you headed in the right direction. They will keep you focused, accountable, and inspired to take the next step of *The Map* (and the next and the next).

How do you feed your dreams? Here are some ideas:

- ***Read them.*** Your intentions are an important part of conscious creating. As you read them, pay attention to your emotions. Are you:
    - *Excited?* Good. You're on the right track.
    - *Disappointed?* You've got some belief work to do.
    - *Indifferent?* Are you sure you want these? Are you sure you believe you can have them?
- ***Write them.*** As you write, imagine that every letter gets you closer to manifesting what you want. Imagine what you will feel like when that happens.
- ***Speak them.*** Saying your intentions aloud will help to strengthen your commitment to them.

For example, I have a ritual with my intentions for my books that I perform each time I sit down to write. I imagine myself breathing in power. I then say my intentions aloud, and light candles immediately afterward as a way to symbolize the passion (fire) within me which is focused on creating the dream (my book).

Feel free to make up your own ritual that speaks to you and your dreams. It's not as much about what you do as how you do it: with conviction, determination, and love for yourself and your dream.

A TRUE STORY OF CONSCIOUSLY CREATING ABUNDANCE

I heard about The Map *while listening to a Jim Harold podcast. Boni was a guest on his show; her approach to and explanation of creating realities sounded interesting, so I figured, "Why not?" I had nothing to lose but a few bucks to buy the book (although, back then, even a few bucks were tough to come by).*

At that time in my life, things were not going very well for me physically, financially, or in my marriage. I had watched The Secret *on Netflix, so I had some idea of what the Law of Attraction was, but I still had my doubts. I couldn't believe that I had created what I was going through.*

I am a cancer survivor of five years. Although I did have health insurance during most of the treatment, I lost it when my employer decided to discontinue our group coverage. I went on my husband's plan; shortly thereafter, he was let go from his job. We had COBRA coverage for eighteen months, which was very expensive—and, after that, no insurance at all.

Expenses were starting to pile up. I was the main breadwinner, working two part-time jobs. Eventually I was able to go full-time with one of the jobs, but the working conditions were not great. I had a lot of responsibility, and had to work in the middle of the office in a hallway! My employers were difficult men to work with, which made things even more stressful for me.

In the meantime, my husband started his own business after his non-compete was up, but he didn't turn a profit. Our finances were so bad that we barely had enough money for groceries. All of our credit cards were maxed out.

The plumbing and air conditioner broke, requiring repairs to the tune of a few thousand dollars. My house was upside down in the mortgage. Even though the cancer was gone, I was having issues with acid reflux, depression, and anxiety. I was seeing a hypnotherapist and a naturopath, since conventional medicine did not help me at all. I had to borrow thousands of dollars from my mother, which left me feeling terrible. I wondered why everything was such a struggle and why nothing ever came easily.

In early 2015, I read The Map *over a weekend. I let it sink in, then began to re-read the book, this time taking notes and creating a journal along the way. Three months later, my life began to change significantly.*

My boss informed me that we would hire another person to help with customer service in the office, which would help lessen the burden on me. A month later, I was told we would be moving to a bigger space, and I would have my own office. Finally, some privacy! (I now have a very nice office with a view and patio.)

My difficult boss suddenly changed. He became spiritual, even Zen! That alone blew my mind.

I received a bonus for organizing the office move. We hired yet another person.

Five months after I implemented The Map, *I asked to be promoted to a position with a six figure salary ... and I got the job.*

Last year, my company offered employees a new group health plan. My husband's business is finally seeing some positive cash flow. My health issues subsided, the stress in my marriage is gone, and I was able to re-finance my house for a smaller mortgage. Things continue to manifest to this day!

I want to be clear, it is not about all of the material things that manifested for me in such a short time. It is about how changing my beliefs changed the way I view my reality.

As soon as I started working with The Map, *I began a journal. I suddenly saw so many signs that things were changing, and I wrote them all down. I felt grateful and thankful for every big and little thing. I wanted to feel safe, secure, excited, and happy. I didn't want to worry anymore. Every time I received a little sign, I felt so happy and grateful for it.*

It became contagious. I started looking forward to each new day, and each new thing that would happen to reinforce my intentions and desires. I worked with my inner child and negative self. I changed my negative beliefs. I read my intentions aloud every day.

When I look back at my whole life, the one truth that is crystal clear to me is that when I really put my mind to something—when I truly wanted something with every fiber of my being—I got it. Good or bad, I got it. It was that realization that solidified the concepts described in The Map for me.

- Kim J.

PS: I'm reading The Map *for the third time now.*

ABUNDANCE-ALTERING TAKEAWAYS

- When you are creating money and other forms of abundance, it's more elegant to *let go of the forms.* This gives the universe many more possibilities to make you happy.

- One of the most important considerations in creating abundance is to be honest about where you are right now. This honest assessment will make the difference between the survival and the death of your "abundant self."

- Living an abundant life requires that you trust the universe to deliver your abundance without you trying to figure out how it will look. This will be much easier if you separate abundance from work in your creation process.

- When you feel happy, grateful, and abundant you get more things in your life that will make you feel happy, grateful, and abundant. It's as simple as that—but it must be genuine. Saying something is good when underneath you hate it won't fool the universe.

- Intentions are more than desires: they are a *commitment to create.* They acknowledge that you may already have some (or all) of what you're intending, but that you want more of it and will continue to create it. They are a strong plan and expectation for something to manifest.

- Follow your heart. Don't let anyone tell you that you can't create your dreams, and don't sell yourself out for anyone. It's your life, and you are living it for yourself.

YOUR NEXT STEPS

- Revisit the early section in this chapter on dreaming the what, why, how, and when of your abundance. Did you see anything that pointed to constrictive beliefs you are carrying around money or abundance? If so, jot them down.

- With regard to an abundance of money, love, joy, health, fun, and great relationships ... How abundant are you right now? Where would you like to be in one year? Five years?

- Write your Overall Intention, Core Intentions, and Specific Intentions for healing your abundance issues, for becoming a stellar conscious creator, and for all forms of abundance.

- Revisit your intentions daily by reading them and deeply feeling their essence. Change and expand your intentions as needed.

- Use the applied kinesiology techniques in Appendix B to test for the constricting beliefs in this chapter. Document the beliefs that need to be changed so you can work with them later, or change them now using a technique in Appendix D.

CHAPTER SIX

Flowing Abundance = Creating Abundance

"Miracles start to happen when you give as much energy to your dreams as you do to your fears."

~ RICHARD WILKINS

Do you know that if you simply stated what you want (i.e. by writing your intentions), and did nothing else, your dream would absolutely manifest?

So why don't manifestation miracles happen all the time for everyone who writes their intentions or states their desires?

Because it's easy to say what you want, but it's harder to keep that energy pure and *not flow energy in opposition to it.*

Here's what I mean ...

Most of us aren't patient enough to allow abundance to manifest according to the universe's timing. This impatience pushes your dream further away, which creates feelings of lack, despair, and frustration.

And, even when we master the art of patience, we may be unconsciously flowing other energies that oppose our dream. This opposing flow slows things down, or even stops them from manifesting altogether.

The energy you put forth attracts realities that match your energy. This is just another way of saying that the thoughts you think, the feelings you feel, and the beliefs you hold are all forms of energy that flow from you—and that energy creates your reality.

In this chapter, we'll start working on the "energy" step of *The Map to Abundance* by figuring out what energy you are flowing toward *non-abundance*—aka lack, scarcity, and struggle.

Are you saying that I'm flowing scarcity? Me?

Yeah, you. And me. And everyone else who has ever been challenged around money and abundance. If you are struggling, somehow, some way, you are flowing struggle. Period. It's the law of this universe.

However, there's good news on this front: you can change what you flow. This change begins when you become *conscious* of what you're flowing.

In *The Map* I wrote about "flow stoppers"—emotions that stop your dreams in their tracks. Now, I'd like to hone in on the flow stoppers that are specifically linked to abundance. I call them …

THE ABUNDANCE STOPPERS

"Abundance stoppers" are emotional states that keep abundance at a distance.

Of course, any negativity could theoretically stop you from creating abundance, but these particular emotions seem to come up regularly around money.

Sometimes, these emotions are subtle energies that run deep within us, such as feeling undeserving, or like we're not enough. Other times, they are relentlessly conscious, such as inescapable fear. And sometimes, our abundance stoppers flip-flop, showing up as conscious one day and nearly imperceptible the next.

All abundance stoppers will stop your abundance, regardless of whether you sense them or not. Becoming conscious of them, and learning how to deal with them, is key to taking your power back.

So, what tops the list of abundance stoppers?

FEAR

Unless you are facing a terminal illness, money is the place where your biggest fears are likely to show up. Your money fears are the broadest-reaching fears you have, and may impact many other areas of your life in ways both obvious and sneaky.

Here are a few examples of these insidious money fears:

- *Will I have enough money for the rent this month?*
- *Can I make it to payday before they shut my electricity off?*

- *What if my child's cold gets even worse? Can I afford to take him to the doctor?*
- *Should I stay with the man I know isn't right for me? What would I do for income if I left?*
- *Should I quit the job I hate? What if I can't make as much doing something I love?*
- *Should I quit school and follow my passion? What if I can't make a living by following my heart?*
- *What if my car doesn't last another year? I can't afford to replace it.*

Fear rears its ugly head more with money than with any other dream out there, and for good reason. Money seems so *real!*

There is nothing more real than an eviction notice tacked to your door, your electricity being shut off, or your car being repossessed. Yes, money seems mighty "real" when you don't have it. And, because you *know* how real that "real" is, the terror of losing money, or never having enough money, is paralyzing.

Yet, you must remember …

Fear Will Tear Your Abundance Into Shreds

Fear *destroys.* It destroys your hopes, your dreams, your passion, your excitement, and your motivation. It destroys your future.

Reading that, you might be ready to wage war on your fear, and do everything in your power to eradicate it. (Or, at the very least, work around it by pretending it doesn't exist.) But before you charge in, there's something you should know:

Your fear is also a priceless gift—as long as you are ready to receive it.

Fear tells you where you're going askew. It tells you when you're flowing energy down the wrong path. It tells you where you're mis-creating. It tells you what your *beliefs* are.

So don't think of fear as your enemy. Think of it as your friend. But as with all relationships, you need boundaries.

What does that mean?

It means be cognizant of fear, but don't let it take over.

Easier said than done.

I know. As I said, money is different—we perceive it as life and death. Fear is a big issue. But you're still the gatekeeper, and you can choose when to let fear in and what to do about it.

Let's look at ...

How To Keep Fear from Freaking You Out

First, it is important to realize that not all parts of you feel fear. The highest aspects of you—your soul and higher self—don't feel fear.

Of course they don't. They aren't living on Earth.

Exactly. But it's not just that. Your soul and higher self know that everything happening on Earth is a reflection of what's happening inside of you. Your higher self and soul know that you create your own safety, security, and abundance. They also know that you created your struggle, your debts, and the financial bogeyman under your bed.

Are you saying I'm freaking myself out?

Well, yes. But stick with me.

Your soul and higher self aren't the only "additional" parts of you. There are others, many of whom aren't so sure that you're in charge of your own safety, security, and reality creation. In fact, they may feel quite the opposite.

Your *child self* likely feels insecure, afraid, and helpless to create much change anywhere in their life. Unless you've worked with him/her already (meaning, if you've done the exercises in *The Map* (or similar exercises)), your child self is likely the cause of a good deal of your fear. Even if you have worked with your child self, new dreams create new fears, and you'll need to work with him/her again.

Your *adolescent self* can also allow fear to take over. Why? S/he looks at your life and at what you, as an adult, are up against, and thinks, "No way can I handle that!" Of course, your adolescent self is right. S/he can't handle it. S/he's just a kid.

Your *younger adult selves* have had experiences that left them scarred. Maybe they lost jobs, had business disappointments, or had dreams they let die. They, too, have a lot of fear—and for good reason.

Later in this book, I will walk you through healing the younger aspects of yourself around the issues of money and abundance. But there is another "fear monger" aspect that lives within you …

Your *negative self* is a certified freak-out specialist. Truly. Your negative self wants you to be mired in fear. It wants you to curl up in a little ball and anesthetize yourself. It wants you to let fear sabotage all your hopes and dreams and take over your life.

Your negative self *sucks*. And yet, you listen to it. You let it take over. You let it run your life.

Why do I do that?

You do it because you *forget*. You do it because you haven't had enough practice giving voice to your negative self and taking your power back. You do it because you're still learning this important new skill called "conscious creation."

And sometimes, you do it because you're afraid of taking responsibility for your life.

Yup, there's no denying it. I've been there, remember?

I know that the idea of creating your entire reality is a big bite to chew. In fact, it's terrifying. You may have secret thoughts like ...

- *What if I can't create my own reality?*
- *What if I mess up my reality?*
- *What if I'm not powerful enough?*
- *What if the responsibility is too much for me?*
- *What if I create the abundance and then can't hold onto it?*

Yes, I've been there. And just like it took time for me to get good at creating my reality, it will take you time to get good at managing your negative self (and all of your other abundance stoppers). It will take time—as well as practice, patience, and a big dose of sheer determination—for you to assume 100 percent responsibility for everything in your reality.

But you *can* do it.

Those fears around taking responsibility often stem from beliefs such as:

- THE CONCEPT OF REALITY CREATION IS A FANTASY.
- I CAN'T CREATE MY OWN REALITY.
- IF I MIS-CREATE SOMETHING IN MY REALITY, I CAN'T FIX IT.
- I AM NOT POWERFUL ENOUGH TO CREATE A LIFE I LOVE.
- I CAN'T HANDLE TAKING RESPONSIBILITY FOR MY ENTIRE LIFE.
- IF I CREATE ABUNDANCE I'LL JUST LOSE IT ALL.

The whole "taking responsibility" thing scared me early on. Oh, I was fine taking responsibility for other people's lives—especially my children's—but the thought of being responsible for my entire world was daunting.

But, as they say, "You eat an elephant one bite at a time." As I changed my beliefs, one at a time, I was able to take responsibility for more and more of my life.

I'm still stretching that responsibility bubble. Now, I'm looking at the lives of those I love, at the lives of strangers, at Earth herself and beyond—not because I want to control them, but because I want to recognize what in me contributes to scarcity and suffering in others.

Your power and impact grow as you grow. It's a glorious thing.

But first ...

To Alleviate Fear, Align With the Right "Selves"

You have a choice. Do you want to allow your wounded child self, your terrified adolescent self, or your destructive negative self to run your emotions (and therefore your life), or do you want to align with your higher self and your soul? It's up to you.

The first step to alignment is to assuage the fears of your younger selves. The next is to listen to—and, as a result, disengage from—your negative self. I'll teach you exactly how to do that in Chapter Seven.

But what if, even after I've worked with my younger selves, I still feel afraid?

If you still feel fear, you have beliefs rooted in your subconscious that are causing that fear. But beliefs, as you undoubtedly know by now, can be changed.

Let's take a look at some …

Fears & Possible Beliefs

If your fear is:

I won't have enough money for safety from anything and everything

Your beliefs might be:

- I AM ALWAYS IN DANGER.
- I CAN'T CONTROL UNWANTED THINGS FROM HAPPENING.

- I DON'T FULLY CREATE MY OWN SAFETY AND SECURITY.
- MONEY IS NOT ABUNDANT IN MY LIFE.
- MY NEEDS MIGHT NOT BE MET.

If your fear is:

I won't have enough money to be free to do as I wish without restrictions

Your beliefs might be:

- I AM NOT FREE AND ABLE TO CREATE ANYTHING AND EVERYTHING I WANT.
- I AM NOT IN CONTROL OF MY FINANCIAL FREEDOM.
- I AM NOT ABLE TO CREATE MY OWN REALITY.
- MONEY IS HARD TO CREATE.
- THERE IS ALWAYS A PRICE TO PAY FOR MONEY.

If your fear is:

My adult children will never get off the "family payroll" and become financially independent

Your beliefs might be:

- MY CHILDREN NEED MY SUPPORT TO SURVIVE (OR HEAL, OR BE SAFE, OR GROW).
- I CANNOT CREATE ENOUGH MONEY FOR BOTH MY NEEDS AND MY CHILDREN'S NEEDS.

- MY CHILDREN ARE KEEPING ME FROM ABUNDANCE.
- IT IS ALWAYS UNLOVING TO SAY "NO" TO MY CHILD.
- THERE IS A LIMITED AMOUNT OF MONEY AVAILABLE TO ME.

If your fear is:

I don't have enough money, and I'll never have all the "good things" in life

Your beliefs might be:

- THERE IS NOT ENOUGH MONEY TO GO AROUND.
- THE LACK OF MONEY PREVENTS ME FROM HAVING THE BEST THINGS IN LIFE.
- I NEVER HAVE ENOUGH MONEY.
- I WILL NEVER HAVE ENOUGH MONEY.
- I NEVER HAVE MORE THAN ENOUGH MONEY.
- THE UNIVERSE IS NOT ABUNDANT.

If your fear is:

If I came into great sums of money, I'd be "forced" to give it to people that I don't want to give it to, instead of giving it by choice

Your beliefs might be:

- I CAN'T CONTROL WHO SHARES IN MY ABUNDANCE.
- IF YOU HAVE MONEY YOU MUST SHARE IT.

- IT'S MOST LOVING TO SHARE YOUR ABUNDANCE WITH THOSE WHO NEED IT.
- HAVING MONEY CREATES PROBLEMS.
- PEOPLE WILL DISLIKE ME IF I DON'T SHARE MY MONEY.
- I CAN'T BE RESPONSIBLE FOR GREAT SUMS OF MONEY.

If your fear is:

If I become very wealthy I will be too visible, and my money (and perhaps more) will be at risk

Your beliefs might be:

- IF I CREATE A BEAUTIFUL, ABUNDANT LIFE, SOMEONE WILL TAKE IT AWAY.
- IF I AM VISIBLE, I WILL LOSE MY PRIVACY.
- IF I AM WEALTHY, PEOPLE WILL BE JEALOUS OF ME.
- BEING WEALTHY PUTS ME AT RISK.
- IF I AM WEALTHY, I WILL NO LONGER BELONG.

Remember beliefs are easy to change. It's sometimes difficult to motivate yourself to change a belief, but you can be the exception to that rule. Just do it.

Once Your Beliefs Are Changed

You will have much less fear once you've dealt with your other "selves" and have changed your beliefs.

Will I still feel fear, though?

Yes, you will still feel fear. You will always dream bigger dreams, and every time you stretch beyond your comfort zone you will feel fear about doing so.

The difference will be that your fears will no longer control you. They'll serve their purpose—to show you what beliefs to change—and then they'll graciously step out of the way. Whatever remains can be easily transformed into *excitement*!

Yes, fear is a natural part of creating bigger realities. And when you've handled all the beliefs and the fear is still yours, not another aspect of you flowing the fear through you, it can easily be shifted directly into excitement.

To do so simply feel the fear, and then choose to feel the excitement of the big leap instead—with all the other possibilities handled, it should shift over in no time at all.

DOUBT

Can this really happen? Can I genuinely create unlimited abundance for myself, now and always? Can I truly stop living in fear and trust that the universe will always provide?

Yes, you can. I know you can. But I don't know if you *will.*

I do know it's possible. I do know it's what you came here to do. But will you do it? Will you take the steps outlined in this Map? Will you never, *ever* give up? That, I cannot answer.

You see, as long as you are physical, doubt will plague you. Your negative self will jump right on that bandwagon, whispering things like, "You aren't headed down that stupid path of 'you create it all' again, are you?"

Or, it will pipe up with something like, "If you do create your reality, why isn't your life perfect? Why aren't more wonderful things happening to you?"

Your negative self is in the business of screwing you up, so it conveniently forgets the little thing called "time lag" which causes things to manifest slowly. It also forgets that it isn't just wishing that causes realities, it's flowing energy (in the form of emotions and thoughts) toward what you desire while simultaneously minimizing or eliminating opposing energy (in the form of unhelpful beliefs).

Your negative self wants you to give up on this "stupid idea" because, in a world where you no longer have sabotaging beliefs, doubt, or overwhelming fear, your negative self is no longer powerful or relevant—until you dream a bigger dream and let it in again.

The fact is, you do create it all. That's how our reality works.

If you let your negative self choose what you create—if you focus on what you *don't* have rather than what you *do*, if you go unconscious and forget about creating an abundance of love, joy, meaning, success, and fun—your life isn't going to turn out well. How could it?

So, when you come down to it ...

What Do You Have To Lose?

Why even debate it? Why give power to your doubt? What potential result is so terrifying, so fear-producing, that you wouldn't keep trying to create the best possible reality for yourself, over and over, until you succeed?

The fact is, once you've done a technique or two from the Map process, you'll always receive signs that it's working within a few days, if not a few hours. It's not like you have to wait for decades to know that your creation is working, or give up your firstborn child, or suffer or sacrifice or struggle in any way. You just have to be patient and keep flowing positive energy as you wait for your signs to appear.

You know in your gut that I'm right, so why the big hesitation? What is so scary about creating your reality?

Oh, I see. Maybe, waaaaay back in the dark recesses of your mind, you're wondering ...

What If It Doesn't Work For Me?

Yeah, I know. I create my own reality. Blah, blah, blah. Sure, I believe it.

Then why aren't you doing the work?

Well, um ... I got busy.

You're too busy to create a better life?

Yeah, you know. Stuff happens.

There is *always* a reason why you don't find time. Sometimes the reason is that you don't really expect that conscious creation can, and will, work for you.

Oh, you totally love the concept. You can't stop reading the books, or listening to other people talk about their successes. But when it comes to really committing to creating for yourself, well ... you just don't do it.

Underneath that doubt is a fear that asks, "What if it doesn't work for me?"

Rather than face that fear, and take the chance that it's actually true, you'll dance around it the rest of your life. Anything is better than giving up the hope that the Law of Attraction is true. If you lose that hope, you lose everything.

Oh, my. I think I hit a nerve there.

But maybe, just maybe, this isn't your doubt. Maybe you know for a fact that conscious creation can work, has worked, and does work for you. And yet, you wonder ...

What If It Won't Work on *This* Dream?

You know it works. You've seen it work. It's amazing how well it works. You've manifested tons of wonderful realities so far, and you'll manifest more in the future.

And yet for some reason, you doubt that your skills will work on this dream. Maybe it's a bigger dream. Maybe it's a dream that is so spectacular you haven't yet dared to try. Maybe you just can't imagine life being quite that good—because, after all, you have so much already.

So, you procrastinate. You settle. And, yet, the whole time, you judge yourself for your lack of focus and determination, because you *really* want this dream. The longer you sit on it, the more that energy of judgment pushes your dream further and further away.

Or, maybe you're contending with a different doubt. Maybe the change you're seeking is big—like becoming absolutely free financially. You know it can happen. You know you are powerful enough. You know you could manifest this dream if you tried. But, you wonder ... What will happen when it *does* manifest? What backlash will your life suffer when this whopper of a dream comes true?

The core of this particular flavor of doubt is ...

- THE UNKNOWN PETRIFIES ME.

Change is scary for everyone. The bigger the change, the bigger your fear of it. This is especially true when you're dealing with that sticky caveat of conscious creation: *You can't control what it looks like.*

For those who have a hard time with change and the unknown, being out of control sucks.

Fear of the unknown will stop you from moving forward. It will keep you mired in mediocrity. It will snip your wings before you can begin to fly.

Yes, if you haven't figured it out yet ...

Doubt Is Debilitating

Doubt is a mask that hides a truer fear beneath it. All of your doubts and fears have a good reason for existing: they are protecting you.

What on Earth are they protecting me from?

They're protecting you from disappointment, shattered dreams, negative repercussions of your success, and any of the other shadowy, unforeseen consequences of your forward motion.

How do you untangle yourself from this mess of doubt? The first thing you have to do is ...

Change the Underlying Beliefs

When you change your beliefs, you will change your world. Literally.

I know. You're sick and tired of hearing about beliefs. But baby, beliefs are the keys to changing your reality. And if you don't have the right ones, your beliefs will stop you from doing all of the other steps of *The Map*.

Because they're sometimes tricky to discover, I am going to point out all the cracks and crevices that your beliefs like to hide in, starting with that lovely little fear …

What if it doesn't work for me?

If you're holding that fear, your beliefs might be:

- I CANNOT CREATE MY REALITY.
- THE LAW OF ATTRACTION WORKS SOMETIMES FOR SOME PEOPLE.
- I AM NOT POWERFUL ENOUGH TO CREATE REALLY BIG DREAMS.
- THE LAW OF ATTRACTION IS A SILLY FANTASY.
- IF WE REALLY DO CREATE OUR REALITIES, EVERYONE WOULD KNOW ABOUT IT.

If your fear is:

What if it doesn't work on this dream?

Your beliefs might be:

- YOU ONLY GET SO MUCH GOOD, AND IF YOU STILL WANT MORE YOU'RE BEING GREEDY.
- IF LIFE GETS TOO GOOD, SOMEONE WILL TAKE IT AWAY.
- I CREATE MY OWN REALITY, EXCEPT WHEN IT COMES TO ________.
- THE LAW OF ATTRACTION HAS EXCEPTIONS.
- I DON'T DESERVE TO HAVE EVERYTHING I WANT.

And if your fear is :

The unknown petrifies me

Your beliefs might be:

- I MUST CONTROL MY WORLD IN ORDER TO BE SAFE.
- SUCCESS COMES WITH A PRICE.
- I CAN CREATE THE SUCCESS ITSELF, BUT NOT THE RESULTS OF THAT SUCCESS.
- I MIGHT LOSE WHAT I HAVE IF I DREAM BIGGER DREAMS.
- THE UNKNOWN IS DANGEROUS.

Whenever doubts enter your mind, examine them closely and discover where they come from. When you change the beliefs that are creating the fear that's fueling the doubt, the doubt will disappear.

But wait, there's another sly little Abundance Stopper to watch out for, and that is …

VICTIMHOOD & SELF-PITY

When I first opened my eyes to my own victimhood and self-pity, I was shocked. I had never thought of myself as a victim (at least, not consciously). I thought of myself as a positive, upbeat, "can do" kind of person—and on the surface, I was.

But then, I looked deeper. Sure enough, I was subtly flowing "victim" energy beneath the surface of my upbeat self.

You see, *all* of our emotions create—not just the ones we show to others, and not just the ones we want to admit to ourselves.

Here are some ways I played the victim, and in doing, counteracted receiving abundance:

- ***I sought sympathy.*** I would sadly, or angrily, or resignedly tell my friends and family my latest "bad news." It was always something: my car broke down, my kids were sick, my adjustable rate mortgage went up again. I sought out others to commiserate with me.

- ***I blamed others.*** Back then my ex-husband was my prime scapegoat. He was the reason I couldn't pay my mortgage, because he had decided to use the child support money to pay our son's medical bills. (Although, technically, he was the reason I couldn't pay the mortgage, I could have processed the anger and moved through it, instead of holding on to the blame.)

- ***I worried.*** Empowered people don't worry about money. They just don't. Even when something goes wrong, they feel the fear (if it's there) and then let the worry go and imagine the situation handled. But back then, I worried morning, noon, and night. I wasn't telling the universe, "I've got this." I was telling the universe, "I don't have this. I'm not strong enough. My world is falling apart and I'm powerless to do anything about it." Worry is a telltale sign of victimhood.

- ***I felt sorry for myself.*** I spent a lot of time crying and feeling powerless back then. I felt hopeless, helpless, worthless, undeserving, and like my life just wasn't fair. It was one big pity party, and my whole reality was showing up for it.

Self-pity and victimhood typically show up together. It's easy to see them when they are blatant (i.e. the minute something doesn't go your way you're on the phone whining to anyone who will listen), but they're more difficult to recognize when you simply become a little "down" when something doesn't go the way you'd hoped.

On the surface, the second option doesn't look like victimhood, but it is—and it will stop your abundance from manifesting.

You simply can't be a victim and be powerful at the same time. You have to choose one or the other.

The way to handle victimhood is to *pay attention*. When you can catch yourself in that energy, you can make another choice. But if you go unconscious and spend days, weeks, months, years even feeling like you're powerless, your reality will agree with you.

Possible Beliefs Underlying Victimhood

If you slip into victim energy, look to see whether you have subconscious beliefs that need to change, such as:

- I AM POWERLESS TO CHANGE MY REALITY.
- NOTHING EVER WORKS FOR ME.
- I MESS UP EVERYTHING I TRY.
- SOMETHING IS WRONG WITH ME.
- I CAN NEVER HAVE WHAT I WANT.
- IF SOMETHING CAN GO WRONG, IT WILL.
- I CAN NEVER GET AHEAD.

Now, it's important to note that not every bad feeling means you're playing the victim. You're allowed to feel sad, frustrated, or even angry. But there's a difference between feeling disappointment because something hasn't happened the way you'd like, and being a victim who has been singled out to receive the booby prize in life.

Whenever you feel negative emotions, you're mis-creating. Regardless of what those emotions are, you've either got to shift out of them and into a more uplifting and positive thought and feeling as soon as possible, or change the underlying beliefs that cause them to keep happening.

But you don't want to stuff your emotions either. Unfelt emotions don't just disappear. Whatever you try to cover up without feeling will simply stay in your energy field and flow that disappointment, frustration, or anger all the time.

When any negative emotion comes up, feel it fully, and then let it go. You can even give it to your higher self to transform into light. But if the same emotion comes up repeatedly, it indicates an underlying belief.

Dealing With Disappointment Without Becoming a Victim

An efficient way to shift your emotions is to give yourself a specific amount of time to feel them, and then force yourself to shift into a more expansive mindset.

Let's say that you interviewed for a job you wanted, but you didn't get it. Of course you are going to feel disappointment. You're human! So spend twenty minutes (or an hour, or even a whole night) wallowing in your disappointment. Whine, complain, cry ... whatever you need to do to get it all out of you. Then, hit the "off" switch, because on the other side of your personal pity party is the fact that you can intend, and create, an even better job that is even more perfect for you.

Time limits prevent self-indulgence, and help you keep your negative emotions from taking over your life. They force you to come back to the table with your conscious creation plans, and do what you need to do to keep your intention alive and fed. If you end up spending more than a day wallowing, do so if you must—but know that your reality will suffer.

Does this sound hard? It's only hard if you believe that you're less powerful than your emotions—which, of course, is another sneaky way that victimhood can show up in your reality.

Of course, you might feel like you shouldn't have to create abundance at all—that you should simply be *given* what you want. If you're feeling this way, you might have a case of ...

ENTITLEMENT

Who, me? Entitled? Don't be silly.

That's what they all say. And yet, when someone with lots of money, resources, or possessions shows up in your life, you might find yourself thinking, "By rights, at least some of that should be mine."

If you don't think this sounds like you—or if you're just not entirely sure what entitlement is—consider the following scenarios:

- Your parents don't have a lot of money, but your sister just borrowed $5,000 to "get her life together (again)." You know she'll never pay them back. It makes you angry that she's getting that money and you aren't.

- Your ex walked out before your son was born, and you haven't heard from him since. But the kid's grandparents are rich. Shouldn't they pitch in since their son won't?

- Your best friend has money to burn and doesn't appreciate it as much as you would. Doesn't she kind of owe you a vacation at her house on the lake now and then?

- Time after time, your deadbeat brother runs to Mom to "fix" things for him. Meanwhile, your car is falling apart, and you can't afford to replace it. The money Mom's spent on him could buy you a sweet ride, and you can't help but wonder, "When is it *my* turn?"

- Your parents are loaded. Shouldn't they take you on vacations with them, share their beach house, and buy you fancy presents every once in a while?

- You go in to work early, stay late, work through your lunch hours ... and yet, another review breezes by with just a 3 percent "cost of living" raise. The jerk in the next cubicle got 10 percent even though he takes "martini lunches" with his friends and shows up late at least once a week. When will management realize what *you* deserve?

- You got laid off. You're halfheartedly looking for a job—but isn't this why they invented unemployment insurance?

- Your daughter is a fancy lawyer and lives in a mansion. Couldn't she use some of that money to make her mother's life a little easier?

- You served in the Gulf War and are pretty sure you suffered from chemical exposure. You spend the next two decades fighting the government for "what's rightfully yours."

- Your ex-husband is very well off, and the alimony and child support ran out way too early. He is living the high life while you and your kids are struggling. He should give you some money. After all, he'll never spend it all.

- Your friend, who has a successful business, always buys lunch. But she can afford it.

- You received a nice bonus last Christmas from your company. You already have this year's bonus money spent in your head.

- You suspect your ex is not reporting her freelance work for what she owes for child support. You are enraged. She's stealing money from your child (and you)!

- You're fifty-five and have struggled for the past twenty years. Your live-in partner is well off, but he won't marry you and refuses to share what he has beyond the weekly dinner and a movie. Why doesn't he understand that he should share his money with you?

- You own a small accounting firm. Your biggest client went bankrupt and left an unpaid invoice of nearly $10,000. You can't stop thinking about where that money was supposed to go.

- You've worked your butt off trying to create abundance for the past five years. You've *earned* it, dammit. So where's the cash?

- You're a therapist. Two of your clients have amassed pretty large bills, but neither has paid you yet. You finally had to stop seeing them, and now they have cut off all communication with you. Every month when it comes time to pay the bills, you think, "If only they would pay me ..."

Wait a minute on that last one. Shouldn't you *expect* people to pay you when they owe you money?

Of course you should. But once someone has indicated they won't, stop counting on it. Feel the disappointment (for an hour). Get angry (for a little while). Take legal action if you choose. But *let it go emotionally.*

Why Entitlement Hurts You

Before you know the consequences, feeling entitled makes sense. There's a possible source of money—money that might even technically belong to you—and you glom onto it. It's there, waiting for you. It's so close. It's only a matter of time (or coercion, or manipulation, or legal action) before it's yours for the spending.

It may very well be true that this money *could* come to you. It's possible that the law would even agree, and would award you the money (should it come to that). But the minute you feel you are "owed," or "should have," or "have a right to" anything from anyone, you have stepped into entitlement—and entitlement is a deadly virus to abundance.

It's human nature to try to figure out how money is "supposed" to come to you. More, you've been taught to fight for what is yours—to grab whatever you can, and stake a claim to anything in arm's reach, lest you lose it.

But this primal mentality doesn't serve you, and it certainly doesn't help you create abundance in your reality.

Here are some ways in which entitlement affects your energy, and thus your abundance:

Entitlement Sends The Universe the Wrong Message

When you feel entitled, you're saying to the universe:

> This *is the way I will receive money because it should (or could) come to me so damn easily!*

The fact that it isn't coming to you may make you angry because someone is stealing your money—and anger is another flow stopper.

What you should be saying is:

> *Universe, I don't always understand how you bring things to me—but I do know that, no matter what anyone around me does or says, money will flow to me effortlessly, elegantly, and abundantly. Sometimes, how it comes (and how it doesn't) will surprise me. When it does, I will know that you have found an even better way to bring me money. Thank you, universe. I'm excited to see what it is!*

Entitlement Keeps You From Focusing On What You Do Want

While you're busy scheming to grab the money pot, or complaining about what you didn't get, you are wasting super-valuable time and energy that you could be using to focus on what you do want. The opportunity costs here are major.

Entitlement Is An Easy Road to Martyrdom & Victimhood

It's a natural progression. You feel entitled, but you don't get what you want. Then, you slide down that slippery slope into victimhood (why me?) and martyrdom (after all I did for him/her!). Resentment, and possibly self-pity, come next. How empowering do you suppose those emotions are?

Entitlement Impedes Gratitude

Entitlement also stops you from being grateful for what you *do* receive. When you're ultra-focused on getting what's "rightfully" yours, you stop paying attention to the abundance you are receiving. Gratitude is a powerful energy, and your entitlement is snatching that tool right out of your toolbox.

Your Negative Self Loves Entitlement

Your negative self jumps on the bandwagon of entitlement and encourages you to fail. Because entitlement is so subtle, and as humans we hate to let go of any "sure thing," the negative self can get an easy foothold here.

Neg (as one of my friends calls her negative self) will prod and poke you, encouraging you to "do what it takes" to receive what is "rightfully yours."

Don't listen to Neg. Neg is a jerk. Or rather, *do* listen to Neg, but only until it tells you what beliefs you're hiding. Then, bust it at its own game.

Entitlement Seeks to Control the Form of Your Desire

Remember, you can't control the *form* of your creations. Entitlement is just another way of trying to control the form of your abundance, which decreases the number of ways it could come to you, increases the time it will take, and raises so many feelings of "Oh my God, what if I never get this?" As we already know, all of these things create greater scarcity.

Yes, entitlement is a subtle but dream-deadly energy. But don't misunderstand …

Accepting Abundance Is Fine

There's nothing wrong with accepting abundance from others. By all means, receive and feel grateful for all the gifts that come your way. Just be careful that you don't cross that line of feeling you are owed those gifts; when you do, you cross the line into entitlement.

Also ...

Helping Those Unable to Care For Themselves Is Fine

You share the planet with people who truly are victims. Some have been disabled, mentally, physically, or emotionally. Others have suffered tragedies of one type or another, and need a helping hand to get back on their feet. It would be a shame not to help people in true need.

People truly in need are entitled to be fed, clothed, sheltered, and kept safe. These are basic human rights that should be inalienable. This is not the "entitlement" that I am writing about. If you are reaching out for help of this sort, you are not acting entitled—and if you offer help of this sort, you are not feeding into someone else's entitlement.

No, it's only when you take on the notion that "Someone should pay/give to/support me in some way ..." that you slow or halt your ability to create abundance.

You May Find It Difficult to Disengage from Entitlement

If you just can't let go of your entitlement and right now you want to scream, "It's mine! Stop trying to convince me it's not!" you may want to consider changing some of the following beliefs.

If you feel you deserve abundance because of how hard you've worked (or how much you've suffered), your beliefs might be:

- I MUST EARN MY WEALTH.
- IF YOU WORK AND STRUGGLE LONG ENOUGH YOU WILL RECEIVE ABUNDANCE.
- I AM UNAPPRECIATED.
- I AM UNLOVED.
- MONEY IS HARD TO COME BY.

If someone close to you has abundance and you don't, your beliefs might be:

- IF OTHERS I KNOW ARE ABUNDANT THEY SHOULD SHARE THEIR WEALTH WITH ME.
- IF OTHERS CREATE ABUNDANCE I DON'T HAVE TO.
- OTHERS CAN CREATE ABUNDANCE BUT NOT ME.
- I AM NOT POWERFUL ENOUGH (OR SMART ENOUGH) TO CREATE GREAT WEALTH.
- THE ONLY WAY I'LL GET CLOSE TO GREAT ABUNDANCE IS TO HAVE [NAME] SHARE THEIRS WITH ME.

If someone legitimately owed you something and reneged, your beliefs might be:

- I CAN'T HOLD ONTO THE SUCCESS I CREATE.
- I ALWAYS GET SCREWED.
- PEOPLE TAKE ADVANTAGE OF ME.

- I ATTRACT DISHONEST PEOPLE.
- IF SOMEONE OWES ME MONEY IT'S MY JOB TO GET HIM OR HER TO PAY.

But, before you can discover and change the beliefs, you first have to …

Release the Constricting Emotions Around Your Entitlement

If you are swimming in entitlement, it's because you feel you've gotten ripped off somehow—and you're angry about that, whether you're in touch with that anger or not.

The first step in healing anything is to let your emotions flow. If you don't allow the emotions to release, you'll simply carry them around with you like a pile of wet blankets. Not only will they interfere with your process of uncovering and changing your underlying beliefs; eventually, they'll start to feel like they're suffocating you.

So, get angry! Feel the hurt. Feel the pain and betrayal if it's there—but in an appropriate way. (For example, you can blow up your boss's house in your meditation, but you can't egg his house in real life!)

What? I could never do that. You keep telling me that my mind is powerful—I'll hurt someone!

No, you won't. You'd be blowing up your boss's house in meditation for the purpose of releasing your pent-up emotion. That act of release won't hurt anyone. In fact, you'll hurt him—and yourself—a lot more if you keep all that anger inside.

Deeply-held resentment and anger will attack its target both energetically and through passive-aggressive behavior you may not even know you're exhibiting.

In other words, expressing your emotions (in appropriate ways) frees you and others from the constrictions of those emotions.

> *But maybe I don't* want *to free that person. Maybe [name] deserves my hate.*

That's the anger I'm talking about—and if you consciously choose to hold onto it, you are consciously choosing to keep creating the *exact same reality* you have now. Let it go.

If meditation isn't your thing (even when it involves explosions), write a "hate letter." Make it mean and hurtful and scathing. Say everything you've always wanted to say, and then some. Don't give it to the person, though; instead, safely burn it. Again, this is for the purpose of releasing your emotions, not punishment.

But what if I still feel wronged?

If someone legitimately owes you money, then ...

Maybe You *Do* Take Legal Action

It's not wrong to sue someone for what you know is yours. But if you emotionally hold onto the entitlement when you're doing so, it will slow your abundance.

How do I know if I should sue or not?

First, release your emotions around the money. Then, change the constricting beliefs. Remember that you create your money, all of it, and if it doesn't come through one path, it will come through another. Really own that wealth; more, own the security of knowing the only way you can be short-changed is if you do it to yourself.

Only once you've released all that need, emotion, and attachment should you consider the possibility of a lawsuit.

Sometimes a lawsuit is appropriate. It can raise your self-esteem, set important boundaries, and be a form of taking your power back. If this is the case for you, go for it.

But if the idea of it feels like a lot of work, and you think your energy would be better spent letting the universe reimburse you, don't file the suit.

There are no right or wrong answers; there are only answers that are right or wrong for you. Whatever you decide, know that you are creating the *results* of that decision as well, because ...

You Create Your Safety, Security, & Abundance

The real damage of entitlement (in any form) is that it is disempowering. No one can give you financial or emotional security but you. Take your power back and grow wealthy—or keep giving it away while you wait for what is "due" to you. It's your choice.

However, there's another tricky little Abundance Stopper that often rides along with entitlement, and that is ...

ENVY

Have you ever yearned for something a friend, acquaintance, or public figure possessed—be it love, style, beauty, success, or a "free ride" with a rich spouse?

Wanting something that someone else has isn't necessarily a bad thing. In and of itself, it doesn't mean you're envious; it only means that you've identified one of your own desires.

> *Envy (n):*
>
> 1. A feeling of discontented or resentful longing aroused by someone else's possessions, qualities, or luck.

Envy goes beyond noticing what someone else has. It means that you're flowing negative emotions because that person has what you don't, and you don't believe you'll ever have it.

While we're at it, let's take a look at what "resentment" means:

> *Resentment (n):*
>
> 1. Bitter indignation at having been treated unfairly.

There is a big difference between saying, "I love what you have and I am going to create that too—thanks for the inspiration!" and saying, "I want that so bad I can taste it and I'll never, ever have it, as long as I live!" (You could even tack on a scathing "That bitch!" for emphasis.)

When your admiration crosses the line to envy, you've got a problem. It's not an unsolvable problem—it's just a problem you need to solve before you can effectively create abundance.

To start, ask yourself why you don't feel you can create what someone else has. Maybe it has something to do with these beliefs ...

- I DON'T DESERVE A SPECTACULAR LIFE.
- OTHER PEOPLE CAN HAVE WONDERFUL THINGS, BUT I CAN'T.
- SOME THINGS ARE BEYOND MY ABILITY TO CREATE.
- I DON'T HAVE WHAT IT TAKES TO CREATE _________.
- I AM NOT LOVABLE.
- I AM NOT WORTHY OF GREAT SUCCESS.

... or myriad other possible beliefs. Feel it out. What is hiding in your subconscious mind?

If one of those beliefs resonates, make note of it. But before you move on, ask yourself if you are longing for a specific reality, or if you want the emotional aspect of what someone else has.

If it's the former, you're setting yourself up for disappointment. If you want someone else's body, money, fame, mate, house, etc., chances are you think that these things will make you feel worthy, loved, and like you are enough. But, dear heart, only you can change the beliefs that tell you that you are not worthy, loved, or enough. Until you do that, all the stuff in the world won't transform your reality.

And if you think having what someone else has will make you happy, well, that's just never gonna happen. Happiness doesn't come from outside of you—it comes from inside of you.

Another thing to remember when it comes to envy ...

Envy Comes With a Hidden Gift

Envy is a message to you. It says:

Everyone in your reality who has what you want is a "sign" to you that you can have it too.

Did you let that in? The very fact that someone in your life has what you want means you can have it, too! Someone else is showing you it's creatable—and the fact that you've created it in your world is a sign that it is within your ability to create it too. Every time you see someone with something spectacular, it's cause for celebration!

I promise, it's true—but only if you get over the big stumbling block of …

DESERVABILITY

You *deserve.*

How could any divine being, any spark of consciousness who is a piece of God and Goddess *not* deserve? Exactly. It's impossible. Because you exist, you deserve. By your very nature, you are deserving.

But, the fact that you are deserving doesn't mean you believe it—and if you don't believe you deserve abundance, *you will not create abundance.*

You'll blame your lack of abundance on the economy, on your parents who didn't give you enough support, on your partner who spends too much, on the lack of opportunity in the job market, or on the jerks who don't see your talent. You'll make excuses as to why you can't make it in the world—from "I don't really want to" to "There is nothing I really feel passionate about"—and you won't even admit that they're excuses.

You'll find a thousand things to do with your time, but say you're "too busy" to change the beliefs you know you have to change and flow energy toward your greatest dreams and desires.

You will do all of these things, and more, because deep down, underneath it all, *you don't believe you deserve.*

But ... you *do* deserve.

Feeling undeserving, not good enough, or unworthy *does not mean* you are undeserving, not good enough, or unworthy. These are beliefs, and only beliefs. They aren't written in stone. They aren't even real—but as long as you keep believing them, *they will affect your reality as if they were.*

Because you're ashamed of feeling these horribly debilitating emotions, you hide them from the world, and from yourself. You ignore them. You work around them. You set intentions with your conscious mind as if they weren't true. But your reality doesn't hide them. Your reality shows them off like the cheap imitation diamonds they are—and everybody sees it but you.

It sounds dire, I know. It is. And it will continue to be, until you take your power back.

Once you do that, it's game on! You can heal the not good enough, the undeserving, and the lack of worthiness. Everything can be healed—but first you need to admit it's there. You need to see that the faucet is leaking before you can make repairs.

Where Does This Lack of Deservability Come From?

Who knows? It's probably not from just one place, but instead from thin blankets of shame, pain, disappointment, and "not enough" that you've picked up over the years from ...

Your Parents

Dad and Mom were our "God and Goddess" when we entered this world. What they felt, said, and did impacted us deeply. We could be cut to the bone by an offhand remark, or receive a signal of "not good enough" from a parent who was preoccupied with something else when we felt we needed them.

That we didn't (and don't) feel deserving doesn't mean that our parents were bad parents, or that they didn't love us—but how could parents who were not quite healed, whole, or evolved teach us to be those things? Chances are, they carried their own feelings of being not enough, undeserving, or unworthy, too.

Authority Figures

As we grew, other gods and goddesses—other male and female authority figures—came into our lives. Uncles, aunts, older siblings, teachers, doctors, and others become the powers in our lives who could wound us with the sword of unworthiness in one fell swoop.

Suddenly, one unthinking remark from your junior high school music teacher (who had just had a fight with his wife and took it out on you) resulted in you becoming a little less whole, a little less worthy, and a little less deserving of the good things in life.

Religion

Whether you were brought up in a traditionally religious household or not, religion has impacted you. The idea that "we are all sinners" doesn't exactly leave anyone with a warm, fuzzy feeling about our inherent value as human beings.

What rambunctious kid hasn't been threatened by a line like, "I'll put the fear of God into you"? When you're five, or six, or seven, you don't reason out the concept of "Why should I fear God, anyway?" or "Why would God find me so bad?" You just accept that you're bad in God's eyes.

How deeply religion has impacted you depends upon on how immersed in religion you were as a child and adolescent—but we are all affected by this cultural phenomenon to one degree or another.

Yes, those in our lives who felt undeserving themselves, or who were trying to do the right thing but were unaware of the deeper impact of their actions, have affected our sense of worthiness.

But, believe it or not ...

There Are People Who *Want* to Keep You Undeserving & Un-Abundant

It's sad, but it's true. There are factions out there that are motivated to keep you powerless and filled with fear. There are those who have a vested interest in keeping your abundance, fulfillment, peace, and joy perpetually out of arm's reach.

Think of the illness industry (ironically called "health care"). How many people, companies, and entire industries would lose out if people took their power back and became responsible for their own health and healing?

Then, there's the cunning fashion and beauty industry, which keeps people wanting what they don't have by changing the "must have" every season. Staying on top of the "latest and greatest" is a full-time job for some people—yet, sadly they never feel as if they truly "make it," at least not for long.

If the fashion industry fails to persuade you that you aren't "enough," the diet and exercise industries will. Beyond the widespread injuries to self-esteem, real crisis occurs when people forgo their ability to have a positive impact in the world and instead obsess about weight and BMI.

Of course, the entertainment industry is right up there, too, with its attempts to rob you of your own passion, lust for life and creativity, and instead replace it with what it thinks you should be passionate about and lustful for (not to mention, spend your money on).

And, don't forget the quiet one in the corner: the insurance industry. This is a multi-billion dollar industry whose sole purpose is to keep you so fearful that you buy their policies to protect against catastrophes that haven't happened, and may never happen. This isn't to say insurance is never a good idea—but to look at it and everything with eyes wide open.

Don't worry. Once you begin to recognize manipulative energy, you can simply say "no"—or, at the very least, make your decisions consciously, by looking past the cleverly-presented coercion. Remember, you are divine and deserving of all good things—so change the beliefs that say you aren't, avoid the sources that try to re-implant those beliefs, and go on to create abundance.

But even once you do this, the act of creating an abundant life, or even your intention to create an abundant life, may bring up something else ...

GUILT

What if you had lots and lots of money, but those you loved continued to struggle and suffer?

Well, I could give them some of my money!

Yes, you could. But if they still wanted to struggle and suffer, trust me, they would figure out a way.

Well, wouldn't giving them money make them happy?

No, it wouldn't. Money doesn't make people happy. Remember, money is nothing more than pretty printed paper. It has no power in and of itself.

Happiness is a choice you make for yourself as you create your reality. Your loved ones can also make that choice—but you can't make it for them.

Many people tie their sense of self worth and value to what they earn. Those in your life who hold those beliefs could be threatened when you start to create abundance with elegance and ease, because it challenges their notion of what is "true" about money and brings up feelings of inadequacies in many.

Now, imagine if you also had other abundances, like love, creativity, joy, success, health, and even fun—but those you love didn't. What happens when you create what others want (but don't create for themselves)?

Guilt happens. And guilt will slow, and eventually stop your abundance, if you let it worm its way into your consciousness.

Guilt (n):

1. A feeling of having committed (a) wrong or failed in an obligation.

What Is Your Guilt Telling You?

Guilt is saying (and believing) things like:

- I HAVE MONEY AND OTHERS DON'T, AND THAT IS WRONG.
- I AM OBLIGATED TO STAY POOR IF THOSE I CARE ABOUT ARE POOR.
- I SHOULD MAKE MY FATHER/BROTHER/HUSBAND/FRIENDS/ETC. FEEL GOOD ABOUT THEMSELVES BY NOT MAKING MORE MONEY THAN THEY DO/DID.

There are infinite variations on this theme, but one thing is always true: guilt tells the universe, "I shouldn't have money."

Let's face it: if you want to create abundance, that is *not* the message you want to be sending.

How to Handle Guilt

Here are a number of ways to work with guilt:

- ***Check to see if you have some anger underneath the guilt.*** The anger would be related to others preventing you from creating abundance—either by guilt-tripping you, or simply by being the reasons you don't allow it. In meditation, confront them and express your anger. Blow things up, yell, scream, hit ... whatever feels right. Make it clear you will create abundance with or without their support and that you will love them unconditionally whether or not they create an abundant life.

- ***Remember (and affirm) the following truths:***
  - Stopping yourself from allowing abundance won't help anyone.
  - You can't control whether others accept abundance for themselves—but you *can* control whether *you* do.
  - When you create abundance, you lift the resonance of everyone around you. This helps them create better realities whether they believe in conscious creation or not.
  - Others may be creating *you* in *their* lives to prove to them that creating money can be easy and fun.

- ***Change these beliefs if you have them:***
  - THERE IS A LIMITED AMOUNT OF MONEY AVAILABLE.
  - I AM RESPONSIBLE FOR [NAME]'S ABUNDANCE.
  - I MUST SHOW MY LOVE BY STAYING IN SCARCITY.
  - [NAME] WON'T LOVE ME IF I AM RICH AND SUCCESSFUL.
  - [NAME] WON'T LOVE ME IF I DON'T TAKE CARE OF THEM FINANCIALLY.

And Remember ...

It's not that you can't be compassionate when people are struggling. You care about those you love, and it's wonderful to express that care. The key to caring without guilt is to detach emotionally from others' outcomes. Allow others to live their individual experiences and journeys in this lifetime. Be an inspiration, but don't allow anything or anyone to detract you from your mission of living an abundant life.

You may want to plan how you'll respond to those who ask you for money[1] once you become abundant—but for now, be aware of what you feel, more than you ever have before. Remember, we're human; we all fall into difficult emotions from time to time. When you do, remember what the constricting emotion does to your abundance, forgive yourself for creating whatever made you feel that emotion, and move forward into the emotions (and the reality) you prefer.

Creating abundance is a skill, but it's also an art. As a "reality artisan," you must become intimately aware of your emotions. If you let it, this can be fun in and of itself. After all, the better you feel, the better you feel—and the better you feel, the better you will create!

(1) You may want to refer to the blog post "How to (Lovingly) Turn Down Requests for Money." Access it at www.LiveALifeYouLove.com/money-requests.

A TRUE STORY OF CONSCIOUSLY CREATING ABUNDANCE

I created the life of my dreams after thirty-one years of working in the medical field as an RN. I loved my patients, but I began to feel suffocated and drained by the administrative aspects of the career, and my heart was increasingly burdened by the corporate emphasis on machines and paperwork over people.

I wanted to take a year off to pray, think, seek God, and find my true path, but I was afraid I couldn't support myself, my daughters, and my beloved pets without working as a nurse.

When I couldn't take it for another second, I tucked my dog-eared copy of The Map *(my favorite book), a fresh new journal, and three new colored pens into my worn, happy canvas bag (the one with a cheery sunshine face on it), and I went to my favorite little Mexican restaurant. As I sat there, I cried, laughed, and closed my eyes to dream. I decided that I wouldn't leave my seat until I came to a resolution.*

I made a mini-vision map in my journal, and I decided to take the plunge. I wrote my resignation letter and turned it in that day.

The very next day, my sister called to offer my girls and me the use of their church parsonage free for six months. We packed up our things, hopped in our car, and moved from Florida to the tiny hamlet of Franklin, GA.

God provided literally everything we needed—right down to cat food and cat litter—for a full six months. The last week of our stay there, I was still in the process of creating my dream life, not entirely sure how I wanted my new life to look, but determined not to run back to my nursing career.

That week, a dear friend called to ask if we wanted to house sit for him for six months. After a three-hour drive to Gainesville in North

Georgia, we found a perfect little green cottage, complete with a fenced yard where our dog Beau could run, and brightly-colored lights strung up along the covered back porch. It was an ideal spot for me to write my stories, dream my dreams, and weave the threads of this brand new life I was creating.

Ultimately, I decided to pursue a career in inspirational writing. The magical stories of manifestation continue, and writing opportunities abound. My daughters have begun to create lives they love as well. As a bonus, I have lost twelve pounds, and finally feel confident in my body. I feel abundant! I feel like anything is possible! I am creatively bringing my dreams to life, and it is magical!

- Donnamarie R.

ABUNDANCE-ALTERING TAKEAWAYS

- Do you know that, if you simply stated what you want (i.e. wrote your intentions) and did nothing else, eventually your dream would manifest—if you didn't flow energy in opposition to it?

- "Abundance stoppers" are emotional states that keep abundance at a distance. Sometimes these emotions are subtle energies that run deep within us. Sometimes they are relentlessly conscious. And sometimes they vary between the two extremes, depending on the day. However, they will *all* stop your abundance.

- You will have much less fear once you've dealt with your other "selves" and changed your beliefs. You will always dream bigger dreams; every time you stretch further, you will feel fear about doing so, but the fear will no longer control you. Instead, it will serve its purpose: to show you what beliefs to change next.

- To handle your doubt, examine it and discover where it comes from. When you change the beliefs which are causing the fear that underlies the doubt, the doubt will disappear.

- Self-pity and victimhood typically show up together—and they can be very subtle. Even when they show up as you being "just a little down," they are both flavors of victimhood, and they will stop your abundance from manifesting. You simply can't be a victim and powerful at the same time.

- It's not wrong to accept abundance from others, but once you expect it from someone (or something), you have crossed the line into entitlement, and are doing yourself and your abundance a grave disservice.

- There's a big difference between saying, "I love what that person has and I am going to create it!" and saying, "I want that so bad I can taste it and I'll never, ever have it, as long as I live!" When your admiration crosses the line to envy, you have a problem.

- How could any divine being, any spark of consciousness who is a piece of God and Goddess not deserve? Exactly. By your very nature, you deserve—but if you don't believe you deserve abundance, *you will not create abundance.*

- Guilt tells the universe, "I shouldn't have money." Let's face it: that's *not* the message you want to be sending.

YOUR NEXT STEPS

- Ask your unseen friends to gently bring to your attention any abundance stoppers you've been indulging in, and to help you heal and change the habit.

- Do you have doubts about your ability to create abundance? What beliefs keep them alive? Write them out so you can change them.

- What fearful scenarios about money and abundance do you replay in your head? What beliefs do they point to?

- What doubts do you have about creating an abundant life? What fears (and beliefs) underpin those doubts?

- Do you have a propensity to feel hopeless, helpless, powerless, and/or that life isn't fair? Do you complain to your friends and family? Do you tend to worry more than not? If so, do you have beliefs that are keeping your victimhood locked in place? What are they?

- Do you feel a sense of entitlement to receive anything in your life? If so, process the constricting emotions, then look for the beliefs that keep your entitlement from being released.

- Do you greatly admire anyone you know? What does that person being in your life tell you about yourself and your ability to create?

- Do you feel envious of anyone you know? What beliefs does that envy show you?

- On a scale of 1-10, how deserving do you feel? Do you have any beliefs regarding deservability that you want to change?

- Does guilt come up for you when you think about creating and having abundance? If so, follow the strategies outlined to deactivate it.

- Use the applied kinesiology techniques in Appendix B to test for the constricting beliefs in this chapter. Document the beliefs that need to be changed, and change them using a technique in Appendix D.

CHAPTER SEVEN

Making Your "Selves" Abundant

"A sense of worthiness is a child's most important need."
~ POLLY BERRIEN BERENDS

You have made a commitment to abundance. You've become clear about what you desire. You've written your intentions. So now, you're ready to create abundance, right?

Not so fast my friend. There's still some prep work to be done.

Why? Because, again, abundance is different. You're not a blank slate when it comes to money. You've been programmed to truly believe that it is beyond your ability to create money out of thin air. You probably also have a slew of failures in your back pocket that prove you can't create it by hard work and desire alone, either.

Wow, that's a hopeless combination, isn't it?

Hopeless? Never. Nothing and no one is hopeless. Remember that.

However, you can't fix a conundrum like your programmed beliefs and experiences around money with the same thinking that created it. You have to step outside the box, and do things in a new way—the *right* way.

And what is the right way?

MOVE INTO ALIGNMENT WITH ABUNDANCE

Whether you realize it or not, you are a complex being. There are more aspects to you than just your adult self—the self who is reading this book right now.

There are higher aspects of you, such as your higher self, your soul, and spirit. These selves are totally in alignment with your desire to create and enjoy abundance, and support anything that makes you genuinely happy and helps you to grow. They are totally hopeful about your future, and 100 percent confident in your ability to create the best life possible for yourself.

There are also aspects of you from your past, like your child self, your adolescent self, and your younger adult selves. These aspects may or may not be in alignment with you about creating abundance—but if they're not, their opposition will sabotage your success.

And then, there's "Neg"—your negative self—whom we met in the last chapter. Trust me, Neg would sooner die than see you create a happy, abundant life.

These aspects are all flowing energy either in favor of or against the abundance you seek. Aligning those selves is critical, because if there are parts of you that don't feel good about and/or empowered enough to create abundance, well, it's going to throw a monkey wrench in *your* ability to do so.

Oh, you may eke out some abundance if you don't do this alignment, but it will be nothing like you could create if all of your "selves" are on the same page.

It might sound like a chore at first, but trust me: this preparatory work makes the entire Map process so much easier and more fun. Imagine how hopeful and joyous it would feel to know that nothing could pull you back into your old paradigm of struggle and lack.

So, where do you begin?

FORGIVE THE PAST

I felt like such a failure when my life was falling apart. There's nothing like creditors calling around the clock to make you feel like a schmuck.

And I couldn't help thinking, "I know better!"

I did know about the Law of Attraction. By that time, I had been reading books about it for fifteen damn years! And so, I kept asking myself, "What the hell is wrong with me that I could create such a dismal mess of my life?"

Of course there was nothing wrong with me. I just hadn't figured out how to create differently. That energy of self-judgment didn't help, though. It never does. I had to learn to let it go, and so do you.

You see, as long as you blame yourself for your past, you send messages to your subconscious mind, which holds them as beliefs like:

- I AM A FAILURE.
- I AM FLAWED.
- I AM POWERLESS.

This is not good energy to put out there if what you want to create is:

- I AM A SUCCESS.
- I AM DIVINE.
- I AM POWERFUL.

You need to forgive yourself for your past.

But, if I forget about the past, I might make the same mistakes all over again!

I didn't say you needed to *forget* the past (although, in some cases, that might not be a bad idea). What I said was that you needed to *forgive* yourself for it—even if "the past" is as recent as yesterday.

Stop defining yourself by what's happened before this moment. Let it go.

The Stories We Tell

Many of us have a tendency to hold on to our stories about why we struggle. We blame our past circumstances, our parents, our environment, our bosses, and ourselves. We let these stories define who we are and what we're capable of.

In other words, we become the victims of our own stories. And, as you'll recall from Chapter Six, victim energy is poisonous to conscious creation.

I remember fighting with my ex over alimony, child support, and the children's medical bills. The way he decided to handle things resulted in me not being able to pay my mortgage and the house going into foreclosure. I was livid with him for putting me in that situation.

One day my very wise teenage son said to me, "Mom, why don't you just stop depending on Dad for money? That way what he does pay will just be icing on the cake?"

It was then that it hit me: I was feeling *entitled* to that money. I held the belief that it was owed to me, and I was afraid I wouldn't get it. I was essentially telling the universe:

- MONEY CAN COME TO ME FROM ONLY ONE SOURCE.
- I AM NOT RECEIVING MONEY.
- I AM NOT IN CONTROL OF WHETHER OR NOT I AM ABUNDANT.
- [NAME, ENTITY, OR SITUATION] IS IN CONTROL OF WHETHER OR NOT I AM ABUNDANT.

Believe me, this is *not* the energy that will create money.

I can hear you fighting this, saying,

But I really am owed money!

I know. But unless you let it go you will not be open to receive all that you could otherwise receive. Does that mean let go of a legal fight? Maybe.

I know a man—let's call him Jacob—whose business provided over a million dollars of work for a major corporation. Then, the corporation decided not to pay him.

Now, to practically everyone on the planet, a million dollars is a lot of money. And yes, Jacob was owed that money. But it was eating his abundance alive.

He spent hundreds of hours lamenting the loss of the money, and hundreds more in lawsuits to recover the money. While this debt was in his life, he was putting forth energy that told the universe, "I don't receive money!"

Not only is Jacob not receiving the money that's owed to him, he's not receiving much else, either. His business has been slower than molasses since the lawsuits began, and for every step forward it takes two steps back.

Now, as we discussed in the last chapter, I'm not saying that suing for what you are legally owed is wrong. I am saying that unless you can energetically let it go, fighting for your money may do you more harm than good.

What does "energetically letting it go" look like?

Repeat after me.

> *I know I am owed this money, but I choose to energetically let it go. I may pursue legal recourse for various reasons, but I am open to money coming to me in the easiest and most elegant manner possible; if it doesn't come from the one who 'owes' me, I choose and allow that it comes to me multiplied by one hundred through other more perfect avenues.*

I've used this approach several times in different situations when I was owed money that wasn't paid to me, sometimes to the tune of tens of thousands of dollars. And, while it feels hard the first time (or ten) that you do it, I know firsthand that letting go frees you.

Letting go allows you to move on. It allows you to spend your energy and emotions on things that make you feel good, not bad. And, if your belief system is in alignment, it allows the money you "let go" to come back to you one hundred fold. (Actually, it was more like one hundred thousand fold for me!)

I've said it before, and I'll say it again: *you can't fool the universe.* If you don't go the legal route, but spend the next ten years wishing you had, it will gnaw away at you, and that doubt will slow down or halt your ability to create abundance. If you do pursue a lawsuit, but don't let it go energetically, it may cost you a lot of abundance because the energy you spent fighting for your money was energy you couldn't spend allowing and inviting money to arrive easily and elegantly from different sources.

Holding onto entitlement or judgments from your past will not bring you abundance. So, make the choice that is right for you right now, and then back up that choice by honestly and truly *letting it go.*

And for everyone …

FORGIVE YOURSELF

Forgive yourself for all of your past financial creations, conscious or not, that were challenging, disastrous, or simply less than you'd hoped. If you can't forgive yourself at this point in time, *set an intention* to forgive yourself; your unseen friends will gently guide and assist you to do just that.

Once you have a clean (energetic) slate, you'll be ready to move forward and create your life of abundance. But first, you'll want to …

GET YOUR "CHILD SELF" ON BOARD

You may not remember your childhood, but your subconscious mind does—every teeny, tiny bit of it. The adult, present-day you has moved on, but your child's energy around money has not.

If you felt or witnessed any lack, scarcity, struggle, guilt, greed, fear, negative thoughts, or negative feelings around money when you were a child, you likely still carry that energy (in the form of beliefs) today. You're not conscious of it, so it seems as though it doesn't exist—but it does, and it's reflected in your reality.

I don't know why it works this way; I only know that it does. We don't lose aspects of ourselves. They stick around for as long as we're residents of this Earth, and maybe even beyond that.

Time machines haven't yet been invented, so we can't go back and physically change the past. However, we can change the past energetically, which is just as good, if not better. And, when we do that, we shift the energy of the present. How cool is that?

Past: *changed.*
Struggle energy: *gone.*
Scarcity energy: *vanished.*
Lack energy: *nil.*

And all of this is reflected in your world.

How does one accomplish such a magical feat? Simple. Go back to your child self in meditation, and have a little chat.

That's it? Seriously?

That's it. Since space and time are illusions, nothing really dies. Your child self still exists, and you can access them within minutes.

But here's the catch: this can't be just an exercise. You must engage your emotions in order for this to work. (Emotions flow energy, remember?)

Even if you feel silly doing this the first couple of times, take this work seriously. It will change your creation capacity, your finances, and your life.

When you step into this work, you'll have three major objectives:

First, you will heal your inner child by allowing them to fully feel and express their emotions around abundance and worthiness.

Second, you'll discover your child self's limiting beliefs around money, worthiness, and deserving. Your child self has beliefs you have no clue they carry—beliefs you have long since forgotten. While you can guess at what these beliefs might be, you'll never know for certain *unless you go back and ask your child self.*

Third, you will improve your child self's relationship with money. This will automatically align you with abundance. My favorite technique for accomplishing this is to give your child a money machine.(1)

What? That's crazy!

Who cares? It works!

Imagine if you'd had a money machine as a child, and all you had to do was press a button for $20 bills or $100 bills (simply flip a switch to choose!) to pop out into your hands. Unlike a gumball machine, this money machine contained an unlimited supply of money. It never had to be refilled. There was no end to the money that you could receive simply by pressing that button.

(1) I first learned this technique from the channeled entity, Galexis. For more information, visit www.GalexisSpirit.com.

Such a machine might have made quite a difference for your child self. You wouldn't have had any worries whatsoever about money. You could have given your parents as much as you wanted, making their lives abundant too. You would have felt powerful. You would have felt as if you lived in an abundant universe.

And, since space and time are illusions, you can give this gift to your child self *now*, and it will change your relationship with money *now*.

Isn't that exciting?

Thought so.

Just one thing: if your child self has some bad feelings about money, you must allow them to feel those emotions before giving them the money machine. Feeling the lack, fear, hopelessness, sadness, or whatever they felt will create the space for the new feelings the money machine will bring: abundance, safety, hopefulness, joy, etc.

Here's how to do it ...

Align Your "Child Self" With Abundance[2]

> Find a comfortable and quiet place to be alone. Lie down, or sit comfortably. Lower the lights. Play some soft music if you like, or light a candle. Close your eyes. As you breathe deeply, imagine yourself drifting into a deeper and deeper state of relaxation.
>
> Imagine yourself in a beautiful place in nature. Sit here for a while. Allow yourself to notice your surroundings. Continue to relax, knowing you are safe.

(2) This meditation, Aligning Your Child Self with Abundance, is recorded and available at www.LiveALifeYouLove.com.

Your higher self comes to join you. Greet them in a way that feels right and true to you, and tell them of your desire: "I want to meet with my child self. I want to talk with them about money and abundance. I want to give them a reality where money is no object."

Your higher self wholeheartedly agrees with this plan. They wrap you in their arms, and you feel a beautiful bubble of love and light form around you. As your head rests upon your higher self's shoulder, you relax into their love. Time passes as you float across time and space. And at some point, you raise your head and open your eyes.

You and your higher self are standing in front of the house you lived in as a child. It could be when you were four, or five, or even as old as nine or ten. Trust that you have come back to the perfect time.

Go inside to find the "you" who still lives in that house. Somehow you know exactly where to look. Your child self is alone, as if they knew you were coming. You go to them, and greet them, or introduce yourself if this is your first time meeting them. You say, "I'm here because I'm creating unlimited money and abundance in my life. And I'd love to know how money and other abundances show up in your life."

Your child self will tell you what they think about how money comes into one's life. They will tell you about their own life. Don't interrupt; just listen. Their emotional reaction may surprise you. They may be angry. They may laugh at you. Let it be what it is and don't try to make them respond in any certain way. Just give them the respect they deserve, and keep listening.

> You may find they're willing and excited to share what they think. Or, you may have to say goodbye and continue in another, later meditation, and win their trust before they open up to you. There is no right or wrong way to do this. Again, trust the process.
>
> Once you feel you have discovered where this younger "you" stands on the topic of money, let them know you can create unlimited money for him or her. Say something like, "Did you know that I can make sure you never, ever have to be concerned with money again? How would you like a money machine?" Then give it to them. Show them how it works. Watch them press the button in delight, and take in their smile that stretches from ear to ear.
>
> Leave the meditation when you are ready. Let your child self know that you'll be back to check in with them—but make them promise not to join you in your reality. You are fully capable of handling your reality as an adult. They don't have to do anything except enjoy their new money machine, and keep smiling.

Once you are out of meditation, jot down what your child said. *Their* ideas about money translate into *your* beliefs about money. (We'll talk more about beliefs in the following chapter.)

Next …

WORK WITH YOUR ADOLESCENT SELF

The process of working with your adolescent is similar, but it won't be the same. You were a different person as an adolescent than you were as a child, so allow this experience to be brand new. Allow your adolescent to feel their "not good enough" and any other feelings they had around money. Give him or her a money machine too. They will be very excited at this new level of power and ability they now have.

Again write down what your adolescent says about money and abundance, because those feelings, thoughts, and ideas translate into beliefs which may need to be changed.

Next ...

VISIT YOUR YOUNGER ADULT SELVES

All of us have past experiences that we wish had gone better. Lost job opportunities, difficult financial situations, and dreams that never manifested (at least, not in the ways we'd hoped).

There is a younger adult self attached to each and every one of those experiences—and every one of those disappointed selves took on beliefs about themselves, others, and the world during these life events. Because of their disappointing experiences and the resulting beliefs, they carry energy that will cause more disappointment if left unchanged.

However, your younger selves don't have to keep defining you or your reality. Just like you did with your child and adolescent selves, you can shift all of their energies to align with empowerment, abundance, and success. All you have to do is go back and give those younger adult selves success instead of failure!

In my early twenties, I interviewed for a position as the marketing manager for a mall. I had a background in window design, and had done some advertising for a large department store, but the job was still a stretch for me. To my twenty-one-year-old self, it was almost "too good to be true."

Amazingly, I landed a second interview. Then, it was down to a decision between me and another, older woman who had much more experience. When I didn't get the job, I tried to be philosophical about the loss, but honestly, it stung.

Bigger disappointments were to come—the biggest of which was, ironically, my first foray into conscious creation work in the mid 1990s.

I had so many positive signs. I had interest from Nightingale-Conant about carrying my tape series in their catalog. I signed a contract for a story to be published in one of the first *Chicken Soup for the Soul* books. I wrote a little book called *A Piece of Chocolate for a Woman's Heart* (this was before a similar book had been published). I secured an agent in NYC and she was excited to sell the book.

Then, Nightingale-Conant decided against carrying my tapes. My story was pulled from the *Chicken Soup* book. And believe it or not, *both the agent and I lost the manuscripts of my book!*

It's obvious to me now that I was not ready for success. But although the present-day me understands why and how I created those setbacks, my younger adult selves were still just as devastated as they were at the moment these reversals occurred.

These parts of me believed that:

- I AM NOT GOOD ENOUGH.
- I NEVER SUCCEED.
- I AM UNWORTHY OF SUCCESS.
- I CAN MANIFEST SIGNS, BUT I CAN'T SUSTAIN THE ENERGY.
- SOME THINGS REALLY ARE TOO GOOD TO BE TRUE.

Needless to say, that was *not* the energy I wanted in my present. So what did I do?

I went to each of those selves in meditation and gave them the reality they wanted. The twenty-one-year-old got the job in the mall. Nightingale-Conant gave my thirty-something a contract for her audio workshop. The *Chicken Soup for the Soul* book contains my younger self's story. And *A Piece of Chocolate for a Woman's Heart* was a *New York Times* best-seller.

Doing this dramatically shifted my energy. Suddenly I felt successful and triumphant—as if no dream were too big!

Was it really that easy?

Yes, it was. This doesn't have to be a long arduous task. You just have to do it.

Once you have all of your younger selves in alignment with abundance, it's time to ...

LET YOUR "NEGATIVE SELF" TELL YOU YOU'RE CRAZY

Your negative self is your inner saboteur, the destructive aspect of your ego, your inner critic, and the least evolved "you" that there is. Your negative self expects you to fail, in fact wants you to fail.

Your negative self is the part of you that speaks in your head about what you can't do, have, and be. It's tempting to just ignore what it has to say and hope it will go away, but here's the thing: this part of you needs to have a voice.

So give "Neg" a voice. Imagine it sitting next to you, in all its ugliness. Let it tell you that you're crazy for trying to create money out of thin air. Let it rant and rave.

The conversation might go something like this:

You: "Hey, I wanted to tell you, I'm in the process of creating financial abundance."

Neg: "What?"

You: "Creating financial abundance. I have discovered I create my own reality. I want to be abundant. So I'm creating that."

Neg: "You poor thing. You're more gullible than I thought."

You: "I'm not gullible. It's a very old concept, and it's easier now than ever before!"

Neg: "Yeah? Prove it."

You: "Well, you can't really prove it. The evidence is more anecdotal. But it does work!"

Neg: "Sure, kid. Good luck with that. Buy me a mansion when you 'create' being a billionaire, will ya?"

You: "I *am* creating it." (Note: It's never a good idea to argue with your negative self. It wants that. And you'll never convince it of anything. Just listen.)

Neg: "You can't create crap, kid. This whole thing is a scam."

You:: "Okay. Thanks for your opinion."

Neg: "I mean it. You're being duped. Get your head outta the clouds and get real. You're gonna die poor."

You: "Thanks for sharing. Anything else?"

Neg: "Yeah, you're pretty stupid for believing this stuff. Oh, and you're ugly too."

You: "Nice. You finished?"

Neg: "Harrumph."

Then, mentally call in your higher self, and ask that it gently take your negative self away to be healed. Then—for a little while, at least—you'll be free.

I suggest working with your negative self daily when you have some big dreams in the works. It has a tendency to creep back into your head at the precise times when sustaining your energy is critical.

But, as far as aligning your energy ...

You Did It!

Once you have cleared the energy of lack in all of the various aspects of yourself, changed the limiting beliefs that were pointed out to you, and introduced the energy of abundance to each self, you will be fully aligned and ready to create true and miraculous abundance.

You will *feel* the difference. The entire concept of conscious creation will feel more true, more real, and more believable. Celebrate this feeling. You are one step closer to creating your totally abundant reality and making your dreams come true!

A TRUE STORY OF CONSCIOUSLY CREATING ABUNDANCE

Recently, I was feeling down about money. My roommate hadn't paid rent in several months, and his financial situation was growing more desperate every week. I didn't want to kick him to the curb because he was my friend.

I was using my savings to pay the bills, so my money was dwindling, too. Instead of getting angry, depressed, or worried, however, I decided to let the situation resolve itself—"with grace, elegance, and harm to none," as Boni says.

Shortly before my bank account zeroed out, I found a new roommate. When I broke the news to the deadbeat roomie that he had to move out, he informed me that he had been offered a room for free by some acquaintances of his that lived only .4 miles from my house. ("Good timing," I thought).

Then, a job found its way to me through my school (without any solicitation on my part). I turned it down at first because I thought it would be too time-consuming. Shortly before my summer break, I was offered the same job by the same person, but in a slightly different capacity that was perfect for me. I happily accepted. ("Good timing," I thought again.)

Just the other day, I received a letter in the mail that said I was going to be paid several hundred dollars for a job I completed almost three years ago. I never in a million years thought I'd be paid for that work!

I thought, "Wait a minute. This must be my *doing, I am creating money for myself!"*

I gave myself a mental high-five, and I happily looked forward to more unexpected windfalls of "creative abundance manifestation" in the future.

Let it rain money! I'll figure out how to spend it later.

- Brandon B.

ABUNDANCE-ALTERING TAKEAWAYS

- Forgive yourself for all of your past financial creations, conscious or not, that were less than you'd hoped. If you can't forgive yourself at this point in time, set an *intention* to forgive yourself, and allow your unseen friends to guide, assist, and gently nudge you to do just that.

- If you felt or witnessed any lack, scarcity, struggle, guilt, fear, greed, negative thoughts, or negative feelings around money when you were a child, you likely still carry that energy (in the form of beliefs) today.

- Work with your child self to discover and heal that child's limiting beliefs around money and deserving. Then, give your child a money machine. When you improve your child self's relationship with money, you'll automatically align the present-day you with abundance.

- The process to improve your adolescent self's relationship with money is similar to working with your child self, but it won't be the same. You were a different person as an adolescent, so allow this experience to be brand new. Give your adolescent a money machine too. They'll be very excited at this new level of power and ability.

- For every past experience we wish could have gone better—job opportunities lost, challenging financial situations, and dreams that never manifested—we have a younger adult self that carries the beliefs and energy of that life event. If this energy isn't changed, it will continue to cause more disappointments.

- Your negative self is the part of you that speaks in your head about what you can't do, have, and be. This part of you needs to have a voice before you can quiet it. You can't just ignore it and hope it will go away, but you can disempower it by letting it rant, and then asking your higher self to take it away for healing.

YOUR NEXT STEPS

- Before you're free to create abundance, you need to forgive yourself for not creating abundance in the past. What less-than-stellar realities do you need to forgive yourself for creating? What realities of scarcity and lack? What hurts or betrayals? Remember: Everything is forgivable.

- Write out what you intend to forgive yourself for. Sign it three times. In a meditation, meet the person you intend to forgive or ask forgiveness from. (Note: this person might be a younger aspect of you.) Meet them at night, around a bonfire of forgiveness. Talk to them. Ask for their forgiveness, and when they've agreed (they will), burn the paper in meditation.

- Come out of meditation, burn the (real) paper safely, and *feel* the freedom of forgiveness.

- Visit your child self in meditation. Talk to them about creating abundance, and listen to what they have to say—witness what they allow themselves to feel. When they are complete, give them a money machine and watch their response. When you come out of meditation, write down what they said, and determine the beliefs underlying those statements. Write those down as well.

- Repeat the above exercise with your adolescent self.

- Make a list of the major financial and career disappointments of your life. One by one, visit with these disappointed selves. Let them vent, cry, complain, and get angry. Allow them free reign of emotion. When they're complete, tell them that they never have to be disappointed again. Give them what they wanted at the time, even if it's something you no longer desire. Watch them for a while—happy as can be in the reality they dreamed of.

- Imagine your "negative self" sitting next to you. Tell it that you're learning how to create unlimited abundance. Listen to what it has to say, until it can say no more. Then, call in your higher self to take your negative self away to be healed.

- Use the applied kinesiology techniques in Appendix B to test for constricting beliefs in this chapter. Document the beliefs that need to be changed, and change them using a technique in Appendix D.

CHAPTER EIGHT

Money & The Masculine

"You can open your mind to prosperity by giving up that ridiculous idea that poverty is a Christian virtue, when it is nothing but a common vice."

~ CATHERINE PONDER

Money is a masculine energy.

I know that sounds more than a little "woo-woo," but bear with me. Ultimately, it doesn't matter if money is masculine, feminine, or androgynous—what matters is your *emotional relationship* with money.

If you fear money, fear having money, fear being judged because you have money, or fear someone will take your money away once you have it, then you won't create it. And, since this book is dedicated to looking under every possible emotional rock to make sure nothing is lurking there which will sabotage your abundance, we are going to delve into your energetic relationship with the masculine nature of money.

WHY IS MONEY MASCULINE?

Ultimately, everything is energy. However, because of the way that energy operates in the world, it can express itself as more feminine or more masculine. (The most effective and fulfilled people have a balance of both energies, regardless of their gender!)

Feminine energy is the "being" energy. It is the space in which transformation can happen—just as a woman's body contains the womb where new life is nurtured. Feminine energy is passive and receptive; it's the "not yet manifested" energy. It's also the energy which connects us to one another and to the divine.

When feminine energy is imbalanced in a person, it shows up as dreaminess, lethargy, and a sense of powerlessness. A person with imbalanced feminine energy is someone who fantasizes about the life they desire but he or she never does anything to make it happen. Pure feminine energy can't create its way out of a paper bag, because it can't take action on its own. It is the proverbial empty womb; it needs to wait for a "trigger" to spark a creation which it can nurture.

Masculine energy, on the other hand, is the "doing" energy. It is goal-oriented and focused. Just as a sperm is required to spark the transformation of an egg in the womb into a new human being, masculine energy is necessary to manifest anything in the world.

Masculine energy is the energy that provides our individuality. When imbalanced, it can make a person ultra-focused on taking action—whether it be through work, exercise, relationships, or making money—but prompt them to ignore the inner aspects of life and steamroll through life without appreciating any of the fruits of their labors. Too much masculine energy can also create a sense of self-centeredness, because there isn't enough feminine connectedness to balance the person's individuality.

Money is masculine because it is one result (measure) of some of the outer actions which characterize masculine energy.

If you have issues with the masculine—in any form—you may unwittingly disrupt your flow of creating abundance. If you push away, or are distrustful of, masculine energy, you will also push away and be distrustful of money (if only on a subconscious level).

How might these masculine energy issues show up in your life? The first place to look is at your feelings and beliefs around …

MONEY AND GOD

What does God have to do with money?

Good question. God has *nothing* to do with money!

This entire life you're living on Planet Earth, and everything you create inside it, is an illusion, a very elaborate dream.

You knew this before you came here, but you chose to forget, and that's okay. One other thing you may have forgotten is that God doesn't care what you dream.

Does God tell you that your night dreams must include, or disallow, certain things? Does He say, "No dreaming about puppies!" "Don't you *dare* dream about skyscrapers!" or "Don't even *think* about dreaming about cherry pies!"

Of course not. God has no interest in controlling our dreams, day or night.

Remember, money is simply energy, like every other energy on the planet. Money is like air, water, fire, and earth. It just *is*, and God doesn't have judgments about money, negative or positive.

On the other hand ...

God Has *Everything* To Do With Money

Who do you think *created* money? Yeah, that's right: God (and Goddess)! Of course He has something to do with money, because He is the money architect and builder.

(Well, technically, God created us and we created money—but that's a minor detail.)

The point is, God and Goddess created *All That Is*. The elaborate blank canvas we've been given to be the artisans of our world was created so God and Goddess could experience more of themselves through our creations.

Money wouldn't exist without God, and yet we have *carte blanche* to create money (and everything else under the sun) in this reality in any way we like.

So, the real question we should be asking is ...

What Do *You* Believe God Has To Do With Money?

Again, it comes back to that sneaky little "b-word"—*belief*.

Our beliefs affect *everything* we create—but the fact that we believe something doesn't make it real. It doesn't matter what money actually is; if we assign beliefs like bad or good, right or wrong, spiritual or heathen to money, our ability to manifest abundance will reflect what we believe, every time.

I'm pretty sure that, right now, God is scratching His imaginary head and thinking, "Seriously? They think one form of energy is better than another? It's all Me! How could one kind of Me be better than another kind of Me? Once they learn to love all of Me, abundance will accompany everything they do."

If you believe that God is judging how much money you have and what you do with it, you're constantly under scrutiny—not by God, but by *you*. That scrutiny will disallow the abundance you seek.

Let's take a look at some possible beliefs about money and God:

- GOD DOESN'T WANT ME TO HAVE MONEY.
- GOD WANTS US TO SUFFER.
- GOD WANTS US TO STRUGGLE.
- MONEY IS NOT SPIRITUAL.
- MONEY IS A SIN.
- MONEY IS EVIL.
- RICH PEOPLE DON'T GO TO HEAVEN.
- YOU MUST SELL YOUR SOUL TO BECOME RICH.

If God is the ultimate "masculine energy" or authority figure in your life, and you believe He doesn't want you to be abundant, chances are you won't be.

The good news is, you can change those beliefs, easily and permanently. You have that power.

While we're on the subject of God and money, let's talk about ...

Tithing

The idea of tithing messes up a lot of people. Ironically, it also works for a lot of people. Whether tithing is good or bad for your abundance depends on—you guessed it—your beliefs about it.

If you *believe* tithing will work for you, it will. But then again, so will wearing yellow underwear (a strange but true prosperity ritual in some cultures).

You could make up your own prosperity ritual. What about the Champagne, Chocolate, and Shopping Ritual that, without fail, results in an income of four times the cost of the ritual (including the shopping spree)? It *would* work—if you believed in it wholeheartedly and without reservation. (I'm tempted to try that one myself!)

The point is, *you create* whether a technique, ritual, or choice works. You create it not working, too. The common denominator is what you believe.

Tithing is a really clever marketing technique for religious organizations to increase their abundance. It's made billions. It's a creation that worked for its creators—but it's up to you to choose whether it will work for you.

That isn't to say that giving doesn't have its place. In fact …

The Flow of Money Creates More Money Flow

Don't hold onto money. Let it go. Let it flow.

But wait a minute … you just said don't give it away.

Au contraire. What I said was, don't be dogmatic. Don't buy into a guilt-trip or a belief system set up to line the pockets of corporate structures (be they religious, new-age, or otherwise).

However, allowing money to flow in ways that support and feel good for you will allow more money to flow. If you are afraid of losing what you have, you won't create security by saving. The more you fear losing it, the more you will create losing it. The same principle applies to everything, from love to success to health.

The golden rule: let it go to let more flow. Give yourself the financial cushion you desire so that you feel secure, but then spend, play, even waste money.

What? Waste money?

Oh, yeah. And why not? It's all an illusion, anyway. It's like Monopoly money: it's there to play with while you're playing the game, but once the game is over, it's worthless. So have fun!

Why aren't you taking this more seriously? What if I spend it all? What if I run out?

Hear this: *nothing from the past indicates the future.* Everything is here and now. The money you created yesterday can easily disappear today, if you create it that way. In the same way, the scarcity you manifested yesterday can be replaced in the blink of an eye by millions of dollars for you to play with, should you create that.

It doesn't really matter what your money looks like on the outside right now. It only matters what you *feel* like on the inside. So feel abundant—and know that as you take on your "resonance of abundance," and as that abundance takes shape in material ways, you'll want to share it in those ways as well.

With a little practice, you will be able to tell which causes are filled with love, light, and expansion. You'll be able to discern how to share the abundance you've created in the most positive, uplifting, and light-filled ways possible. I hold these as some of my financial intentions, and you might want to as well.

Your relationship with God and tithing isn't the only way money and masculine energy intersect in your beliefs. You will also want to look at ...

YOUR RELATIONSHIP WITH "DAD" (OR OTHER AUTHORITY FIGURES)

Let me make this simple: If you had issues with your father (or your "father figure," whether that person is male or female), you will likely have issues with money.

If your father (according to you) didn't love you enough, wasn't there for you, disappointed you, etc., it's likely that money will treat you the same way.

Why?

Because if your relationship with the masculine is one of struggle, strife, guilt, animosity, or abandonment, your relationship with money won't be great, either.

How can you change this? By changing your relationship with your father (or whatever authority figure represented masculine energy in your life).

Go back to the origin using the techniques for connecting with your child and adolescent selves that we covered in the last chapter. Let the former "yous" express their emotions regarding the disappointment, betrayal, rejection, etc. they endured from that authority figure.

Really *feel* this. Emotion is key to creating, and you can't fake it. If feeling the emotions of your younger selves is too much to handle, or if you have major issues with Dad or other authority figures to heal, consider getting professional help to heal your past—but make sure that help will actually heal your wounds. This doesn't have to take years, and it doesn't have to plague you for the rest of your life. You *can* heal this, and be done with it forever.

After you've felt and released the anger, frustration, pain, rage, and sorrow, give the past "you" the relationship he or she wanted with your dad (or authority figure). Imagine this relationship as loving, supportive, and as perfect as you possibly can. Then, watch as that past "you" revels in the love, guidance, and true caring that he or she always wanted.

Healing your relationship with your father and other authority figures will free you to have a healthy relationship with the masculine, and therefore with money. This won't negate the other steps you still need to take—it won't be the "magic wand"—but this healing will show up in your financial world.

YOUR RELATIONSHIP WITH THE MASCULINE AND FEMININE WITHIN YOU

Whether you're a man or a woman, you carry both masculine energy and feminine energy. You need both—but unless your masculine and feminine energies are both healed and whole, you will not be able to consciously create on the fully-empowered level of which you are actually capable.

Masculine energy is the aspect of you that is outwardly-focused. It's the part of you that makes things happen in the physical world; the part of you that manifests everything in your illusion; the part of you that is focused, individuated, and goal-oriented. Your masculine energy is *action, planning,* and *execution*.

But, here's the thing: in order to fully embrace and use your masculine energy, you must heal and empower your feminine side. Feminine energy is the aspect of you that is inwardly-focused. It's the part of you that is not differentiated, but instead fully connected to the whole. It is that which holds the space to create; it is the energy of Source. The feminine energy is the *space where creation happens, the pause between actions*, and *the receiving of the fruits of those actions.*

Healed and whole masculine and feminine energy look like the ancient symbol of yin and yang. They are cooperative, balanced, and strong both inside and out. They create a healed and healthy sense of self without the negative aspects of ego.

A healed and whole person will recognize the power of creation they hold inside themselves, and do the inner work required to access that power (feminine). Then, they will comfortably and excitedly take action in the world to create what they desire, without falling victim to a sense of inflated ego or a desire to compete with others (masculine).

To be as powerful and abundant as you can be, you must have a balance of healthy masculine and healthy feminine within you. This is something you will likely work on for your entire lifetime, as different life situations will require you to shift and reassess to maintain that balance.

You can begin by healing your child self and adolescent self, and giving voice to your negative self (all covered in Chapters Six and Seven, and in *The Map*). You also may want to consider whether you have any of these beliefs:

- IT'S NOT SAFE TO BE/SHOW MY TRUE, WHOLE SELF.
- IT'S NOT SAFE TO BE VISIBLE IN THE WORLD.
- IT'S UNMANLY TO HONOR/SHOW MY FEMININE SIDE.
- IT'S UNFEMININE TO HONOR/SHOW MY MASCULINE SIDE.

Divine masculine energy is not aggressive or egotistical. It is sure, powerful action in the world balanced by the divine feminine—the knowing that despite being individuals we are also *all one*. That positive masculine energy, when balanced, is combined with a healthy and loving connection to God, Goddess, and everything that they have created together.

A TRUE STORY OF CONSCIOUSLY CREATING ABUNDANCE

I awoke one morning not too long ago with a feeling of trepidation. My finances were a mess. My business was failing. I had nothing left in the bank and only ten days until my rent was due. I was behind in my bills and I couldn't shake my fears of being evicted, dealing with creditors, and hitting rock bottom.

I'd long understood the Law of Attraction from an intellectual perspective. I truly believed in it, but I had never been a conscious creator—at least, not for long.

Feeling physically ill from the worry and fear, I began searching for a way to calm myself. I tried a meditation session. I tried listening to some of the positive audio tracks that I had amassed over the years. Nothing worked. I just couldn't calm my mind.

Then, I remembered that I had listened to The Map *a few months before. I decided to visit the www.LiveALifeYouLove.com website, where I found the post "In Case of Financial Emergency, Read This!"* [1]

Deciding that I had no other choice, I followed the instructions in the post—and afterwards, I did *feel better.*

I began thinking about my beliefs about money, and suddenly realized that I had a deep-seated belief that the only way to get money is to

(1) You can read this article in Appendix A of this book

earn it. I began thinking about how things didn't need to be that way, and that money can come from unlimited sources as long as I am willing to allow it. I thought very hard about that and began trying to convince myself that this could happen for me.

I went for a long walk in the late afternoon. While I walked, I kept thinking about the unlimited sources of money. As I walked along the path, I found a dime lying on the ground. I stopped and picked it up. A smile came over my face and my heart felt much lighter—was this the universe responding to my plea? The rest of my walk felt joyous. I relished the fresh, clean air, and the quiet of the park where I walked.

I arrived home shortly after 6:00 p.m. and set about preparing dinner. Having temporarily forgotten about my money worries, I enjoyed my meal and relaxed with a book afterwards. I felt at peace.

At about 7:30 p.m. my phone chimed, letting me know I had received an e-mail. As I read it, tears welled up in my eyes. The e-mail was from the owner of a business website where I had, more than a year prior, purchased a lifetime membership.

I had never found the site as useful as I'd anticipated when I bought the membership. The owner informed me that he was shutting down the site, and he would be returning most of my membership fee. All he needed was to know what e-mail address to use for the e-transfer.

I could never have imagined this source of money … ever!

I wasn't out of the woods yet, but I could clearly see that I had to relax about my financial issues. I needed to trust in the universe to provide first what I needed, and then what I wanted. It can all happen so quickly! All I needed to do was be willing to receive.

Since that night, things have turned around for me completely. I created a good job, which allowed me to catch up on my bills—and on July 7, 2015, I opened my own business.

The universe has continued to supply me with a wealth of learning opportunities, and I can see how truly wonderfully everything can, and will, work out for me. I have begun to truly enjoy the journey, and look forward to what each day brings.

- Don. F.

ABUNDANCE-ALTERING TAKEAWAYS

- Money is a masculine energy. If you have issues with the masculine (even unrelated to money) you may unwittingly disrupt your flow of creating abundance.

- If God is the ultimate "masculine energy" or authority figure in your life, and you believe He doesn't want you to be abundant, chances are you won't be. But you can change those beliefs, easily and permanently.

- You create whether a technique, ritual, or choice works—and you create it not working as well. The common denominator is what you believe.

- The more you fear losing it, the more you create losing it. This principle applies to everything: money, love, success, health, and happiness.

- As you take on your "resonance of abundance," you'll want to share that feeling with others. And as that abundance takes shape in material ways, you'll want to share it in those ways as well.

- If your father (according to you) didn't love you enough, wasn't there for you, disappointed you, etc., it's likely money will treat you the same way.

- Whether you're a man or a woman, you carry—and need—both masculine energy and feminine energy. The more your masculine and feminine energies are healed and whole, the more empowered you'll become.

YOUR NEXT STEPS

- Do you feel that tithing (or giving financially in some way), is required of you when you allow your abundance? What underlying beliefs do you want to change with regard to this?

- In the past, did you feel loved, cherished, and supported by:
  - Your father?
  - Other authority figures (teachers, bosses, mentors, etc.)?
  - God?

  If not, complete the exercise to heal those relationships and give your past selves a new experience with the masculine.

- Use the applied kinesiology techniques in Appendix B to test for constricting beliefs. Document the beliefs that need to be changed, and change them using a technique in Appendix D.

CHAPTER NINE

Beliefs: The Game-Changers

"There is little sense in attempting to change external conditions. You must first change inner beliefs, then outer conditions will change accordingly."

~ BASHAR

I kicked my legs high into the air, feeling the summer breeze on my face as I played on the swing set in my backyard. As I swung, a pickup truck pulled up in front of the house, and a man got out of the passenger side. His entire torso was wrapped in gauze bandages.

It took a while for it to register in my mind that this mummified man was my father.

My dad was a roofer in the summertime, and a machinist in the winter. The money was better in roofing, and he took advantage of it as best he could, working sunup to sundown, seven days a week, to ensure our family of six wanted for nothing.

Maybe he was tired that day, or dizzy due to lack of sleep—I guess at this point I'll never know. But when he attempted to cross a narrow gully on the flimsy board which served as a makeshift bridge—all while carrying two buckets of boiling tar on a broomstick balanced across his shoulders—he fell. And the boiling tar fell on top of him.

A quick-thinking coworker grabbed a garden hose and sprayed him down, cooling the tar that was cooking him alive. Not wanting to frighten my alarmist mom, my father refused to be taken to the hospital until he stopped at home to let her know he was okay.

Six weeks, several operations, and one near-amputation later, my father finally returned home. By that time, we were living on the charity of church, family, neighbors, and a kind and patient landlord. Of course, that didn't stop the worries of my parents; they knew the money would need to be paid back.

My seven-year-old self felt everything—all the worry, all the fear, and all the lack.

What did I conclude from that experience?

- IT'S AN UNSAFE WORLD.
- MONEY DOESN'T COME EASILY.
- YOU MUST SACRIFICE IN ORDER TO HAVE MONEY.
- MAKING MONEY IS DANGEROUS WORK.
- BAD THINGS HAPPEN THAT CAN TAKE AWAY EVERYTHING.
- ONCE YOU DO GET AHEAD, SOMETHING AWFUL WILL HAPPEN.

My father never returned to roofing. He spent his remaining working years in a factory. My mother encouraged him to accept as much overtime as he could get; at time-and-a-half, those extra hours made a big difference in the family budget.

When I was fifteen, I found my dad sitting alone after a fight with my mother. He looked at me sadly and said, "No matter how much I make, it's never enough. You'd think she'd want me to spend more time at home with her and you kids, but the only thing she cares about is how much overtime I can get." As he spoke, tears rolled down his cheeks.

I didn't know what to do with a crying father. It scared me to see him this way. If he couldn't figure this out, how on Earth could I?

And what did I conclude from that experience?

- WANTING MONEY MAKES YOU UNHAPPY.
- THERE IS NOTHING MORE IMPORTANT THAN MONEY.
- IT IS IMPOSSIBLE FOR EVEN THE MOST POWERFUL PEOPLE TO CONTROL MONEY.
- THERE IS NEVER, EVER ENOUGH MONEY.
- THE DESIRE FOR MONEY MAKES YOU DO BAD THINGS.
- MONEY IS RESPONSIBLE FOR RELATIONSHIP DIFFICULTIES.

Of course, I didn't know then what I was internalizing. I certainly didn't know that those beliefs would cement my experiences with money for decades to come—but they did. And yours did, too.

The beliefs we learn as children are the building blocks of our creations as adults. However …

It's not actually what you experience that forms your beliefs. It's what you *decide* about that experience.

Two people can grow up with exactly the same experience and end up with two opposing beliefs from the same event.

Imagine Sara and John, twins, who experienced their father losing his job. Dad was jobless for a while, but finally landed another job, even better than the one he'd lost.

Sara could end up with beliefs such as:

- LIFE IS UNFAIR.
- EVENTUALLY EVERYTHING GOOD GOES AWAY.
- THERE IS NO REAL SECURITY.
- MONEY IS A STRUGGLE.
- YOU CAN'T TRUST ANYTHING.

while John could end up with beliefs such as:

- LIFE IS AN AMAZING GIFT.
- ULTIMATELY EVERYTHING TURNS OUT WELL.
- WE ARE EACH SECURE WITHIN OURSELVES.
- MONEY IS ALWAYS THERE WHEN YOU REALLY NEED IT.
- IF YOU ARE PATIENT ENOUGH, THE GOOD WILL COME.

It doesn't really matter whether you grew up as John or Sara. What matters is that you figure out what your beliefs are, and change any that aren't in alignment with what you desire.

I've said it before, and I'll say it again …

BELIEFS RULE REALITY

I don't know how to say it stronger than that. Your beliefs are keeping you where you are—not your past choices, not your family history, not your environment, and not the world at large.

If you believe in struggle, *you will struggle.*

If you believe money is tough to come by, *it will be tough to come by.*

If you believe you are powerless to change your "luck," *you will be powerless.*

Your past does not have to dictate your future—but it probably will, unless you change the unhelpful beliefs stored in your subconscious mind.

Lots of people grow up poor and stay poor. Comparatively few people grow up poor and use that experience to forge a prosperous life—but I did, and you can too.

WHERE TO BEGIN WITH BELIEF WORK

If I've heard it once, I've heard it a hundred times, "Boni, I followed everything in the book, and it just isn't working!"

"It *always* works," I counter.

Still, it hadn't worked for them—and it may not be working for you. If it isn't working, there is a reason.

Of course, I can't tell why your particular dream hasn't manifested. It may be that you're stuck in a flow stopper[1] like self-pity or martyrdom. It may be that you stopped flowing positive energy toward your desire, and are only paying attention to what you don't have (which means you're actually creating not getting your dream).

But sometimes, you are doing everything right, and your dream still hasn't manifested. You're not even getting a sign here and there.

The likely culprit?

(1) The concept of "flow stoppers" was introduced in *The Map—To Our Responsive Universe, Where Dreams Really Do Come True!* The flow stoppers common to stopping abundance are discussed in Chapter Six of this book.

Your Foundational Beliefs

Foundational beliefs are beliefs about beliefs themselves, beliefs about creating reality, and beliefs about your ability to create your reality and/or change your beliefs. If they aren't positive and empowering, they will sabotage your belief-changing work and ultimately your entire dream.

Foundational beliefs are beliefs such as:

- IT IS IMPOSSIBLE TO CREATE MY OWN REALITY.

If you hold that belief, no matter how many books you read or how much work you do to create your world, that belief will make it impossible!

These beliefs must be changed before any other beliefs in order to successfully and easily move forward.

I have broken down these "mothers of all beliefs" into categories to make them easier to identify:

It is not possible/easy:

- WE DON'T REALLY CREATE OUR OWN REALITIES.
- I CAN'T CREATE MY REALITY.
- I CAN'T CHANGE MY BELIEFS.
- IT IS DIFFICULT TO CREATE MY REALITY.
- IT IS HARD TO CHANGE BELIEFS.
- I CAN'T EASILY DISCOVER MY SUBCONSCIOUS BELIEFS.
- I CAN'T CHANGE MY BELIEFS ABOUT __________[MONEY, LOVE, MEN, WOMEN, HEALTH, WORK, ETC.].

It works for everyone else but me:

- EVEN IF I "CHANGE MY BELIEFS," MY WORLD WILL NOT CHANGE.
- NOTHING EVER WORKS FOR ME.
- I DON'T HAVE WHAT IT TAKES TO CHANGE MY BELIEFS, AND THUS MY LIFE.
- I DON'T HAVE THE POWER OR ABILITY TO CREATE MY WORLD.
- IT IS HARD TO CREATE WHAT I WANT.
- I AM NOT POWERFUL ENOUGH TO CHANGE MY BELIEFS.

It is wrong/unspiritual to create my reality:

- IT IS WRONG TO CHANGE MY BELIEFS.
- I'LL BE PUNISHED IF I CHANGE MY BELIEFS.
- ONLY GOD CAN CHANGE MY BELIEFS.
- IT IS UNSPIRITUAL TO CHANGE MY BELIEFS.
- ONLY GOD CAN CREATE MY REALITY.
- IT IS BLASPHEMOUS TO BELIEVE I CAN CREATE MY OWN REALITY.

I'm not ready:

- I'M NOT READY TO CHANGE MY BELIEFS ABOUT __________[MONEY, LOVE, MEN, HEALTH, WORK, ETC.].
- I'M NOT READY FOR THE SUCCESS THAT WILL HAPPEN WHEN I CHANGE MY BELIEFS.
- I CAN HAVE THE REALITIES I DESIRE ONLY AFTER I CLEAR OUT ALL MY BLOCKAGES.

- I'M NOT HEALED ENOUGH TO CREATE MY REALITY.
- IF I SUCCESSFULLY CREATE MY OWN REALITY, THE RESPONSIBILITY OF MAINTAINING IT WOULD BE TOO MUCH FOR ME TO HANDLE.
- I'M NOT _________ [OLD, YOUNG, WISE, CAPABLE, SEASONED, EXPERIENCED, SMART, ETC.] ENOUGH TO CREATE MY OWN REALITY.

It's not safe:

- MY SUCCESS THAT HAPPENS AS A RESULT OF CHANGING MY BELIEFS WILL MAKE PEOPLE I CARE ABOUT FEEL BADLY ABOUT THEIR OWN LIVES.
- IF I CHANGE MY BELIEFS ABOUT _________[MONEY, LOVE, MEN, HEALTH, WORK, OTHER PEOPLE, ETC.] AND MY WORLD CHANGES, SOMEONE I CARE ABOUT WILL BE HURT.
- SOMETHING BAD WILL HAPPEN IF I CHANGE MY BELIEFS.
- IT'S NOT SAFE TO CREATE ALL THAT I WANT.
- IF I BELIEVE IN THIS INFORMATION OTHERS WILL RIDICULE ME.

Can you understand how debilitating these beliefs are, and how they can stop you from moving forward before you even get started?

The most important work you will ever do in conscious creation is changing your beliefs. Nothing will shift you forward faster when you do it. Nothing will hold you back longer if you don't.

How do I tell if a belief is mine?

I have asked that question myself, and for a long time my only answers were:

"If it is reflected in your world, it's yours," or,

"Use your gut to determine if it's yours."

But sometimes, it isn't that easy to tell. That's why I teach how to use applied kinesiology to determine whether someone holds a belief. It's pretty exciting to realize that your body can determine whether or not a belief is yours. It may take a bit of practice, but your body can tell you what's in your subconscious mind.

I have outlined two methods of testing for beliefs in Appendix B of this book. I suggest that you familiarize yourself with both methods, and test with both methods as you make your way through this book. Eventually, you'll develop a favorite—one that you can use in all of your belief work, forevermore.

Who Should Test For Foundational Beliefs?

Everyone should test for foundational beliefs. Even if you're creating some success, there may be a part of you that doesn't believe you're powerful, that you create it all, or that beliefs can be easily changed. Or, you might hold another foundational belief that, if changed, would make your work so much easier.

Life should be a joy. So should this work. Changing your beliefs is one important way to accomplish that. So, have fun with this, and watch your world (finally!) begin to shift!

The next beliefs you'll want to closely inspect are your ...

Beliefs About Money

Unless you are currently creating more money than you know what to do with, you do have beliefs about money that you'll want to change.

Below is a non-inclusive list of the beliefs you might consider changing. I've separated them into categories to make them easier for you to identify. I suggest testing yourself for these beliefs (maximum ten at a time), using both of the techniques in Appendix B.

Beliefs about the value of money:

- MONEY IS THE ROOT OF ALL EVIL.
- MONEY IS DIRTY.
- MONEY IS A CURSE.
- MONEY IS POWER.
- MONEY IS FREEDOM.
- MONEY IS EVERYTHING.
- MONEY MEASURES WORTH.
- MONEY MAKES YOU DESIRABLE TO OTHERS.
- MONEY MAKES YOU HAPPY.
- RICH PEOPLE ARE BETTER THAN POOR PEOPLE.
- POOR PEOPLE ARE BETTER THAN RICH PEOPLE.

Beliefs about you and money:

- I DON'T DESERVE A LOT OF MONEY.
- MY SPOUSE/PARTNER CREATES MONEY BUT I DON'T.
- I CAN'T HANDLE HAVING MONEY.
- I CAN'T HAVE MONEY.
- I CAN'T SAVE MONEY.
- I AM ALWAYS IN DEBT.
- I DON'T HAVE ENOUGH MONEY TO SHARE OR GIVE AWAY.

- I AM SMART AND TALENTED, THEREFORE I SHOULD GET MORE MONEY.
- I WORK SUPER HARD, I DESERVE MORE MONEY.
- I DON'T KNOW HOW TO MAKE MONEY.
- I DON'T KNOW HOW TO CREATE MONEY.
- I CAN NEVER GET AHEAD.
- I HATE MONEY.
- I AM A FAILURE WHEN IT COMES TO MONEY.
- I WOULD FEEL GUILTY IF I HAD MORE MONEY THAN [NAME].
- OTHERS CAN CREATE MONEY BUT NOT ME.
- THE ECONOMY IS RESPONSIBLE FOR MY MONEY PROBLEMS.
- [NAME, ENTITY, EVENT] IS RESPONSIBLE FOR MY MONEY PROBLEMS.
- IF I DON'T WORRY ABOUT MONEY SOMETHING BAD WILL HAPPEN.

Beliefs about the ease with which money comes to you:

- YOU HAVE TO EARN THE MONEY YOU MAKE.
- MONEY COMES WITH INCREDIBLE STRUGGLE.
- MAKING MONEY TAKES A LOT OF HARD WORK.
- IT TAKES MONEY TO MAKE MONEY.
- THERE IS NEVER ENOUGH MONEY.
- THERE IS ALWAYS JUST ENOUGH MONEY.
- THERE IS NEVER MORE THAN ENOUGH MONEY.
- MONEY IS HARD TO COME BY.
- I NEED TO EARN MY MONEY.
- THERE IS NOT ENOUGH MONEY TO GO AROUND.

- THE UNIVERSE IS LIMITED IN ITS ABUNDANCE.
- MONEY ONLY COMES TO ME THROUGH MY JOB.
- ONLY A SELECT FEW GET TO HAVE MONEY.
- IF A LOT OF MONEY COMES EASILY, IT MUST BE ILLEGAL.
- YOU NEED TO BE SUPER SMART TO MAKE A LOT OF MONEY.

Beliefs about what you have to give up to get money:

- IF I AM FINANCIALLY ABUNDANT, I WILL HAVE TO SACRIFICE MY HAPPINESS.
- IF I AM FINANCIALLY ABUNDANT, I WILL HAVE TO SACRIFICE MY FAMILY.
- IF I AM FINANCIALLY ABUNDANT, I WILL HAVE TO SACRIFICE MY FREEDOM.
- IF I AM FINANCIALLY ABUNDANT, I WILL HAVE TO SACRIFICE MY INTEGRITY.
- IF I REALLY LIVE MY TRUTH, I'LL END UP BROKE.
- IN ORDER TO BE RICH, YOU MUST SACRIFICE YOUR FREE TIME.
- YOU CAN'T HAVE MONEY AND HAPPINESS.
- I WILL HAVE TO DO WHAT I HATE IN ORDER TO HAVE MONEY.
- MONEY WILL CHANGE ME FOR THE WORSE.
- YOU HAVE TO DO LOTS OF THINGS YOU DON'T LIKE IN ORDER TO HAVE MONEY.
- MONEY ALWAYS COMES WITH STRINGS ATTACHED.
- IT TAKES MONEY TO MAKE MONEY.

Beliefs about what it means when you have (or don't have) money:

- IF A LOT OF MONEY COMES EASILY, IT MUST BE ILLEGAL.
- BEING RICH IS A SIN.
- HAVING MONEY IS GREEDY.
- WANTING MORE MONEY IS SELFISH.
- MONEY SPOILS YOU.
- RICH PEOPLE ARE SNOBS.
- RICH PEOPLE ARE EGOTISTICAL.
- RICH PEOPLE ARE SELFISH.
- RICH PEOPLE ARE EVIL.
- RICH PEOPLE ARE CORRUPT.
- RICH PEOPLE BECOME WEALTHY BY TAKING ADVANTAGE OF OTHERS.
- THERE IS NOBILITY IN BEING POOR.
- MONEY EQUALS POWER, AND POWER CORRUPTS.
- IF YOU DON'T HAVE MONEY, YOU'RE POWERLESS.

Beliefs about what you have to do to keep money:

- I MUST BE SUPER CONSCIOUS OF EVERY SINGLE DOLLAR TO BE SURE I DON'T LOSE THE MONEY I CREATE.
- I MUST SACRIFICE TO SAVE MY MONEY.
- IF I AM NOT HYPER-VIGILANT SOMEONE WILL TAKE MY MONEY.
- I MUST HIDE THE MONEY I CREATE.

Beliefs about what happens when you get money:

- ACCEPTING MONEY OBLIGATES ME.
- WHEN I AM RICH, I WON'T HAVE TIME FOR MY SPIRITUALITY.
- WHEN I AM RICH, I WON'T HAVE TIME FOR MY FRIENDS.
- WHEN I AM RICH, I WON'T HAVE TIME FOR MY FAMILY.
- WHEN I AM RICH, I WILL BE TIED TO OBLIGATIONS AND STRESSED OUT.
- WHEN I AM RICH, I WON'T BE ABLE TO HANDLE THE RESPONSIBILITY.
- PEOPLE WILL LOVE ME ONLY FOR MY MONEY.
- PEOPLE WILL SCORN ME BECAUSE I HAVE MONEY.
- MONEY COMES WITH A LOT OF RESPONSIBILITY.
- PEOPLE ARE MEAN TO RICH PEOPLE.
- IF I HAVE MONEY, I'LL JUST LOSE IT ANYWAY.
- IF I HAVE MONEY, I'LL LOSE ALL MY FRIENDS.
- IF I HAVE MONEY, PEOPLE WILL BE AFTER ME FOR MY MONEY.
- IF I HAVE MONEY, PEOPLE WILL BE JEALOUS OF ME.
- IF I HAVE MONEY, PEOPLE WILL JUST WANT ME FOR MY MONEY.
- IF I HAVE MONEY, OTHERS WILL BE GOING WITHOUT.
- IF I HAVE MONEY, I'LL BE MORE VISIBLE.
- IF I HAVE MONEY, I'LL BE HELD TO PUBLIC SCRUTINY.

Beliefs About Success & Work

Beliefs about whether and how success comes to you:

- I CAN'T HANDLE SUCCESS.
- OTHERS ARE RESPONSIBLE FOR MY SUCCESS.
- IF I AM SUCCESSFUL, PEOPLE WILL HATE ME.
- SUCCESS IS DIFFICULT.
- I CAN'T BE SUCCESSFUL AND TRUE TO MYSELF AT THE SAME TIME.

Beliefs about what happens when you're successful:

- IF I AM TOO SUCCESSFUL, SOMEONE WILL TAKE IT AWAY.
- IF I AM TOO VISIBLE, SOMEONE WILL MAKE ME PAY.
- IF I AM SUCCESSFUL, PEOPLE WILL HATE ME.
- IF I AM SUCCESSFUL, I WON'T BE ABLE TO KEEP IT UP.
- I CAN'T HANDLE SUCCESS.

Beliefs about work:

- I CAN'T MAKE THE KIND OF MONEY I WANT BY DOING SOMETHING THAT FILLS ME WITH JOY.
- I CAN'T MAKE ENOUGH MONEY DOING WHAT I TRULY LOVE.
- IT'S A DOG-EAT-DOG WORLD OUT THERE.
- MOST ENTREPRENEURS FAIL, THEREFORE THE ODDS ARE STACKED AGAINST ME.

- IN ORDER TO HAVE THE WORK I DESIRE, I HAVE TO GIVE UP SOME THINGS I VALUE.
- I DON'T KNOW WHAT MY PASSION IS.

You may have a lot of money beliefs to change. I changed hundreds of them. And it's important for you to know …

CORE BELIEFS ARE THE ROOT OF YOUR UNDESERVABILITY

All of our experiences (or, more accurately, what we believe about our experiences) gel together to form and strengthen beliefs about ourselves that will color every interaction, every creation, and every dream we ever have. They form our core beliefs about who we are.

What are core beliefs?[(2)]

Core beliefs are your bottom-line beliefs about you. They are the beliefs that shape your entire life—including the amount of success and abundance you allow yourself.

Let's face it: if you don't value something, you're not going to treat it well, which means you have a belief that it's not worth treating well.

Imagine your car is a rusted, banged up, barely drivable 1975 Ford Pinto. How would you treat it? If one car had to stay out in the snow, it would be the Pinto, right? There would probably be trash in the back seat. The car would never get washed because, why bother? Basically, that car would get no lovin'.

Now, imagine yourself driving the latest, coolest Porsche—yeah, the one whose price tag is close to a million bucks. That car might score two spaces in the garage—just to be sure no one

(2) Core beliefs are also referred to as Level Three beliefs in *The Map—To Our Responsive Universe, Where Dreams Really Do Come True!*

dings it by parking too close. And I'll bet it would not only be washed, but also detailed regularly and lovingly. You'd feed it top-quality gas and service it like clockwork.

We take care of what we value—be it furnishings, cars, homes, or people—but far too many of us don't value ourselves. That lack of value is just a piece of the devastating impact that negative core beliefs have on us.

If we believe we are flawed, or not good enough, or unimportant, or unworthy, we won't think we deserve to live lives we love, and we certainly won't think we deserve abundance.

Guess what that does to our ability to create? Yup—it pretty much kills it.

But wait, I really do *believe I deserve it, but my life still sucks.*

Maybe your conscious mind believes you deserve, but what about your subconscious mind? It's not only possible, but highly probable, that you have conflicting beliefs—that you are holding two seemingly opposite beliefs at the same time.

So, which belief manifests?

That depends on a lot of factors, but generally, the stronger belief manifests, even if it's a belief that you've forgotten about for a long time. That's why testing for beliefs comes in handy.

Uncover Your Core Beliefs

Once your foundational beliefs are tested and the constricting ones are changed, take a long, hard look at whether one or more of these core beliefs are yours.

Core Beliefs *(Note: this list is non-exclusive)*

- I AM NOT GOOD ENOUGH.
- I AM FLAWED.
- I AM UNWORTHY.
- I AM NO GOOD.
- I AM UNSUCCESSFUL.
- I AM NOT VALUABLE.
- I AM INFERIOR.
- I AM NOTHING.
- I AM INVISIBLE.
- I AM INSIGNIFICANT.
- I AM UNLOVABLE.
- I AM UNACCEPTABLE.
- I DON'T MATTER.
- I AM UNIMPORTANT.
- I AM A MISTAKE.
- I DON'T BELONG.
- I AM UNWANTED.
- I AM UNWELCOME.
- I DON'T FIT IN ANYWHERE.
- I AM UNBALANCED.
- I AM A FAILURE.
- I DON'T DESERVE.
- I AM A LOSER.
- I AM INADEQUATE.

How to Tell If You Have a Negative Core Belief

Core beliefs are a little trickier than other beliefs to nail down and change.

Most everyone has difficulty seeing the core beliefs they hold.

Why?

First, no one wants to admit that they believe such awful things about themselves.

Second, these beliefs are very, very old, and we've had many decades of practice in hiding them from everyone, including ourselves.

Think about it: if you have a belief like …

- I AM FLAWED

… you obviously believe it. You also fear it—because what if it's actually true?—and you fear others discovering it and using it against you. So, you might hide your belief by judging others before they judge you, or by getting angry at others' weaknesses (or strengths). You might also avoid being seen, being vulnerable, or becoming too close to others. You don't allow success, abundance, or any depth of love, because deep down you believe you're flawed, and you don't deserve it.

Yes, core beliefs can be tough to discover, but here are some clues:

- You had a shame-based childhood.
- You came from a dysfunctional family.
- You were abused as a child.
- You are a child of an alcoholic or addict.
- You didn't feel loved as a child.
- One or more parents were narcissistic.
- You do all the work, but can't seem to move beyond a certain plateau of success.
- The idea of being visible terrifies you.

As with your foundational beliefs, I recommend using applied kinesiology to test for core beliefs. Ultimately, though, when you get really quiet and still, and peer inside to the deepest part of your being, your gut will tell you what you truly believe.

Once you've discovered your core belief(s), take the time you need to change it/them.[3] It will take a while, but it will be *so* worth it.

I urge you to take core beliefs seriously. They not only hamper your ability to create abundance, but also hold you back from creating and reveling in lots of other awesome realities.

THIS MAY BE THE MOST IMPORTANT WORK OF YOUR LIFE—AND YET, YOU WILL RESIST IT

This is critical, my friend. Belief work will literally change your life forever. It will make your life easier, more abundant, fun, successful, and so much more. And yet, you will find this work the most difficult thing you've ever done.

Why?

Well, not because it is difficult. It's actually relatively easy.

You'll find it difficult because you'll put it off, dismiss it, procrastinate, ignore it, diminish it, and do everything you can to ensure it never ever gets done.

I find it fascinating that we're so reticent to change beliefs. Bashar, channeled through Darryl Anka,[4] teaches that negative beliefs are resistant to change. We subconsciously feel threatened if we mess with fundamental aspects of ourselves such as the beliefs that (seemingly) define our world and our place within it.

(3) Learn how to change beliefs in Appendix D.
(4) More information at www.Bashar.org.

I don't know for sure what the reason is, but that explanation makes sense to me!

I do know that, for everyone who has engaged with this work (myself included), changing beliefs is fraught with challenges despite the fact that the process itself is relatively easy and straightforward.

You will have to overcome your internal resistance in order to change your beliefs. I have come to accept, for myself, that:

- Changing beliefs will never feel fun and exciting.
- I won't want to change beliefs.
- I will have to force myself to sit down and do the belief-changing exercises.
- I won't expect the beliefs to change.
- When I'm on the other side of the belief, I won't be able to imagine why I ever thought the negative belief was true.
- After I've changed my beliefs, my life will change with little to no effort at all.
- I will wonder how I could have ever resisted such an amazing process in the first place.

So, my friend, when it comes to belief work, your best approach is to just do it. Trust me, you will be extremely grateful that you did.

A TRUE STORY OF CONSCIOUSLY CREATING ABUNDANCE

I didn't have much growing up, and when the opportunity came to become co-owner in a local diner, I grabbed the chance. I really rocked at the restaurant business. I was great with people, I created the menus, and developed the food. I was the first one to arrive and the last one to leave.

It was the first time in my life that I felt like I had something to contribute. I felt loved, accepted, and like I was worth something. I hadn't found that up until that point—when I realized I had skills I felt good about. People liked me. And I loved caring for them.

Then, the unimaginable happened: we lost the restaurant. I felt like a failure. I felt that it was my one shot at success; I'd worked so hard to make it happen, and now it was over.

My life partner and I both worked there, so we lost both our incomes and our insurance all at the same time. But the loss was so much greater than the income. My identity was wrapped up in that restaurant, and now, it was over—and in some ways, I *was over.*

That's when The Map *came into my life. Even though everything in* The Map *was brand new to me, it was very easy for me to believe what you wrote. It was like a "coming home" for me.*

One of the most profound thoughts was, "It takes a very strong mind to be able to feel that you already have what you don't." Another was, "Begin with finding things to be grateful for."

So, instead of feeling bad that we had to ask our family for financial help, or that we couldn't buy things for our new baby, we flipped it. And we began to feel grateful for the things that were going right instead, as few as they were.

We had a new baby! We were able to stay in a place without rent. We had a hard time paying the utilities, but we didn't focus on that, we focused on the fact that we lived rent-free. We had a yard. Every single thing that we could find to feel grateful for, we did.

Much to my surprise and delight, my reality began changing almost immediately.

I learned so much about myself. I had been angry and bitter—more than I'd realized. You taught me how to test for beliefs, and I was surprised at the beliefs I held that I didn't realize I had. It was like an excavation of myself.

I had never thought of myself as someone who "played the victim," although in the restaurant situation I sure felt like one. Your book brought to light many things that I didn't realize I was doing. A lot of them were subtle. I am still sometimes surprised (and excited) about what a big difference subtle changes can make.

Just three years ago there were days I would have to stay home because I didn't have enough gas to go anywhere. I would feed my family and say I wasn't hungry to make groceries last longer.

Now we have a new vehicle. My partner started his own subcontracting business and has just purchased a work van. I'm able to buy organic groceries and have fresh flowers every week. So much has changed. I'm truly grateful for The Map, *and I can't wait to see what we create from here!*

- DeAnna W.

ABUNDANCE-ALTERING TAKEAWAYS

- It's not actually your experiences that form your beliefs—it's what you decide about those experiences after they happen. Two people can grow up with exactly the same experience and end up with opposite beliefs from the same event.

- Lots of people grow up poor and stay poor. Comparatively few people grow up poor and then use that experience to forge a more prosperous life. I did, and so can you—but first, you must look closely at your beliefs.

- The most important work you will ever do in conscious creation is changing your beliefs. No other work you do will shift you forward faster. Nothing will hold you back longer if you don't.

- Foundational beliefs are beliefs about beliefs themselves, beliefs about creating reality, and beliefs about your ability to create your reality and/or change your beliefs. Negative foundational beliefs will sabotage your belief-changing work—and, ultimately, your entire dream.

- Applied kinesiology (also called "muscle testing") can show you whether you hold a belief. It allows the body to indicate a true or false response when presented with a statement. You can learn how to use applied kinesiology to test for beliefs in Appendix B of this book.

- You can easily hold two opposing beliefs at the same time. The conscious "you" may believe something, such as "I create my own reality," but if a subconscious part of you does not believe it, that will show up in your testing. That's why it is a good idea to test negative beliefs rather than positive ones.

- Unless you are currently creating more money than you know what to do with, you do have beliefs about money that you will want to change.

- Core beliefs are your bottom-line beliefs about you. These beliefs shape your entire life—including the amount of success and abundance you allow yourself. Let's face it: if you don't value something, you're not going to treat it well, which means you have a belief that it's not worth treating well.

- Belief work will literally change your life. It will make life easier, more abundant, fun, successful, and so much more—and yet, you'll put it off, dismiss it, procrastinate, ignore it, diminish it, and do everything you can to ensure it never ever gets done. My advice: do it anyway!

YOUR NEXT STEPS

- Use the applied kinesiology techniques in Appendix B to test for constricting beliefs. Test ten beliefs at a time, with a five-minute break between sets.
    - Test for the foundational beliefs listed in this chapter.
    - Test for the core beliefs listed in this chapter.

- Document all beliefs that need to be changed, and change them, ten at a time, using the techniques in Appendix D.

CHAPTER TEN

Techniques: The Moneymakers

"It's time we put thoughts of lack behind us. It's time for us to discover the secrets of the stars, to sail to an uncharted land, to open up a new heaven where our spirits can soar."

~ SARAH BAN BREATHNACH

Abundance is a resonance. And as you follow *The Map to Abundance*, it will help you to create a resonance of abundance that will make techniques unnecessary.

Ultimately you will simply *be* abundant, and everything will flow to you in perfect timing. You will dance through life joyfully, expecting that all of your needs will be met.

But while you're working on your resonance of abundance, consciously flowing energy toward your dream of abundance will come in handy. These techniques will help you move toward that abundant state of being, and also help you create the specific things you desire.

As you work with these techniques, start with smaller dreams, and build up to bigger dreams. Your dreams have to be believable (to you) before they can materialize.

Most of all, have fun with this! And with that in mind, here's a great place to begin:

THE "ONE-MINUTE MANIFESTOR" TECHNIQUE[(1)]

Who doesn't love a technique that you can complete in sixty seconds?

And my friend, this isn't some wimpy, no-results technique, or a warmup for the big game. This technique is *powerful*—and it works! That's probably why versions of it have been taught by channeled beings like Lazaris, Seth, and Abraham for years.

Preparation

Choose something you want to manifest. You don't need to know the specifics of how it will come to be, only how you'll *feel* when you get it.

Then, imagine the scene when you realize that this "dream" has fully manifested. Obviously you're smiling, maybe even laughing. Perhaps you're on the phone, calling someone to tell him or her about it. Maybe you're holding something which symbolizes this dream—like a paycheck, a letter, or an engagement ring.

Fix this picture in your mind, as if looking at a photograph of yourself. Realize that the you in the picture feels so joyous because this dream has just become real in your life.

(1) The One-Minute Manifestor Technique has been recorded and is available for sale at www.LiveALifeYouLove.com.

The Technique

> Set a timer for twenty-three seconds. At the very start of those twenty-three seconds, close your eyes and visualize that joyous picture of yourself. *Feel* that joy, that excitement, that unadulterated happiness. *Know* that you have your dream.
>
> Hold that picture, and that "over the top" emotion, until the timer goes off at exactly twenty-three seconds. Then, quickly open your eyes.
>
> Take two deep breaths, reset your timer, and repeat.

You should see "signs" of your dream manifesting within a few days. Watch for them, and respond to them positively. (I'll teach you more about how to do this in Chapter Twelve).

And, for goodness sake, *keep doing the technique.* If you want to do this several times a day, by all means do so! You could focus on just one dream or different dreams throughout the day. There is no "one and done" in manifesting—and there are no excuses not to do something that will literally change your life and takes just one minute from start to finish.

THE "YOUR ABUNDANT FUTURE SELF" TECHNIQUE

The Your Abundant Future Self Technique is a meditative technique that puts you in touch with the "future you" who is already fully, joyously, and beautifully abundant.

There is a "you" who already has the abundance you seek. That "you" has mastered the art of conscious creation, and absolutely loves every minute of life.

(There is also a "you" who never mastered the art of conscious creation. You have many possible future selves; it's up to you which one you become.)

As you seek out the brightest possible future, and begin to hang out with that future you who is delighted with life, you will be lifted into that resonance. More and more, you'll find your life mirroring the life of your most abundant future self—and, before you know it, *you will be living that life.*

The Technique

Find a place where you can be alone. Turn off your phone, and lower the lights. You might light a candle, or play some soft music in the background. Sit comfortably or lie down in a comfortable position, and close your eyes.

Now, let relaxation flow through your body.

Begin with your toes. Feel the relaxation spreading from your toes into your feet. Allow your feet to become heavy. Allow the relaxation to gently move into your ankles, your calves, and up to your knees.

Let the relaxation gently make its way into your thighs, and then into your pelvic region. Feel the lower half of your body become heavier and heavier, sinking into the floor as all of the tension in your muscles, bones, and tissues is released.

Beautiful relaxation flows like a morning mist into your belly and chest. Soon, it makes its way gently into your shoulders, down your arms, and into your hands and fingertips.

Finally, the relaxation curls its way into your neck, and up into your head. As your head becomes heavy with the beautiful energy of relaxation, your face becomes relaxed also. You feel the tension draining from your mouth, cheeks, eyes, and scalp as you sink into a state of total and complete relaxation.

Now that your body is fully relaxed, allow yourself to drift. Feel yourself lifting out of your body, and floating like a balloon up to the ceiling, through the roof, and into the sky.

You drift in a state of blissful peace and tranquility. Any thoughts that enter your mind are allowed to drift away as quickly as they come.

You float, loving this feeling, until it feels like it's time to stand. Just as you have the thought, your feet are suddenly on the ground, and you are standing.

Open your eyes. As you look around, you're amazed by the beauty of the trees around you. This place in nature fills you with a sense of joy, safety, and peace. This is a beautiful place—it's *your* beautiful place.

There is a path directly in front of you, and you follow it, happily. You don't have a destination in mind—it feels wonderful to simply follow your feet. The path meanders this way and that. As you walk, you are struck by the beauty, serenity, and peacefulness of this place.

Suddenly, your path is blocked. A huge tree has fallen in this forest, and it's lying directly across the path, blocking your way. You can't see a way to go around the tree, so you carefully climb over it.

You're a little scraped and dirty from this adventure, but you press on. As you travel, you remember what your life has been like for you financially. You remember the struggle and the fear. Although there were a few times when you were happily surprised by the way money turned up in the nick of time, more often than not, money perplexed you, disappointed you, and left you feeling weak and vulnerable.

As you think those thoughts, you realize your feet are sticking in mud as you walk. The mud gets thicker and thicker; soon, it feels more like quicksand than mud. The quicksand threatens to pull you under. You struggle for footing, and see a boulder not too far away. You barely manage to scramble to the huge rock—but you pull yourself up, and from there jump from rock to rock until you reach solid ground.

You're a bit shaken and a lot dirty, but you press on. You hear the trees quaking in the wind, and before you know it, the sun has set, and darkness is upon you.

But then, up ahead, you see a glow. As you get closer, you realize it's the light from a bonfire. You come upon the fire and reach out your hands to warm them as you stand before the blaze.

Once you've warmed up a bit, you stuff your hands into your pockets—where, much to your surprise, you find a handful of papers! The papers resemble extra-large confetti. Each is a little strip with something written on it.

You pick one and smooth it out to read it. It says, "Money is difficult to create." You throw it into the fire. The fire crackles in return.

You look at more of the papers. All of them bear similar, constricting messages about money, like: "This world has limited abundance." "It is greedy to want more money." "You must sacrifice in order to receive a lot of abundance."

After a while, you stop reading the papers because you know they're all the same: ideas about money that you've had since you were a child. You throw all of them into the fire. As you reach deeply into your pockets, you pull out more, and more, and more. All of them go into the blaze.

You find hundreds of these little slips of paper, maybe thousands. You find pockets that you didn't even know you had—and every pocket is chock-full of these antiquated, limiting ideas.

You throw them all into the fire, handful by handful, and every time you reach back into your previously empty pockets, you find they are full again. You empty them over and over, until finally the bonfire is blazing and your pockets are empty.

Just then, you hear a rustling in the woods. As you look up, you see a silhouette. As the person gets closer, you recognize the familiar face of your own future self. You can barely believe your eyes. S/he is radiant and smiling from ear to ear.

It's obvious that your future self is delighted to see you, and you gratefully fall into a firm, loving hug. Then you both sit down next to the fire and begin to talk.

You listen as your future self tells you about your future. Money comes so easily, almost as if by magic. Oh, it didn't happen overnight—and learning to have patience was the hardest thing—but it *did* happen. It really did.

"The funny thing is," your future self tells you, "once I have something in mind that I desire, I don't tend to think about it much after that because everything manifests so easily and so elegantly. I only think about having fun, being creative, and loving my life."

Your future self goes on to say, "I would tell you exactly how it came to be so easy and fun, but you wouldn't believe me. It's better that you don't know, because allowing it to happen without expecting it to look a certain way is what really creates it anyway. What I *do* want you to know is that it's really fun being so free. It's amazing to know that the money stuff is all handled—but it's not just the money. It's the other abundances as well. Opportunities fall in my lap one after the other. Ideas come out of nowhere. Doors open that I didn't even know were there. You're going to *love* this!

You ask your future self, "What is the one thing I most need to know or do right now to create the future you live in?"

Your future self tells you. Listen for the answer.

Then, your future self hugs you, hard, and you feel the boundaries between you disappear. You merge together ... and now, you *are* your future self. You *feel* what it feels like to have unlimited abundance. You *feel* the relief and security of having everything you need and everything you want—maybe not the form, but the essence for sure.

Close your mental eyes and feel what life is like for you when you are abundant. You have no preoccupation with money because there's no need for it. You live in joy, and love your life.

And then, suddenly, you aren't *seeing* your future self's life. You are *living* it.

Stay here in your abundant life as long as you like. When you're ready, open your eyes, and expect your world to mirror back your new essence of abundance.

THE "HOUSE OF ABUNDANCE" TECHNIQUE

The House of Abundance technique gives your abundance a form. When you change that form—when you make it bigger, more light-filled, more beautiful, or more exciting—your reality will respond.

The Technique

Choose a place and time where you can be alone and undisturbed. Close your eyes and get comfortable. Allow yourself to relax. Feel the relaxation spread through your body as you let go of any tensions or concerns from the day.

Imagine that you're sitting in a beautiful place in nature. Hear the birds sing, watch the clouds move gently, and feel the breeze on your face. Know that you are in a place all your own; a place that is absolutely safe, a place where your higher self will meet you.

As you look over the beautiful landscape and bask in the sense of safety, you imagine what it will be like when your higher self arrives. You imagine the feeling of being totally loved. Your higher self has been with you, lifetime after lifetime, and knows you like no one else. Your higher self's love is complete and unconditional.

As you sit in reverie, you see a figure in the distance, and you know it is your higher self. Your joy and excitement build as your higher self comes closer.

When s/he arrives, greet your higher self in whatever way feels right to you.

You sit together for a while as you tell your higher self what you'd like to create. You might say, "I want an abundant life. I want ease and elegance, I want freedom, I want joy, and I want fun. Will you please help me create those things?"

Delighted to help you, your higher self stands and lifts you to your feet. As you stand together, face-to-face, your higher self wraps you in a cloak of love. You rest your head upon his or her shoulder, and dreamlike, you float. You're in a state of total bliss, of indescribable love and peace.

Before you know it, you're standing again. Your higher self gently unwraps the cloak. As your eyes adjust to the light, you see a house before you.

The house may be new or old, fancy or simple, beautiful or ugly. You and your higher self stand in front of this house, and your higher self says, "This is your house of abundance. How would you like to improve your house?"

"Let's make it bigger," you say.

Your higher self laughs and replies, "That's fine with me. Let's imagine that."

And you do. You imagine the house stretching taller, wider, and deeper—and as you imagine it, you see it happening right in front of you! Slowly at first, and then a little bit faster, the house is growing before your very eyes.

You glance at your higher self. S/he is staring at you with a big grin. You know *you* are doing this, and your higher self is helping. Oh, this is fun! Together, you stretch the house until it has doubled in size.

"Now what?" your higher self asks.

"What if we make it more beautiful?"

So, you do. Landscaping appears as if by magic. The colors become more vibrant and beautiful. The house transforms from mediocre to magnificent.

When the transformation is complete (for now) you and your higher self go inside.

From the outside, the house looked like any other house. However, as you walk through the front door, you realize it's anything but. The only thing you can see is a very long hallway, lined with doors on either side.

You and your higher self begin to walk down the corridor. You notice there are signs above each doorway. Each room represents a different kind of abundance. There are rooms for money, time, love, creativity, freedom, joy, and more.

Today you want to visit the room of money. Your higher self opens the door, and you both step through.

The room is old, musty, and dirty. The ceilings are low, and the paint on the walls is grimy and faded. Old furniture, broken, decrepit, and yellowed, is lying about, some of it overturned. The light fixture hangs crookedly from the ceiling, and the draperies are moldy and falling from the windows.

"Let's clean this place up and make more room for money in your life," your higher self says.

Slowly, your higher self raises his or her hands. As they do this, the ceiling rises, too. As your higher self brings his or her hands together and then spreads them wide, the walls magically expand in either direction.

"Your turn," your higher self says. "Why don't you expand the other walls?" Excitedly, you mimic your higher self's movements, and the walls miraculously widen.

Together, you do this until the room is double, triple, and then *quadruple* its original size.

"Now," says your higher self, "let's give your monetary abundance a wonderful place to live." S/he points a finger at the walls. Miraculously, the walls are covered with sparkling, shimmering new color. All the dirt and cobwebs are gone. You watch, amazed, even as you smell the new paint.

Your higher self waves a hand from left to right. Instantly, the old, mangled furniture disappears. The flooring is replaced with gleaming hardwood.

Your higher self turns to you and asks, "Would you like to decorate together?"

Somehow—you're not exactly sure how—you do it. It seems as if all you have to do is *think* about beauty, and beauty shows up: beautiful furnishings, beautiful accessories, beautiful art on the walls, and beautiful flowers in vases scattered throughout the room. There is a soft, fragrant, scent wafting throughout. You didn't notice it before now, but there are notes of gentle music in the air.

When the two of you are finished, the room is spectacularly beautiful. The sun is shining through the many windows, and when you look out, it's the most beautiful view you've ever seen.

"And now," your higher self says, "let's make it even brighter!" Before your very eyes, everything in the room lights up from within.

"This is your room of money," your higher self says. "Your relationship with money has now changed. When you want more money to come into your life, simply come here and hang out for a while. Expand the room a bit, brighten it up even more, and soak up the beauty."

You thank your higher self and say farewell. Then, you close your mental eyes, and open your physical ones, knowing that your room of money will be there whenever you want to visit and create greater abundance!

THE "I CAN AFFORD EVERYTHING HERE" TECHNIQUE

If you're like most people, you enter several retail establishments every week. Oftentimes, when you enter a store, you think, "I can't afford this." This technique is about changing that energy.

There are many stores you enter—like your local Starbucks, grocery store, gas station, bookstore, or even shoe stores—that offer items at low and moderate prices. Nine times out of ten, you could afford any single item in that store you wanted to buy.

This technique focuses on what you *can* afford, instead of what you can't. It focuses on your abundance, not your lack.

The Technique:

> From now on, every time you go into a store that offers moderate pricing, you will think, "I can afford everything in this store."
>
> You really *can* afford everything in this store. Maybe not all at once, but you could afford to purchase any individual item. So the truth is, you can afford to purchase everything in this store! Feel that. Let it in!
>
> For this technique, the key is to feel how abundant you are as you walk around each store and look at all the things you could buy. Own your abundance. Allow your excitement to build as you recognize, and thereby focus on, what you can buy. As you do this, you'll be creating more money to spend as you desire.

THE "ABUNDANCE RITUAL" TECHNIQUE

As I've mentioned elsewhere in this book, money really is one of the easiest things to create. I didn't believe it for a long time—and, of course, my reality reflected that belief. Once I figured out *how* to create money, though, I knew it was true: money is a snap to create.

This technique is designed to help you shift your resonance around money, so do it as often as you'd like. It is also designed to grow with you as your receptivity to abundance (of all kinds) increases.

Preparation

Gather the following items:

- 3 white candles (any size)
- A metal or glass bowl
- Matches or a lighter
- Two strips of paper with these phrases written on them:
    - "Money is hard to come by; it doesn't grow on trees."
    - "Money is easy to create. It's as if it grows on trees!"

The Technique

Find some time to be alone. Play soft music while you assemble the ingredients in front of you on a table.

Take a deep breath, and on your exhale let go of the day's thoughts, feelings, and concerns.

Take another deep breath, and on your exhale let go of all preconceived notions of the outcome of this ritual.

Take a third deep breath, and on your exhale remind yourself of who you are: a divine spark of consciousness from God, Goddess, and everything that is.

Light the first candle, and say (aloud or in your mind), "Higher self, I invite you to join me in this ritual, to add your love, healing, and energy and to add your dreams for my abundance."

Light the second candle, and say (aloud or in your mind), "My soul, I invite you to join me in this ritual, to add your love, healing, and energy and to add your dreams for my abundance."

Light the third candle, and say (aloud or in your mind), "Angel Gabriel, I invite you to join me in this ritual, to add your love, healing, and energy and to help me to release and heal any negativity that may be in the way of receiving prosperity and abundance."

Close your eyes and feel the presence of your higher self, your soul, and the angel, Gabriel. Feel their love, their support, and their belief in you and your ability to create abundance. Spend a few minutes basking in this love. Allow any insights as to which beliefs to change, which actions to take, or which inspiration can guide your next steps to gently filter into your consciousness.

Open your physical eyes, and hold the slip of paper that says, "Money is hard to come by; it doesn't grow on trees." Think about the effect this belief and others like it have had on your reality. Think about the struggle, scarcity, and sacrifices this belief has caused.

Now, forgive yourself for everything—for all the lack, fear, pain, and worry, and all of the doing without. You did the best you could at the time. Say, aloud or in your mind, "I forgive myself for believing I was less than powerful and abundant."

Hold the paper over the bowl and burn it, allowing all of the negativity, constriction, and old patterns to be released as the paper turns to ash.

Pick up the slip of paper that says, "Money is easy to create. It's as if it grows on trees!" Read it aloud or in your mind.

Imagine the change that would take place in your world if you allowed this new belief to take hold in your subconscious mind. Think about how your life would be different if you never, ever had to worry about money again, for as long as you live.

Close your eyes, and imagine yourself in a beautiful, serene place in nature, sitting under a huge deciduous tree. Allow the tree's leaves to sway in the wind. Feel the gentle breeze upon your face. This is your private place. Maybe it's your yard, or maybe it's a secret place no one knows about but you.

Lie down underneath this beautiful tree. It's a warm summer day, and the grass is soft and cool beneath your body. It feels wonderful to lie beneath this magnificent tree.

You don't know how or when, but eventually you drift off to sleep. When you awaken, you look up into the tree. What you see astonishes you.

A *dollar bill* is falling from the tree!

You have no idea exactly where it is falling from—but it falls, slowly, drifting down before your very eyes to land at your feet.

You pick up the dollar. You turn it over and inspect it. You wonder if you're dreaming, and realize you're not. You thank your unseen friends for assisting you in bringing this abundance to you in this most fun and unexpected way.

Then, it hits you. If you can create *one* dollar bill falling out of a tree, you can create *one hundred* dollar bills falling out of a tree. Sure enough, just as you finish that thought, another dollar bill floats down as if from heaven.

Another follows—and another, and another. Soon, you are standing in a gentle rain of abundance. Why, there must be a hundred one dollar bills all around you! Stay here for a while. Play in the money. Gather it. Think about what you will do with it. Then, when you're ready, open your physical eyes.

Watch for signs in your world that your abundance is shifting. Once you see a sign of $1 or more, the next time you do this ritual, $5 bills will fall. Then look for signs of a bigger nature; next time, $10 bills, then $20 bills, and then $100 bills will fall like rain!

As always, change any beliefs that crop up as a result of thinking about and focusing on money.

THE "LOVING MONEY LEAVING" TECHNIQUE

Most people hate the thought of money leaving their lives. They cringe when the bills come in, and resignedly write checks at the end of the month. What they don't realize is, every time they think of money and feel lack, *they are pushing away financial abundance.* Every. Single. Time.

It is as natural for money to come in and out of your life as it is for the tide to ebb and flow. When money leaves, it is a great time to feel as if it will return to you multiplied.

The Technique

When you write a check or hand over cash for anything, practice thinking, "I release this money into the universe, and it will return to me multiplied."

Imagine that money coming back to you twofold, threefold, or even tenfold! Write a little dollar sign in the notation area of your checks. When you do, imagine every little dollar sign you write is "ordering" the check amount multiplied by the number of dollar signs you have written. If you write one dollar sign, expect double your money back. If you write ten dollar signs, expect the universe to send you ten times your money back. You might even write your dollar signs with exponents, ordering the check amount squared, cubed, or to the fifteenth power.

As with every technique, this should *feel* wonderful! You'll begin to look forward to bill paying because it feels fun to "order" more abundance in your world. Soon, you'll learn to love when money leaves your life.

Can it be that easy?

Yes. It can. If you have trouble believing that, you likely have a belief that it can't be that easy, or you aren't powerful, or you don't create your reality. Change those beliefs right now.

HOW TO USE THESE TECHNIQUES[2]

Techniques are a very personal thing. Don't use them just because I suggested them. Don't use them because your friend loves them. Use them because they speak to your heart and mind. Use them because they feel *right*.

You see, it's not the technique itself that creates your reality. It's you. Always. If a technique doesn't feel right to you, it won't produce the feeling necessary to create what you want.

As Bashar[3] says, "Any technique is only a permission slip to allow you to claim what is already yours."

(2) Some techniques have been recorded. Visit www.LiveALifeYouLove.com for more info.

(3) To learn more, visit www.Bahsar.org.

If you'd rather create your own techniques, by all means do so. Or, look for another teacher's suggestions. The bottom line is that techniques should help you focus and project your energy in a fun and enjoyable way.

As for when to use them, dive in when it feels right, fun, and exciting to do so. Oh, I know—that only happens in a perfect world. Sometimes, you *need* something to manifest, and so you reach for the quickest solution. That's okay. But ideally, do your techniques for the fun of it—for the excitement of the process, and the surprise of the result.

Now, go forth and create!

A TRUE STORY OF CONSCIOUSLY CREATING ABUNDANCE

I have been consciously creating for a couple of months and recently started focusing all my thoughts, energy, and time on creating money. I decided to set my computer wallpaper as: "Today is a delightful day. I am attracting money in expected and unexpected ways."

Then, the magic happened.

Since I started doing this, I have been experiencing higher and higher returns through my investments (I actively trade the equity markets). Just last week, as I was doing my accounting for the month, I realized I had two thousand dollars worth of shares I had miscounted. They were just sitting in my account—and, to top it off, they had grown 9% from their purchase price! Talk about money coming in through expected and unexpected ways!

Rest assured, I am not changing my wallpaper anytime soon.

- Mansi G.

ABUNDANCE-ALTERING TAKEAWAYS

- Abundance is a resonance. And as you follow *The Map to Abundance*, it will help you to create a resonance of abundance that will make techniques unnecessary. Until then, flowing energy toward your dream of abundance in the form of techniques will help you move toward that state of "being abundant" and create the specific things you desire.

- Remember to start with smaller dreams and build up to bigger dreams. Your dreams have to be believable (to you) before they can materialize.

- It's not techniques that create your reality; it's you. Always. If a technique doesn't feel right to you, it won't produce the feeling necessary to create what you want.

YOUR NEXT STEPS

- Imagine yourself being surprised by unexpected abundance. Imagine a picture of yourself smiling, remembering you made this happen. Do the One-Minute Manifestor Technique twice a day for seven days with this picture in mind. Write down your results.

- Pick another technique from this chapter that resonates with you, and do it. Then, write about your experience. How did you feel before the technique? How did you feel afterward? What changes did you see in your reality as a result of the technique?

CHAPTER ELEVEN

Action: Bring Your Commitment Into the World

"Dreams pass into the reality of action. From the actions stems the dream again; and this interdependence produces the highest form of living."

~ ANÄIS NIN

Action is a *requirement* in order to manifest abundance. Taking action tells the universe, "I am getting ready, because this kick-ass dream of abundance is about to materialize!" Action is a super-strong message that you believe in your dream, and truly expect it to happen.

Keeping your dreams of abundance in your head without taking action is like setting up a storefront but never unlocking the front door, or building a robust website and never letting it go "live." It's getting 90% of the way there, but never actually bringing it into the world so that you can reap the rewards.

Why would you get so far down the road to your dream and then sit down and refuse to move—or even worse, turn back?

The reason for your failure to act could be …

You're Afraid

It can be scary to open those doors, turn on that website, or to act on your dream of abundance if your subconscious mind is constantly asking, "What if I fail?"

Some people never take action for fear that the final step in creating abundance will prove what they've feared all along—that they will fail at creating abundance. Once they've proven, definitively, that they can't create it, their hope will die along with their dream, and that would be truly devastating. Better to soothe themselves with little white lies, like "I'll take action soon—maybe tomorrow—but today I'm too busy."

If you're hesitant to take action toward your dream of abundance, take a look at your beliefs. Your hesitancy is showing you something. So pay attention, change your beliefs, and then act!

If you're confident that your beliefs are in alignment, and you still don't feel like taking action, it's possible that, just maybe …

You Don't Really Want What You Think You Want

I'm not saying you don't want abundance. I believe that everyone on the planet (if they're honest with themselves) wants abundance. But maybe you don't want abundance to come to you in the way you *think* you want it.

For instance, if you say you want to become a successful real estate investor, yet every time you go to take action you get side-tracked by social media, you might want to take a look at whether real estate actually floats your boat.

And remember …

Not Just Any Action Will Do

Acting for the sake of action—aka doing "busy work"—won't result in attracting abundance. Your actions must be *inspired.*

Inspired action is action that you are excited to take, that moves you closer to your dream, and that sends the clear signal that you truly expect your dream to manifest. It's something you do after you've taken the first steps of *The Map* (owning your divinity, clarifying your dream, and flowing appropriate energy) to physically prepare for the abundance you're seeking.

WHAT "INSPIRED ACTION" *DOESN'T* LOOK LIKE

I was newly divorced and had just moved into a new home with my two sons. At that time I had enough money to get by, but I dreamed of financial freedom. I dreamed of surrounding myself with beautiful things, being able to take vacations, being able to afford any seminar I wanted to attend, and buying whatever clothing I fell in love with.

A friend suggested I supplement my income by doing something "arty," since I loved to express myself by creating. My local supermarket had a great flower shop within it, but the pots they sold were unimaginative, and some were downright ugly.

I decided to take action by painting some pots and selling them to this store. I went out and bought several dozen plain terracotta crocks, and the paint and other decorations I would need to create pots that would sell.

But, here's the thing: I wasn't motivated by joy. I was motivated by need. The action wasn't "inspired," because it didn't feel fun. In fact, it felt like work, and I didn't enjoy it much at all.

Of course, the pots didn't sell, and I ended up dragging them with me through two moves before I finally donated them to Goodwill. I hated those stupid pots. They cost me money I could ill afford at the time, and they hadn't made me one single dime. I wished I had never listened to my friend.

WHAT "INSPIRED ACTION" *DOES* LOOK LIKE

By the year 2010, I had known for twenty years that I wanted to teach people how to create a life they loved. I had already created a beautiful life for myself, and my dream was to help others do the same.

And so, despite having a company to run during the day and a loving new husband waiting at home for me, I decided to offer a series of workshops.

I didn't have much structure to these classes. I didn't prepare. I didn't even have a definitive topic. And yet, it felt right to offer them.

I sent out invitations. I left the cost of the workshops up to the individuals. I knew I had to charge something, or the participants wouldn't perceive it as valuable, but it felt good to me to let my students define that value. "Bring me something in exchange for the class," I suggested. "It can be whatever you want."

I received a half-eaten bag of candy, some loose change, a potted plant, a couple of little crystals, and a gift certificate to a palm reader, among other things. But this action wasn't about making money. It was about opening up to the part of me that yearned to teach the information I found so fascinating.

People learned a lot at these workshops, and so did I. I learned that I really was passionate about this topic, that I could trust whatever information was needed to flow through me, and that I wanted to keep moving forward with my dream.

That action didn't make me any money (well, except the spare change), but it did move my dream one step closer.

Sometimes, Inspired Action Will Seem Less Than Prudent

A couple of years later, I knew it was time to begin teaching full-time. I wanted to sell my marketing company and begin to write. I was trying to do both, but it wasn't working; I needed to be free to write every day and my marketing company split my energy.

So, I set a deadline. I would put my business up for sale, and if it didn't sell within six months, I would shut it down.

This was a big step, and I knew I couldn't do this alone. I asked my (then) husband whether he would step in and help me out with some of the liabilities (like the mortgage due on the commercial building I owned, and a lease on a digital printer) if the worst happened and I had to close the business down. Thankfully, he agreed.

In the end, I didn't need his help for the mortgage and lease, because I *did* sell the company. It didn't happen exactly within the deadline I'd given myself, but it was pretty darned close.

This action was bittersweet. Closing one door to open another isn't always easy. Part of me hated saying goodbye to the company I'd founded and the people who had worked with me for more than a dozen years. Another part of me, though, was excited for my new adventure.

My business broker told me, "You know, I could have gotten you a lot more money for the business if you'd given me more time to sell it." But money wasn't the goal; *freedom* was. I was ready to move on.

Inspired actions feel right no matter the downsides. Of course, you still want to be as savvy as you can, but don't keep putting off action until the time is "right." It will never *be* right if you keep looking for the absolutely perfect moment.

HOW TO KNOW IF YOUR ACTION IS INSPIRED

How can you tell if the action you want to take is inspired?

It Feels Good

Inspired action *always* feels good. When I founded my marketing company in my spare bedroom, I was having a ball! I loved every minute of it—answering the phones, taking orders, dreaming up new products, and working with the vendors. It didn't even matter (much) that I didn't take a paycheck for the first six months. I was just having fun.

If your action doesn't feel great when you think about doing it, flow some more energy toward your dream (i.e. do techniques). If it *still* doesn't feel great, take a look at whether you still really want this dream or if you really believe you can have it.

Another way to test if your action is inspired is ...

You Would Do It in a Heartbeat If the Dream Came True

Inspired action is the action you would take if you were 100 percent sure that your dream would manifest. It is the action you might take *after* the dream has manifested, but is equally appropriate to take *before* it's manifested as well, because you're sure your dream will manifest and inspired action is simply getting super-ready for the dream!

But, always ...

It Is Safe to Do

Taking action as if your dream will absolutely come true doesn't mean putting yourself at risk should it *not* manifest. Don't rent a building if your company is only making $1,000 a month. Don't max out your credit cards because you intend to be a millionaire. Begin where you are, and then create the ability to take the bigger steps. But *do* begin.

Start Small, But Start Somewhere

When my financial world went belly-up after my divorce, I dreamt of owning my own multi-million dollar corporation—but I was without a job or income. Rather than sitting around and complaining, or waiting for the "perfect" opportunity, I took what I could get: a job as a temp two days a week for $10 an hour. It wasn't a big step, but it was a step—and that's enough to start with.

Because you can't (and shouldn't try) to control how your dream manifests, you may find that inspired action leads you down roads you never imagined. If I hadn't taken that temp job, I might not have gotten my full-time job with the mortgage company. If I hadn't gotten that full-time job, I might never have been part of that startup. And if I hadn't been part of that startup, I might never have been in the position to found my company and create my dream of being a multi-million-dollar business owner.

Of course, if you are changing your beliefs, flowing energy toward your dream, and staying away from Abundance Stoppers, your dream could (and will) manifest in any number of different ways. But waiting for the "perfect" way is trying to control the outcome—which, as we know, messes with your ability to create.

So don't be afraid if your most inspired actions look a little odd. As long as they feel right, and you're excited about them, go for it!

EXAMPLES OF INSPIRED ACTION

I asked my readers what their dreams of abundance were. Below are some of the answers I received, along with the action steps they might take.

If the dream is:

To become debt-free

The action steps might be:

- Join a debt-reduction support group.
- Choose a debt reduction approach.
- Read a book on becoming debt free.
- Investigate investment strategies (for when you have no more debt).
- Plan what to do with the extra cash.

If the dream is:

Afford my daughter's education

The action steps might be:

- Send for the school application(s).
- Visit the school(s) your daughter could attend.
- Look into financial aid for the school(s) she is interested in.
- Gather information on college financing.
- Discuss with your daughter what she will be taking with her to school.

If the dream is:

Be a highly-recognized artist

The action steps might be:

- Read about other artists who have made it big.
- Study art marketing.
- Visit possible galleries/studios for rent.
- Determine how to submit art commissions for big cities.
- Plan what you might wear to your next awards ceremony.

If the dream is:

Travel with my family and friends

The action steps might be:

- Make a list of your top ten destinations.
- Sign up for Facebook or e-mail updates on the places in the world you intend to visit.
- Join an online travel forum.
- Plan (and implement) some local travel excursions.
- Visit a luggage store and choose the luggage that will best suit your travel needs to the destinations on your bucket list. (Hint: if it doesn't feel inspired, you don't actually have to buy the luggage yet!)

If the dream is:

Own my own home with an in-ground pool and flowers everywhere

The action steps might be:

- Take advantage of open houses to visit homes that match your criteria. Imagine yourself living there. Try not to think about the price of the house—don't even look at it if you can avoid it.

- Plant some flowers in pots at your own home. (You can always take them to the new house.)
- Take some trips to in-ground pools (friends, family, or public). Imagine they're yours.
- Learn about gardening online or through books.
- Decide the neighborhood you'd most like to live in and investigate schools, restaurants, shops, and facilities. Hang out there as often as possible.

If the dream is:

Build a dojang to host martial arts seminars and classes

The action steps might be:

- Draw up plans for your future dojang complete with lists of the details (bathrooms, office, windows, etc.).
- Visit all the dojangs you can find within a day's trip. Make notes of what you like and what you don't.
- Build a website and maybe a blog and capture contact information of people interested so when yours is open you're ready.
- Attend the seminars put on by others.
- Take a survey of your friends and contacts to find out what they would most like to see in a new dojang.

If the dream is:

Have a community center where people could get clothes, learn skills, have access to healthy food, and nourish their spirits

The action steps might be:

- Volunteer at a similar shelter, church, or organization.
- Research what it takes to form a non-profit corporation.
- Investigate the need for this type of service in your community.
- Find out about grants for this type of facility and what the requirements are.
- Start a list of family, friends, and acquaintances who are interested in volunteering.

If the dream is:

Grow our small business and run it full-time as a couple

The action steps might be:

- Investigate the local Small Business Association (SBA) and sign up for classes.
- Make a list of employees and job descriptions you want to have five years from now.
- Visit possible locations for expansion.

- Take an online marketing course.
- Make a list of why your company is different than your competition and how you plan for it to be even more unique.

If the dream is:

Have enough money to eat healthy food regularly

The action steps might be:

- Investigate local food co-ops.
- Subscribe to blogs about eating healthily on the cheap.
- Start an herb garden in pots.
- Investigate local organic farmers who might sell roadside or at farmers' markets.
- Gather healthy recipes you intend to try.

Wait a minute—a lot of your action steps seem to indicate "settling" for a lower income and being frugal instead of creating wealth.

Just because you take action steps in the direction of your dream now, that make sense for the income you have, doesn't mean you are settling for your current level of wealth.

What you *don't* want to do is to postpone your dream until you create more money.

I hear lots of people say in words and actions, "I will live my life when I get my dream!"

"Hogwash!" I say. "That's just an excuse not to do the work and to stay stuck where you are."

You'll notice the dreams of the people I interviewed really have nothing to do with money itself (even though each of those interviewed began with "I want lots of money because"). Their dreams consist of what they believe money can finance.

However …

YOU MIGHT BE SURPRISED

There are many ways for dreams to come true without actually creating cash to finance them. Being abundant doesn't necessarily mean having lots of money. It means having "access to resources."[1]

Allowing your dream to manifest in the easiest and most elegant way possible may result in the dream manifesting in a way you didn't expect, and couldn't have anticipated in a million years. Expect to be happily surprised.

I was astonished when the startup I worked for closed its doors after six months. But instead of an ending, it was a beginning—and it took only $50 and some inspired action for me to start another company.

I had built-in customers, a functional website, and procedures in place for marketing and fulfillment. I couldn't have anticipated or planned for that turn of events, and yet it worked out perfectly and gave me my dream: owning my own company.

Of course, I worked at it and created magic for it for the next twelve years to grow it into the company it became—but it

(1) Definition of abundance from Lazaris. Learn more at www.Lazaris.com.

did manifest. And the same goes for you: if you have a dream, and your beliefs are in alignment, it will manifest.

While you wait for your dream to take form, take lots of action steps that don't require all of the money you need to fully manifest. Those actions will help your dream manifest. They'll also give you the feedback necessary to determine if your dream is what you really want—and, if it is, inspired action will bring your dream to you more quickly.

A TRUE STORY OF CONSCIOUSLY CREATING ABUNDANCE

My boyfriend and I have a blended family, and together we have six children. Both of us went through divorces about four years ago, and neither had good credit. My vehicle was a '99 Toyota Corolla, and he had a Chevy Silverado. We could never go anywhere with the whole family unless we wanted to take two vehicles. This was a big issue for us, and prevented us from a lot of family activities.

After reading The Map, *I wrote out some intentions and began creating a vehicle that would be affordable and that our whole family could comfortably ride in.*

We focused our attention on having a Honda Pilot, but left it open if something else would fit what we needed. I thought about this car a lot. Every time I would see one on the road, I'd visualize myself having one, and that visualization made me so happy.

Within a couple of months, my boyfriend got a raise (bringing in more money was also an intention), and we started looking for a car. Even though we didn't have decent credit and had no down payment, we began looking anyway.

My boyfriend found a dealership that approved him for a loan (the first miracle) so we packed up the kids and drove an hour and a half to the dealership. When we arrived, our truck was almost out of gas, but we were running late, so we decided to wait until we were done to fill it up.

My boyfriend befriended the sales manager, who also had a blended family. They were both from the same area of Texas. Because of their new friendship, the dealership made us an offer to trade in our old truck as a down payment. The truck was realistically only worth about $2,500 to the dealership, but they gave us $4,000 (the second miracle).

The first approval didn't go through, so they had to find another finance company. The only reason this second loan worked was because of the money from the trade-in.

Five hours later, we took all of our stuff out of the old truck and put it into our new Honda Pilot. Before we left, the dealership even filled up the tank.

And—get this—the difference between the payment for the old truck and the new Pilot was exactly the amount of my boyfriend's recent raise.

The synchronicity of this whole experience was nothing short of magical. Now as I drive down the street, I look at what I am driving and see our whole family sitting in the back, and I know that I really can create my universe.

- Amanda

ABUNDANCE-ALTERING TAKEAWAYS

- Action is a requirement in order to manifest abundance. Taking action tells the universe, "I'm getting ready, because this kick-ass dream of abundance is about to materialize!" Action sends a super-strong message that you believe in your dream and truly expect it to happen.

- If you are hesitant to take action toward your dream of abundance, take another look at your beliefs. Your hesitancy is showing you something—so pay attention, change your limiting beliefs, and then act!

- Inspired action is action that you are excited to take, that moves you closer to your dream, and that sends the clear signal that you truly expect your dream to manifest. It's something you do after you've taken the first steps of *The Map* (owning your divinity, clarifying your dream, and flowing appropriate energy) to physically prepare for the abundance you're seeking.

- Inspired action always feels good. If your action doesn't feel great when you think about doing it, flow some more energy toward your dream—and if it still doesn't, take a look at whether you still really want this dream, if you really believe you can have it, or if you are afraid of the consequences of the dream coming true.

- Taking action as if your dream will absolutely come true doesn't mean putting yourself at risk should it not manifest. Begin where you are, and then create the ability to take the bigger steps.

- Start small, but start somewhere.

- There are many ways for dreams to come true without actually creating cash to finance them. Being abundant doesn't necessarily mean having lots of money. It means having "access to resources."

YOUR NEXT STEPS

- Write out the answers to these questions:
    - When you think about your dream of abundance, do you find yourself getting excited?
    - When you think about taking action toward your dream of abundance, do you feel inspired to take action?
    - Do you have any hesitancy toward taking action? If so, can you trace it back to the beliefs or the wrong dream that might be causing it?
- Make a list of the actions you'll take in the next 30 days toward your dream. Then, schedule time to take them.

CHAPTER TWELVE

See the "Signs" & Make Them Grow

"Prosperity is a way of living and thinking, and not just money or things. Poverty is a way of living and thinking, and not just a lack of money or things."

~ ERIC BUTTERWORTH

The universe *always* responds.

Everything you see, hear, touch, taste, and experience "out there" is mirroring the thoughts, feelings and beliefs inside of you.

As you shift and change, your reality will too—but not necessarily all at once. It will likely happen slowly, and you'll receive "signs" to indicate that it is, indeed, changing.

Signs are not an "out there," "woo-woo" kind of thing. Signs are indications of impending movement. You can see signs of change for just about everything on the planet. The more you pay attention to the signs, the more you will attract the reality they indicate to you.

For example, you might get a sign of a cold coming on in the form of a tickle in your throat, slightly swollen glands, or scratchy eyes. When you notice the signs, you can dive straight into the belief that "I have a cold"—after which you'll likely become sicker by the hour—or, you can head the cold off at the pass by figuring out why you created it and responding to the message of the cold (oftentimes we create colds because we need to slow down) and giving your body what it needs (such as Cold Snap—love that stuff!).

The weather holds signs that precede a change. Remember the rhyme, "Red sky at night, sailor's delight; red sky at morning, sailors take warning"? I'll bet the old-time mariners paid close attention to those signs, and took action to embrace or avert them as necessary.

Signs occur before relationships change, children change, jobs change, and realities change. If you learn to pay attention to those signs, they can tell you whether you're on track or not—and with that information, you will become more empowered.

SOMETIMES, THE SIGNS ARE NOT SO SUBTLE

A friend of mine was telling me how much fun she had recently when her sister came to visit. The two of them spent a few days in a quaint little town in Colorado called Blackhawk, a former mining town turned gaming destination.

My friend's sister (we'll call her Marie) was quite new to the concept of reality creation, and my friend had been teaching her about it.

As they sat down at the slots to try their "luck," Marie said, "I don't know why I gamble. I never win."

"Don't say that," my friend replied. "Say, 'I haven't won *yet*'!"

Marie laughed and said, "Okay, I haven't won *yet*! Hey, wouldn't it be great if I won enough money to cover my plane fare out here?" With that, she turned and put a coin in the machine.

Jackpot! Marie won 60,000 nickels—$300! Her plane ticket had cost $301.65.

Astonished, she turned to my friend, "I can't believe this!"

My friend replied, "It's amazing, isn't it? Now, can you allow yourself to receive even more than the cost of the plane ticket?"

Grinning, Marie walked away to cash in her winnings. When she came back, her grin had grown even wider.

"What's up?"

"You're not going to believe this!"

"What? Tell me!"

"When I got to the machine to turn my nickels into cash, there was a $100 bill already in the tray!"

Why did it happen so quickly for Marie?

She didn't have any attachment to what she was creating. She wasn't trying to *prove* it worked—she was just having fun with her sister. She was lighthearted about it, and delighted when she won the money to cover the plane ticket—so the universe responded by giving her more. (And maybe, just maybe, she got a little help from her unseen friends who wanted her to pay attention to this concept.)

Now, granted …

IT DOESN'T USUALLY HAPPEN INSTANTLY

Normally, things take a little longer to manifest.

Why? Because of *time lag.*

Time lag is the time between your request for what you want and the point when the universe responds with a reality.

It's important to remember that time lag is here because we *need* it. Until we learn that we are creating our realities, we aren't paying much attention to our thoughts and feelings, and, let's face it, we don't have a clue about what we believe. If our unchecked thoughts, feelings, and beliefs manifested instantly, we'd live pretty short lives.

Because time lag is built into Earth's system of creation, it sometimes takes a while for the universe to line things up and deliver them to our doorstep.

But there's another reason it usually takes time for a reality to manifest:

MOST PEOPLE AREN'T FLOWING CONSISTENT ENERGY

If you had a positive flow of energy *all* the time (including your thoughts, feelings, and beliefs) all of your dreams would manifest all of the time. Not instantly, perhaps, but they would manifest.

Most people don't flow consistent energy. They get excited, then disappointed. They believe it will happen, then they doubt themselves.

Especially in the beginning, you will forget to think about what you want, and slip into thinking about what you don't have. You'll start to feel frustrated, and wonder if you've failed and if you'll ever create your dream. These thoughts and feelings push your dream away. Then, perhaps, you'll read a book, or attend a seminar, or hear about a friend's success, and you'll get serious (again) about making your dreams come true.

It's an ebb and flow. Your dreams come closer, then you push them away. Closer, then away. If something doesn't change, this can go on for a long, long time, and you'll become very frustrated. Even worse, you'll begin to feel powerless, and even hopeless, because you'll be under the impression that this whole reality creation thing isn't working for you, and that you don't have what it takes—which, by the way, is absolutely, totally untrue.

There is a way out of this spiral of disempowerment. You just need to ...

ACKNOWLEDGE THE SIGNS

The universe will *always* respond when you put forth a strong flow of positive energy toward what you want.

Negative energy is weaker, so it takes much more to make negative realities manifest (thank goodness)—but positivity is powerfully strong. When you flow strong positive energy, you will receive signs that the universe is responding to your flow within days, if not hours, of putting it forth. How exciting is that?

You don't have to wait for months or years to get the first pieces of your dream. You don't have to wonder if you're doing it right. The universe will give you a metaphorical high five every time you flow strong, certain, excited, imaginative, joyful energy in the direction of your dreams.

So ...

What Does a Sign Look Like?

A sign is something that happens in your life that is related to your dream. For instance, if your dream is to double your income, and you do a powerful technique toward that end (such as one of the techniques in Chapter Ten), the signs you receive might be:

- You receive an unexpected tax refund from your property taxes.
- You run into a friend at the grocery store and he tells you about a mutual friend who's made it big.
- Your annual review is called back by corporate and declined. Corporate decided it wasn't enough and doubled the intended pay increase.
- You read an article about a blogger who makes $50,000 a year writing a few hours a week.
- Your spouse receives a small inheritance.
- You turn on the TV. The channel just happens to be playing a show on self-made millionaires.
- You win a free weekend in the mountains in a raffle.
- You receive a copy of *Worth* magazine in the mail.

But some of those things don't actually bring me any money.

No, they don't—but they're still signs that abundance is coming your way. They're indications that your energy is shifting.

You aren't hearing stories of friends who have become homeless. Your wife didn't get a speeding ticket she has to pay. You didn't get a tax bill for a special assessment tax. No, you're hearing stories of success—and that tells you something about *you*.

When you receive an indication that your abundance is changing, it is super-important to …

RESPOND POSITIVELY TO THE SIGNS

It can be tempting to see someone else having the things you desire and become disheartened because you don't have them yet. But if you're seeing *any movement at all* around the area of your dream, try to see if you can find a positive message in the event.

You may have to stretch your imagination to see a way to interpret it positively, but that's okay. You're learning to shift your energy (i.e., thoughts, feelings, and beliefs) to "always positive," and sign interpretation is a great place to practice.

Here are some possible "signs" for some of the dreams outlined in Chapter Eleven. See if you can stretch your "positivity muscle" to accept them as indications that the dream is manifesting.

If the dream is:

Become debt-free

After you did a powerful technique, the signs might be:

- A call from a headhunter inquiring as to whether you are open to switching jobs, but for the job they have in mind your salary would decrease.

You may be tempted to blow this one off since the job being offered is below your current pay level. But remember there are no accidents—your energy allowed or created this call. And who knows what it might turn into in the long run? Take it as a win, whether or not you are interested.

- An offer to refinance your mortgage.

Oh come on—who doesn't get an offer every other week to refinance their mortgage?

Maybe millions—but that doesn't matter. What *does* matter is that you are shifting your energy and you got the offer to potentially reduce your debt. In this case, it might make sense to take a little "action," and see if it does, in fact, make financial sense to refinance!

- You save a record amount (with coupons) at the grocery store.

Seriously? Clipping coupons is a sign?

No. Saving a *record amount* with coupons is a sign.

- Your best friend invites you to vacation with her at her timeshare in Cabo San Lucas.

This might be such a fun and exciting offer that you forget that it might be a sign, too. However, abundance is abundance. Be grateful to your friend, but also high-five yourself for the creation!

- Your son gets a scholarship to soccer camp.

Sure, maybe you weren't even certain you were going to send your son to camp, but the important thing to focus on is the abundance. Getting something of value for nothing is a fabulous sign!

If the dream is:

Afford my daughter's education

After you did a powerful technique, the signs might be:

- Your daughter's new teacher at the public school is the best one she's ever had.

You may be happy with the current situation, but secretly worry that this "good year" will make you complacent about creating a private school education for your girl. "After all," you think, "this is unlikely to last. Next year, her teacher will probably be horrible."

If you react this way, you are missing the *essence* of your dream. You want a good education for your child. Demanding that it can only come through a private school is trying to control the outcome.

And, believe me, private schools don't guarantee a good education. My son had the worst teacher of his life when I pulled him from public schooling and enrolled him in a private school I thought would be better. The teacher had a nervous breakdown after losing his wife to cancer, and my son had a horrible experience.

So, remember the reason you want the abundance, and celebrate every sign that gives you a taste of that.

- You read an article about the decline of the public school system.

Some would read that article and despair that things are getting worse and their child is still in the public system, letting their energy spiral downward. Don't be that person.

Sometimes, you need to *decide* what your sign means. This sign is clearly related to the dream, and you could take it to mean that the need for better education is receiving attention, which will result in positive changes. That is a good sign!

- You decide to sell some old toys on Craigslist and are shocked that people will pay good money for them.

How is selling used toys possibly a sign?

You were inspired to act (inspired action, remember?) and then you were pleasantly surprised at the amount of money you made. How is this *not* a sign?

- Your homeowners association is shot down on their proposed special assessment and you don't have to pay an extra $875 this year after all.

But that probably would have happened anyway. It was always a long shot that they'd be approved.

By taking that attitude, you, my friend, are giving your power away. Every time you can take credit for a good reality, take it. The world is your oyster, and everything is coming up roses. (Enough clichés for you there?) Seriously, though: each and every time you can say, "This is good news, and I created it," you step a little bit closer to living in a reality that is all abundance, all the time.

- You win $10 from your office fantasy football league.

The signs that produce "a little extra money" often go ignored. But pay attention, because they add up—and if you respond positively they will lead to more and more money coming in.

If the dream is:

Be a highly-recognized artist

After you did a powerful technique, the signs might be:

- A fan of your work asks you for your autograph.

It would be hard to argue this isn't a sign; the challenge is actually recognizing it when it happens. You need to train yourself to do so.

- Your friends encourage you to submit your art to a juried show.

But my friends aren't qualified to judge good art. They just want to support me.

Maybe so, but you have created them in *your* world—which suggests that you are good enough for the show.

However, let me add a note: don't let your ego take over here. Feeling "better than" others, even professionally, can come back to bite you in your reality. Creating success doesn't mean you're better than anyone. It only means you're *willing* to be successful.

- You read an article about Carmen Herrera, who became a famous artist at ninety-four.

But I would be scared if I read that. I don't want to wait that long for my success!

Of course you don't—but your reaction illustrates the danger in seeing a good sign as bad. Your emotions create. So instead, look at her success and think "It can happen to anyone, so why not me?" Then, you can flow joy instead of fear.

- You get a promotion at work.

I know I should be excited about this, but this also brings up fear. What if I'm so seduced by the "job with the money" that I never break free and really go for my dream?

First, it's wonderful that you can be emotionally honest. If you acknowledge your feelings, you are halfway to healing them. The next step is to ask yourself what belief is behind that fear. Maybe it's something like:

- I CAN'T MAKE AS MUCH MONEY AS AN ARTIST AS I CAN AT A "REAL JOB."

If so, that belief can be easily and unconditionally changed.

- You finally sell a piece that you created ten years ago.

You may be tempted to think of this in the negative, like, "Gosh if it takes me ten years to sell my paintings I'll never make it big!" Instead, view it as an energy shift. Yesterday you didn't allow success, but today you do!

If the dream is:

Travel with my family and friends

After you did a powerful technique, the signs might be:

- You tell your friend about your dream and he tells you about a book he saw, *How to Become the Jack of All Travel: A Beginner's Guide to Traveling the World for Free.*

But I don't want to volunteer. I want to make enough money to travel first class.

That may be so. But this is still a fabulous sign that travel is creatable by everyone.

- You decide to Google "amazing travel opportunities" and spend the afternoon reading about paid and unpaid jobs that offer chances to travel.

How is that a sign when I proactively decided to do it? It didn't just happen to me.

It's a sign because the search was your idea. The interesting websites and possibilities could or could not have happened—but you created them appearing on your screen.

- You get a new job that pays you more money, but you have two weeks less vacation a year.

More money to travel with, but less time to travel? That would bum me out!

I suggest you practice looking at the good side of everything (except perhaps, when you're scouring your subconscious for unhelpful beliefs). You don't know how the universe will deliver your dream, you only know that it will—and this is a sign that it is. Who knows: you could save for a year and then have a life-changing job offer as a travel companion! The important thing here is that you created more money, and money can be used for travel.

- You flip on the TV and a famous actress is talking about her trip to Africa.

Of course she could travel to Africa. But I'm no famous actress!

You *do* want to travel, though. And you created someone close to you (right in your living room) who is traveling. It's a good sign. Take it.

- You find a five-dollar bill on the street.

I know, five bucks won't get you enough gas to get across town. But it's still a sign—so acknowledge it, expect more, and strengthen your flow.

If the dream is:

Grow our small business and run it full-time as a couple

After you did a powerful technique, the signs might be:

- You spend a full day in your business and have the most fun you've ever had at work.

What? Just having fun in my little company is a sign?

Yes, it is. It indicates you're headed toward your greatest excitement. The more fun you have, the more fun you'll create. Having an awesome day at work should tell you the choice is a good one for you. As long as your beliefs are in alignment, the money will follow.

- One of the entrepreneurship blogs you subscribe to ran an article about a couple who quit their jobs, started a company together, and grew it to earn ten times what they made in their former professions.

I can't help thinking, why not us?

That's the point. It is you. You created that article! If it has happened to anyone, it can happen to you. Simply tell the universe, "Thank you. I'm next!"

- An opportunity presents itself to collaborate with another company that would generate a lot of income. Then, the opportunity falls apart.

I know what you're thinking—how disappointing! But remember, signs are not "the dream." Do you hear me? Yes, sometimes you'll jump to creating the dream without even a sign, but don't expect that to happen every time.

A sign is a sign. With each one, expect that the dream is coming. When the opportunities (read: signs) come, simply say, "This or better please, universe," and really feel that. Be okay with opportunities coming and going, and allow each and every one to get you more excited because you're closer than ever to your dream!

- Your spouse gets a new boss at work who he despises.

Yes, this is a sign that you've changed the energy and the dream is looking better and better. Now is a great time to test for beliefs such as:

- I MUST BE FORCED TO QUIT MY JOB AND FOLLOW MY HEART, BECAUSE JUST QUITTING IS TOO SCARY.

Remember, you can create an easy transition to your new life that is a win-win for everyone concerned.

- Your little company's major competitor releases a new blog, and it's fabulous.

It's tempting to see the genius of others—especially competitors—and feel envious. But you've created them in your life because you have brilliance, too, and yours is closer than ever! Celebrate the brilliance of others, and you'll attract more brilliance of your own.

WHEN YOU RECOGNIZE A SIGN

When you do see a sign in your reality, acknowledge your impact. You made that sign happen ... and you will make the next sign happen, and the next, and the next, until your dream has fully manifested.

Then, celebrate your success. Get excited about what you have created, and even more excited about what you can create from here. You're a powerful reality creator—and the more you let that in, the more powerful you will become.

Finally, every time you recognize a sign, strengthen your flow toward the dream. Do another technique, imagine your life as you desire it, write about the changes that will occur in your new life, or use your success as fuel to change some more beliefs. Signs are there to motivate you to continue on your current trajectory.

Keep track of your signs and creations in some type of success journal. It will help you to remember the impact you've had on your reality in the past. Each time you read back through your old successes, you strengthen the belief that you are in control of your world.

Recognizing signs can help lift your creations to the next level, but you have to see them and own them in order for that to happen. As with anything, the more you practice, the better you'll get!

TRUE STORIES OF CONSCIOUSLY CREATING ABUNDANCE

Finances have been a bugaboo for me for a while now, so as I've read and followed The Map's "conscious creating" steps, financial abundance has been high on my list of things to create.

On Monday, I closed on the refinancing of my home. As a result, I have some extra money because I won't have any mortgage payments for two months. Also, in February, I'll receive a quarterly annuity check that will help my finances considerably, and by the end of February I expect I'll be getting a good-sized tax refund.

For a couple of weeks I've been thinking to myself, "This is going to be a great period of abundance. I can do a few things I've wanted to do but couldn't afford lately, and I can buy a few things I've needed, but felt I couldn't afford."

I also simultaneously (and almost unconsciously) thought, "And after February, things will go back to normal."

Tonight, I was sitting at the computer and I had an "a-ha!" moment that almost lifted me out of my chair. "Wait," I said to myself. "This IS the abundance I've been working toward! My dearest creative self, accept this as the beginning of an abundant life. If you think this is a momentary diversion from 'life as usual,' you are missing the point and adding an unnecessary limitation to the process!"

I got up from my chair yelling, "I've got it! I think I finally get it!"

I find it interesting that my picture of "how it will look when it's working" is different than how it looks in reality!

- Linda H.

Every day I'm receiving little signs of abundance. I was out delivering some pamphlets this morning to earn some much-needed extra money, and found a twenty dollar bill just sitting there waiting for me. I'm grateful and loving it.

- Andrew D.

My intentions have been to receive a check in the exact dollar amount to pay off my debt.

I just started using the One-Minute Manifestor technique, and today I saw a post on Facebook from a friend who said that she had received a check from an anonymous source for a dollar amount that was exactly what she needed.

I also received a bigger paycheck this past payday due to a bonus that I was not expecting. I know that when you start to manifest what you desire you will see signs all around. So true!

- Melissa K.

I am so excited to see the signs that I am manifesting abundance. I was in a rush this morning and stopped to grab breakfast at McDonald's (which I normally do not do). I received two instant-winning game pieces for food prizes. Then, I went online and input my game codes and won again! Everything is falling into place as I am creating my new world!

-Bobbie

Before leaving my apartment, I thought about how, when I first started consciously creating, things seemed slow, but then they really picked up. I remembered that I have to keep flowing energy to see results.

I went to Starbucks. While standing in line, I imagined receiving a free drink. Less than a minute later, the elderly gentleman in front of me placed his order and said he'd cover my drink as well! Pretty sweet!

- Jay

Just two weeks after changing my beliefs about money, I received a check in the mail from a company I had never before dealt with in any way—and the check was addressed to me!

Although I notice subtle changes every day, this sign could not be clearer: a check for me for no reason at all, other than that I now believe I deserve it! I know this came about because I let go of how it should happen, and opened myself up to limitless possibilities!

- DeAnna W.

ABUNDANCE-ALTERING TAKEAWAYS

- As you shift and change, your reality will too, but generally not all at once. It will likely happen slowly, and you'll receive signs that it is, indeed, changing. Signs are not an "out there," "woo-woo" kind of thing. They are real indicators of change.

- Time lag is the time between your request for what you want and the universe responding with a reality.

- If you had a positive flow of energy (including thoughts, feelings and beliefs) all of the time, ALL of your dreams would manifest ALL of the time. Maybe not instantly, but they would manifest.

- The universe will always respond when you put forth a strong flow of positive energy toward what you want. You will receive signs that the universe is responding to your flow within days, if not hours, of putting it forth.

- It can be tempting to become disheartened when you see that someone else has the things you desire. But someone having what you want is a very positive and powerful sign that you can have it too. You've created it close to you—the next step is it showing up for you!

- Recognizing signs can help lift your creating to the next level, but you have to see them and own them in order for that to happen.

YOUR NEXT STEPS

- Read your previous entries in your success journal (or start one if you don't have one already). This journal can be a simple computer document, a paper notebook, or a formal journal. Write down any signs you have received thus far but haven't recorded.

- Do a technique from Chapter Ten. For three days, pay attention to the signs that occur and write them down.

- Consider working with a partner to discuss dreams, signs, beliefs, and creating. Sometimes another person can see signs that you have missed.

- Use the applied kinesiology techniques in Appendix B to test for the constricting beliefs in this chapter. Document the beliefs that need to be changed, and change them using a technique in Appendix D.

CHAPTER THIRTEEN

Meanwhile, As You Wait for Your Abundance ...

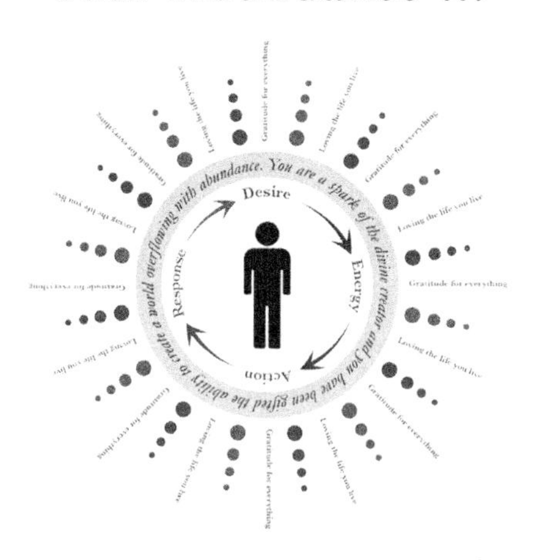

"Those who have not found their true wealth, which is the radiant joy of Being and the deep, unshakable peace that comes with it, are beggars, even if they have great material wealth. They are looking outside for scraps of pleasure or fulfillment, for validation, security, or love, while they have a treasure within that not only includes all those things but is infinitely greater than anything the world can offer."

~ ECKHART TOLLE

I learned the most important lesson of my life when I gave up on creating abundance.

(Yes. You read that correctly.)

When I found myself at my lowest point ever, financially—when the creditors were calling, foreclosure notices were arriving by certified mail, and I had no job or income whatsoever—I gave up on creating abundance.

It wasn't working. I couldn't manifest anything but more bills. I was drowning in debt, and there seemed to be no viable solution.

So I said, "Screw it."

Being worried every waking moment sucked. I felt awful about my future, my situation, and myself. I felt ashamed that I had allowed my life to spiral out of control. I felt hopeless about my future, and helpless to change anything. And the worst thing was, *I had been trying this whole time to consciously create my reality!*

"Imagine how bad things could have been if I *hadn't* been trying!" I thought.

I think what hurt the most was that I was supposed to be *good* at this creating stuff. I mean, I'd been studying it for years, and I'd spent a ton of money learning everything I could about it—and yet, here I was, feeling absolutely powerless to change my circumstances.

And so, I gave up trying to change anything. I gave up feeling bad. I even gave up *thinking* about my situation.

Instead, I chose to make my emotional state my only priority. It hurt too much to feel bad, so I decided to let that go and simply feel good, regardless of what was happening in my life.

THE CHOICE THAT CHANGED MY LIFE

I only expected that choosing to feel good would, well, feel good. I *hated* feeling bad. I wanted a break from the incessant worry. And so, I chose to be happy instead. I figured that, if I had to be a homeless person, at least I could be a happy homeless person!

That choice rocked my world.

First, I felt immediate relief. I had forgotten how much joy there could be in just being. I had forgotten that I had value beyond the things I possessed. Happiness set my world-view straight.

But it was more than that. There was also a huge amount of relief in not caring about my future. And I don't mean I didn't care about myself: I did. But I no longer cared about the specifics of what happened in my life. I didn't care what manifested. I only cared that I enjoyed each and every moment.

"Just be happy" is easy to say—and, when you really commit yourself, it's easy to do. But when you're wrapped up in trying to make something happen, it can also feel incredibly hard.

One of the biggest keys to abundance is to let go of desperately wanting it. Manifestation works best when you relax and allow the universe to deliver your dreams in its own perfect timing.

Once you stop obsessing about whether your abundance will manifest, and how it will show up, you open the way for abundance to enter. Instead of hanging around waiting for the doorbell to ring, peeking out through the curtains every five minutes, you throw open the door and say, "Show up anytime, abundance. I'm here, just doing my thing and loving life!"

With such a joyful standing invitation in place, abundance *will* enter—if you've worked *The Map* to this point by changing your negative or constricting beliefs, working with your younger selves, and let go of trying to control how abundance shows up.

But if I've worked The Map *up to this point, abundance should show up, right?*

Yes, it should—and it will. But not if you are desperately wanting and clinging to it. Because if you're desperately wanting and clinging to it, you still have a fear (read: belief) that it won't come when you need it.

So, instead of waiting by the door and driving yourself crazy while you wait for abundance, just have a blast living life!

You see, most people have it backwards. They think you need to create a wonderful job, money, opportunities, etc. in order to have an abundant life.

But, you see, you already *have* an abundant life. You just haven't realized it, or begun to enjoy it yet.

You have a life in which you are a god. You literally create your world. That, my friend, is the epitome of abundance. If you are creating it all (and you are), you can create *unlimited abundance.*

Once you let that in, and you begin to enjoy—and I mean really enjoy—every single minute of your life, the stuff you want comes automatically. Stuff is a side effect of living your abundant life, not a condition for it!

HAPPINESS CREATES ABUNDANCE

I didn't choose happiness to create abundance, and neither should you. You should choose happiness because it's a beautiful way to live your life. That happiness can open the doors to spectacular abundance is just a really cool side effect.

This lifetime is like an invitation to a really fun party. If you decide to come to the party, you'll have a blast. You'll discover who you truly are, and what your talents and gifts are. You'll enjoy the party down to the tiniest detail—and you'll even get a goodie bag.

This "goodie bag" contains the things in the world (or as Lazaris calls them, the "trappings"): cars, houses, money, jobs, opportunities, successes, people, friendship, and experiences.

The goodie bag is given to you for attending the party. But the goodie bag is not the party. The party is your fabulous life!

You won't get the goodie bag unless you attend the party—at least, not without a lot of struggle. And you won't receive true abundance without embracing, with your whole being, this amazing lifetime you've been given.

But I don't know where my next dollar will come from. How can I be happy?

You can be happy for so many reasons. You can be happy because nature is breathtaking. You can be happy because there is goodness in the world. You can be happy because there are amazing people in your life, right here, right now to be grateful for. You can be happy about the stuff you already have, even if it isn't (yet) the stuff you dream about.

And, you can be happy for no reason at all! Happiness is a choice. When you live your life with the intention to be happy all the time, no matter what happens around you, you open the doors to magic, miracles, and opportunities that you can't even imagine right now.

It's not just the energy you flow when you're doing techniques or working on your dream that counts. It's the energy you flow *all day long.*

Speaking of which, there is another emotion that will supercharge your ability to create abundance, and that is …

GRATITUDE

The word gratitude is so overused that, for many people, it's lost its meaning—and its ability to rock our lives.

I'm not talking about some guilt-ridden credo of "gratefulness" like, "Say thank you to Grandma for your birthday gift," or, "Be grateful you have food. There are children in Africa who are starving!" I'm talking about *true* gratitude—a deeply-felt love and appreciation for something or someone in your life.

Trust me, when you start flowing gratitude, it can …

Change.

Your.

Life.

Think about it. Your thoughts and feelings create your reality, so feeling good literally draws to you *more things to feel good about!*

I'm usually all about focusing on the future by thinking about what your life will be like and feeling the feelings you'll have when you have the dream. Gratitude is different because it focuses on the present—but either way, good feelings generate good realities. That's the way our universe works.

And, gratitude has extra power. It's supercharged. When you feel grateful about things in your life—be it your love life, your finances, your health, this Earth, whatever—that's because those things *are already in your life*. They have already manifested.

That feel-good energy acknowledges that you have received this great gift. All of the hesitancy, disbelief, and "will this ever happen?" energy within your dreams for the future is eliminated by gratitude.

Gratitude also strengthens the belief that you are the creator of your world, that your universe is benevolent, and that good things come to you.

When you flow gratitude, it feels wonderful. When you feel it, you're resonating pure, unadulterated joy, love, and thankfulness. In this way, gratitude may be the most powerful "technique" ever.

But wait, there's more.

Gratitude also connects you with the rest of the world in a way nothing else can. It is a connecting energy that opens your heart and connects you to your soul. It lifts you to a higher resonance, and reminds you that *we are all one.*

Another Little Reminder

When you ignore the good things that are happening in your world (read: when you don't feel grateful) you're sending a signal to the universe that says, "Don't send me more of this."

Emotion attracts. You've seen it happen in your life. Positive emotion attracts. Negative emotion attracts. But neutral emotion does nothing.

So, if good things happen, and you ignore them, you, my friend, have missed a great opportunity to double your order from the universe.

Five Ways to Allow Gratitude to Create Abundance In Your Life

1. ***Make gratitude a habit.*** Make time every day to count your abundant blessings. Write in a journal, or in a gratitude document on your computer. Review your gratitudes in the shower, or while getting dressed, or while in the car—but do it regularly.

2. ***Make gratitude specific.*** The more specific you are, the more the magic of gratitude will be present.

Why? Because when you get specific, you will feel it more, and specificity deepens the gratitude. Instead of, "I am grateful for my paycheck," you could think or write, "I am so grateful for this piece of paper with my name on it. This check represents my ability to consciously create my reality. I didn't have this money yesterday, and today it's in my life. I *made this happen*, and it's only the beginning. I know that if I can create a nickel, I can create a dollar. And if I can create a dollar, I can create $1,000."

3. ***Spread gratitude across your life.*** Be grateful for *all* of the abundance in your life. Don't stop with being grateful for your paycheck, or the money that shows up. Be grateful for your home, your relationships, your family, your car, your clothes ... the list goes on. The more things you can find to be grateful for in every category—large and small—the more you'll stay in that energy of gratitude all day long, and the faster your life will change.

4. ***Take time to savor gratitude.*** I know you're busy, so this may be much easier said than done—but every so often, take ten to thirty minutes to just sit still and feel deeply grateful. Life isn't perfect, and never will be, but there are always things to feel grateful about. Gratitude is a spiritual experience more than a human one, and it will connect you more deeply to your higher self, soul, and other unseen friends.

5. ***Be grateful in advance.*** Once you have gratitude down in the here and now, imagine wonderful things happening in the future, and feel immensely grateful for them. You don't even have to know what they are! Just imagine yourself tomorrow, next week, or a year from now, sitting and thinking, "Oh, my gosh! This day/week/year has been amazing. I never could have imagined things turning out this wonderfully. I am *so* grateful."

Be grateful for gratitude. It's more than just an exercise: it's a way to create your reality, deepen your spirituality, and connect more deeply to yourself, your unseen friends, and every other good thing in your life.

And yet …

You Might Hesitate

When I was first introduced to the power of gratitude, I was conflicted. On one hand I could (and did) acknowledge the wonderful people, opportunities, and things that showed up in my life.

On the other hand, I feared that, if I felt grateful, I'd be saying to the universe, "This is enough for me"—that I would somehow close the doors to additional abundance. There was a belief underneath that conflict, of course:

- IF I ADMIT I RECEIVED SOMETHING GOOD, I WON'T RECEIVE ANY MORE GOOD.

Gratitude should feel great, especially when you remember that, by feeling it, you're creating more to be grateful for. If it doesn't, find the limiting belief and change it.

The emotions you feel in your day-to-day life are the emotions that create your world. So stay conscious of how you feel, embrace your life, and live as fully and completely as you can. Attend this party you've been invited to. Dance, sing, and celebrate like there's no tomorrow—and, if your beliefs are in alignment, that goodie bag full of abundance will be ready and waiting for you.

A TRUE STORY OF CONSCIOUSLY CREATING ABUNDANCE

This past Thanksgiving, I had to get my car inspected. (I live in Virginia, and we have to get our cars inspected annually). I took it in on a Saturday, and discovered it wasn't going to pass inspection. The dealer was going to charge $1,200 for the repairs needed.

With the holidays approaching, plus our personal property taxes due, I didn't have the extra cash for this expense. Long story short, my boyfriend was going to front me the money to get the work done.

Then, miraculously, my brother-in-law offered to do the work (and then some) for less. Of course, I agreed.

I was sitting on the couch that Sunday, reflecting on our financial situation, and said to myself, "I have so much to be grateful for that this does not matter. My family is healthy, I have a life full of people that love me, and God blesses me every day!"

My parents called me that evening to say hi, and I told them what was happening. I didn't ask for the money or make it seem like I was in trouble financially, but they sent me a check for the full amount of the repairs!

I truly believe that changing my attitude about the situation and feeling grateful made the money come back to me immediately! What a blessing!

- Melissa K.

ABUNDANCE-ALTERING TAKEAWAYS

- Once you stop obsessing about whether and how abundance will manifest, and just have a blast living life, you open the doors for abundance to enter—and it *will* enter, if you've worked this map to this point by changing your beliefs, working with your younger selves, and letting go of controlling how abundance shows up.

- Once you really and truly begin to enjoy every single minute of your life, the "things" will come automatically. The things are a *side effect* of living your abundant life.

- I didn't choose happiness to create abundance, and neither should you. You should choose happiness because it's a beautiful way to live your life.

- You can be happy for many reasons. You can be happy because nature is breathtaking. You can be happy because there is goodness in the world. You can be happy because there is a boatload of stuff to be grateful for in your life, right here, right now. You can be happy for no reason at all. Happiness is a choice.

- Gratitude is supercharged. When you feel gratitude about anything in your life, that thing is already in your life. It has already manifested.

- When you feel gratitude, you are resonating pure, unadulterated joy, love, and thankfulness. In this way, gratitude may be the most powerful "technique" ever.

YOUR NEXT STEPS

- Make a list of things that make you happy. Refer to it often when you find yourself slipping into an unhappy place.

- Every hour, check your emotional state. To remind yourself to do this, set an alarm, tie a ribbon around your wrist, or set up some other reminder mechanism. If you're less than happy during your hourly check, ask your higher self to help with a request like this one: "Higher self, please help me shift into the emotion of happiness." Then, remember you are the divine creator of your world, and make the choice to be happy.

- Start a gratitude journal. Every morning or evening, set a timer for five minutes and write down everything you're grateful for. It could be gratitude for that day, or for your life, or your gifts, or your body. Whatever you choose, feel the gratitude as deeply as you can.

- Use the applied kinesiology techniques in Appendix B to test for the constricting beliefs in this chapter. Document the beliefs that need to be changed, and change them using a technique in Appendix D.

CHAPTER FOURTEEN

Meet Your Financial Partners (aka Your Unseen Friends)

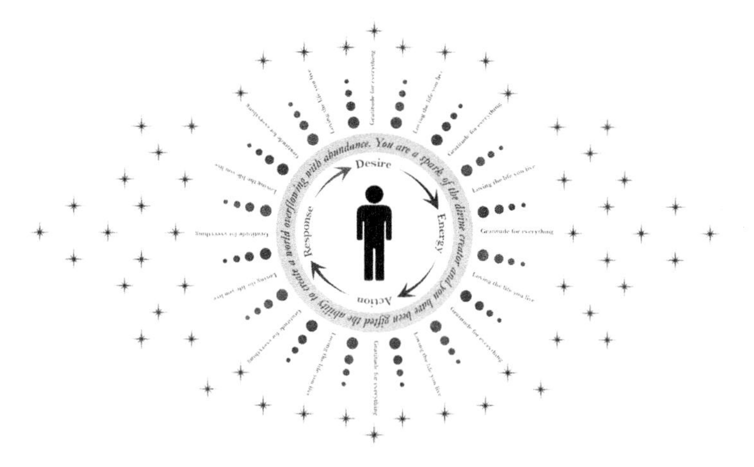

"Allow yourself to lean ... to lean upon the love. Allow yourself to receive ... to receive the love. You are strong enough to lean ... you are powerful enough to receive. Allow."

~ LAZARIS

Creating abundance is a paradox.

On one hand, it takes you, and *only* you, to create and allow abundance. I can't do it for you. Your spouse, boss, parents, and friends can't do it for you. Neither can your unseen friends. Abundance must be your choice—and you must make that choice over and over again, every single day, until it becomes so natural that you can't imagine your life without abundance.

On the other hand, you *can* ask for help. You can learn from books (like this one), teachers, friends, and colleagues. You can also receive help from your unseen friends.

Unseen friends are those to whom you are connected on "the other side." They are your spirit family, which includes your guides, counselors, higher self, soul, spirit, and, of course, God and Goddess.

We all have these "basic" unseen friends. Oftentimes, we also gather more guides along the way, some of whom specialize in our areas of interest or expertise. Think of your unseen friends as older, wiser, more powerful mentors who love you unconditionally and want only your highest good.

Now when I say "more powerful," that is saying a lot, because you are *absolutely* powerful. After all, you create 100 percent of your reality!

But your unseen friends are even more powerful than that. They can override the rules of conscious creation on this planet and instantly "gift" you with a reality. They can drop ideas into your mind, place a book or a teacher in your path, or lift an energy that has been keeping you bogged down. They can help you in unlimited ways, but ...

You Have to Participate

Your unseen friends won't do it for you.

The phrase, "Let go and let God," is popular, but misunderstood. Many want to give away their power with that phrase, thinking, "If I turn my life over to God, He will make everything work."

But you came here to this planet to learn how to create your reality. Yes, God (and Goddess) gave you life, but they know you want to figure this out yourself, and they won't take that opportunity from you no matter how you beg them. But they will help, and so will your other unseen friends.

Early in my spiritual growth journey, I did a lot of praying. I wanted someone—God, my father, my husband, my boss, or the lottery—to rescue me. I was so mired in self-pity and victimhood that, in hindsight, it isn't surprising I didn't get rescued. Who wants to deal with that kind of neediness?

However, when I started taking responsibility for my life, and asked my unseen friends for help, they always responded. Sometimes it took a day, or even a week, but whenever I asked for their help, I magically came across the right books, the right teachers, and the right techniques. More, I was able to ask myself the right questions to move forward.

The more earnestly you want to discover your deepest truths and take responsibility for your life, the more your unseen friends will help. They love nothing more than helping you grow!

During my first Lazaris intensive in 1990, I meditated for the very first time. The intensive was called, "Your Soul's Path, More Deeply Revealed," and I was excited to actually receive information in my meditations.

The final meditation of the weekend was about traveling to the temple of your soul and "seeing" your soul's path. I was thrilled to "see" a key, a sun, and a dove.

"Yay!" I thought, "I can go home now. I saw my soul's path."

"Open further," Lazaris said.

"Yikes!" I thought, "I don't know if I can." But I tried anyway.

And suddenly I *knew* that the "key" to my soul's path was what I saw next: a sun with a dove superimposed over the top. Of course I had no idea what that signified, I only knew I saw something in meditation and felt happy that I did.

I headed to the airport happy and triumphant. Those feelings didn't last. Soon my negative self was piping up.

"Come on," it goaded, "You don't really think that was real, do you? You made that up. It means absolutely nothing. Don't be a fool."

"Wow," I thought. "What if it was just my imagination?" (I had very little experience with my negative self at that point, and didn't know its sneaky and undermining nature.)

But instead of going too far down that self-defeating path, I asked my higher self for guidance. "Higher self," I said mentally, "Send me a sign that the meditations I've been doing are real." And then, I let it go.

The plane landed at the Buffalo International Airport. My husband and young sons were waiting for me. After we got home and put the boys to bed, my husband asked me about the workshop. I wanted to keep this new experience private for a while, so I said it was fine and asked him about his weekend.

"It was strange—I felt so insecure."

My husband at the time was a rather macho Italian type. Insecurities were rare, and talking about them was even rarer.

"Really," I prodded. "How so?"

"I don't know why, but I felt emotionally insecure, and I couldn't shake that feeling. But then luckily something happened that made me feel great."

"What was it?"

"I went to see Judy."

Judy was the owner of a new age bookstore I frequented. She was also my husband's advertising client.

"She wanted a new logo," he said, "and I thought and thought about it. I came up with something, had the art department work it up, and took it to her. She loved it! She hugged me and jumped up and down, and it made me feel so good."

"Wow," I said, "I'd love to see it."

"I brought it home to show you," he said. "It's a picture of a sun with a dove superimposed over the top."

I was shocked. *Shocked.* I had never felt so heard by my unseen friends in my life.

But that's not the end of the story.

Two months later, another Lazaris workshop was announced. I had just spent over $1,000 (which was a ton of money to us) on the previous workshop, so to think of attending another one so quickly was ridiculous. Plus, it was in California, which felt so far away that it might as well have been on the other side of the world.

But I had this nagging feeling I should make it happen, so I said, "Okay, higher self. If I'm supposed to attend this workshop, send me a sign. Make it one I can't ignore."

An hour later, I went to get the mail. One of the many catalogs in the pile was from the Metropolitan Museum of Art. On the cover was a sun, with a dove super-imposed over the top.

"I guess I'm going to the workshop!" I thought.

A few days later, I recounted the story to a friend. "You're kidding," she said, "I got that catalog too, but mine doesn't have that on the cover!"

I did attend the workshop, and I worked magic to create the money to go. The experience was life-changing—as, of course, I knew it would be.

When I got home, I had the cover to that catalog framed. It hangs in my magic room to this day as a reminder that my unseen friends are only a thought away.

ENGAGING THE HELP OF YOUR UNSEEN FRIENDS

Your unseen friends are always with you. You only need to think of them, and they will be there. But there are ways that you can strengthen that relationship even more, and to learn to hear them when they offer their guidance:

Ask For Help

I have one request for my unseen friends every single night: "Help me fulfill my destiny. Help me do what I came here to do."

I believe it is *everyone's* destiny to learn how to consciously create a life they love, so I figure my nightly request will help me do that, and continue to get better at it. Beyond that, though, I know each and every one of us on the planet has a personal destiny—a choice made with our soul before we came to Earth.

I want help with that destiny, too. I know that if I follow that path, I'll be the happiest, most successful, and most fulfilled person I can possibly be.

No matter how good my life gets—and it's pretty great—I will never stop asking for help to make it better. I know that my unseen friends can see further than I can, so even if I feel in every fiber of my being that "I've got this!" I'm humble enough to know that they understand my ideal life path even better than I do.

So, I ask, and ask, and ask.

I encourage you to ask, too. Your unseen friends honestly can't help much unless you ask. But when you do ask, sometimes they'll knock your socks off with their answers.

How do you ask?

My two favorite ways to ask for help are:

1. ***Simply thinking the thought.*** Mentally ask for help before bed, first thing in the morning, or anytime in between. It doesn't have to be fancy; it just needs to be sincere.

2. ***In meditation.*** This can be a formal meditation, like the ones I've recorded[1] or it can be merely sitting quietly, closing your eyes, and seeing your unseen friends in your mind's eye.

   If I say, "Think of an orange," you do, right? You can see it, feel it, and imagine the smell as you rip open the rind. Maybe you can even taste it as you bite into its juicy goodness. All you needed to conjure up this image of an orange was a simple directive.

   When you close your eyes and open to your higher self, soul, guides, angels, or other unseen friends, it's no different. They may appear as ovals of light, as geometric forms, or in human forms. Or, you may simply feel their energy wrap around you like a warm blanket. Allow your impressions to reach you in their own timing, and allow them to change and transform as you get used to contacting them this way. Above all, trust your results if they feel trustworthy.

Make Time to Listen

Your unseen friends won't text you their advice. They won't tweet it or e-mail[2] it either (at least, not usually)! You have to make time and space to listen for it. It doesn't have to be in meditation; you can listen while alone in nature, while sitting and daydreaming, while taking a bath, or during any other solitary activity.

(1) Visit www.LiveALifeYouLove.com for more information.

(2) You may want to sign up for my Messages from Your Unseen Friends weekly e-mail at www.LiveALifeYouLove.com/email-sign-up.

Your unseen friends can, and do, communicate in other ways—like books falling off bookshelves, during night dreams, and through other "signs." But the communication will always be smoother and clearer if you do your part and listen.

Sebastian, my unseen friend and male counselor, told me decades ago, "It (the dream) will happen when you least expect it." I had been complaining about my dream "not showing up" as quickly as I thought it should.

That was one of the best pieces of advice I've ever gotten. My reality has proven his words to be true time and again. Remember, when you let go of needing it to happen now, paradoxically, you allow it to happen.

Your unseen friends have lots of good advice to share. Listen to what they say—but always make sure their advice agrees with your own inner knowing. The negative self (aka Neg) has been known to dress up as your unseen friends on occasion, so don't follow any crazy "advice" without thinking and feeling it through.

Your unseen friends will never give you ultimatums. They will never tell you there is only one solution. They will never encourage you to sacrifice yourself, and they will never be upset if you don't take their advice. They know that this is all a learning process, and they won't abandon you.

Watch for Signs

When you expect to receive and clearly understand your unseen friends' guidance, you will be amazed at how clearly and loudly they "speak." But, as I've said before, they don't often speak in words. Instead, they speak in *symbols*.

That's why your night dreams are sometimes so cryptic, and it's why it's important to watch for messages from your unseen friends in your daily life, especially if you've asked for help.

Your unseen friends communicate best through signs, so you'll need to learn to understand their language. This takes practice—but once you get it, you will be amazed at how much they have to share!

Now, it's important to note that your unseen friends may have a different method of communication than my unseen friends, or your friends' unseen friends. As your unseen friends come to understand what you "see" most easily, they will use those methods of communication before others.

For instance, my unseen friends know that one particular tarot/astrology website never fails to give me the clarity and guidance I seek. Is it the website that's great—or is it that my unseen friends are helping me decode and translate the information in a way that gives me what I need?

I really don't know, but I suspect it's both. What I do know is that this website is one of their favorite ways to communicate with me. Your unseen friends will help you find your favorite way to communicate as well, if you just give them the chance, ask, and listen!

HOW YOUR UNSEEN FRIENDS HELP YOU CREATE ABUNDANCE

Your unseen friends *want* to help you create everything you desire. They want you to be sublimely happy, and they want to help you fulfill your destiny.

I'll tell it to you straight, though: they won't be as supportive if you are unwilling to grow spiritually. Don't get me wrong: they aren't nasty authority figures bent on keeping you from abundance. *You* are the ultimate authority in your life, and you will keep yourself from abundance if your ego is keeping you from learning something your soul wants you to learn on a higher level.

There was a time when human beings could manhandle abundance into manifestation, but that time period is rapidly ending. For those with a spiritual destiny, that time never existed; they never could "force" abundance into being, because it wasn't what they were here to do.

So, call on your unseen friends to help you get clear about your destiny and the best way for you, personally, to create abundance. Call on them to help you discover and change your limiting beliefs. Call upon them for guidance and spiritual growth in general. Remember: growth, fulfillment, and joy are the *true* abundances. Let your unseen friends help you acquire abundances of every type, and you'll soon be overflowing with the abundance you've been dreaming of.

A TRUE STORY OF CONSCIOUSLY CREATING ABUNDANCE

Since reading The Map *for the first time (as well as other new-age and metaphysical books), incredible things have happened. My business went from earning $500 – $800 a month to earning $8,000 – $11,000 a month. I'm now a month into renting a new home, and in the process of getting out of a negative marriage. The house is absolutely perfect for me in every way! It feels like "home" to me. Plus, it's just blocks away from where my kids go to school. My ex-husband and I still get along, and this all just feels right. I can't imagine a better way that all of this could have happened or be happening.*

I know without a doubt that these amazing things have come from reading The Map *and doing the work and techniques—and I barely got into the book! I can't imagine what life will be like when I really get serious about going further into my beliefs!*

Oh, but there's more! Last year, as I drove my old minivan around town, I would picture that I was driving a new vehicle. I would feel what it felt like to be driving it, how I felt like a "rich-bitch" sitting higher up from the road, etc. Well, a few months ago, I purchased a beautiful pre-owned SUV. I love it. I love the color. I love the sunroof. I love the auto-start! This is just so amazing!

And, even more great news. On Sunday, I sat down and wrote out a list of all the crazy, far-out ways I could think of for my newest intention to manifest (i.e., random people coming to my house and dropping off the most beautiful, luxurious furnishings and décor for my new place, luxurious furnishings sprouting from the ground as if planted from seeds, you name it!). On Monday, I had two people contact me with incredible business offers! Both offers are perfect add-ons to my current products, and one will lighten my workload significantly. Both will bring in new revenue. You should have seen me jumping up and down and squealing like a kid. My teenage daughter thinks I'm nuts.

And then, how about this: I opened up my Creation Journal[3] *yesterday. I ordered it a while ago, and had only gotten as far as writing a few intentions. (Honestly, I'd forgotten I had even done that.) What were the intentions?*

1. *A new home in the perfect location, close to family and school with a beautiful, peaceful, free, and positive atmosphere, an office so I can keep business separate from our home, and a beautiful patio where I can enjoy nature.*
2. *A beautiful patio/outdoor living space that makes me feel closer to nature, free, safe, and luxurious.*
3. *A new car.*

Pretty cool, huh? House? Check. Car? Check. The patio and office are still to come—but I have all winter to play with those intentions.

I've read a lot of books on Law of Attraction, metaphysics, etc., but I always come back to The Map. *It's a no-nonsense, easy to follow, well … map. Incredible work!*

- Kay B.

(3) Creation Journals are available at www.LiveALifeYouLove.com/creation-journal-2.

ABUNDANCE-ALTERING TAKEAWAYS

- Unseen friends are those you are connected to on "the other side." They are your spirit family, which includes your guides, counselors, higher self, soul, spirit, and, of course, God and Goddess.

- The more earnestly you want to discover your deepest truths and take responsibility for your life, the more your unseen friends will help.

- Your unseen friends are always with you. You only need to think of them and they are there. That said, there are ways that you can strengthen that relationship and learn to hear them when they offer guidance.

- Your unseen friends have good advice, so listen to what they say—but make sure their advice agrees with your own inner knowing. The negative self has been known to "dress up" as your unseen friends—so don't take any crazy "advice" without thinking and feeling it through.

- Your unseen friends will never give you ultimatums. They will never tell you there is only one solution. They will never encourage you to sacrifice yourself. And they will never be upset if you don't take their advice.

- Your unseen friends communicate best through signs, so it's highly advisable that you get good at understanding their language.

- Your unseen friends want to help you create everything you desire. They want you to be sublimely happy, and they want to help you fulfill your destiny—but they won't be as supportive if you are unwilling to grow spiritually, and it is time for you to do that.

- Call on your unseen friends to help you gain clarity around your destiny and the best way for you, personally, to create abundance. Ask for their help to discover and change limiting beliefs, and for guidance and spiritual growth in general. Remember: growth, fulfillment, and joy are the *true* abundances.

YOUR NEXT STEPS

- What (besides creating a life you love) do you think you might be here on Earth to do? What are your unique talents, strengths, and gifts? How might you incorporate this destiny with creating/allowing abundance?

- How well do you know your personal unseen friends? How willing are you to get to know them better? Commit to setting aside at least 30 minutes a week to meet with them meditatively (at least your higher self, and one male and one female guide). Write about your experiences in your journal or in a computer document.

- Every night and every morning, ask your unseen friends for something important to you. During this time you've set aside for "asking," make note of the signs you've received from them in response to your request.

CHAPTER FIFTEEN

Abundance Trip-Ups

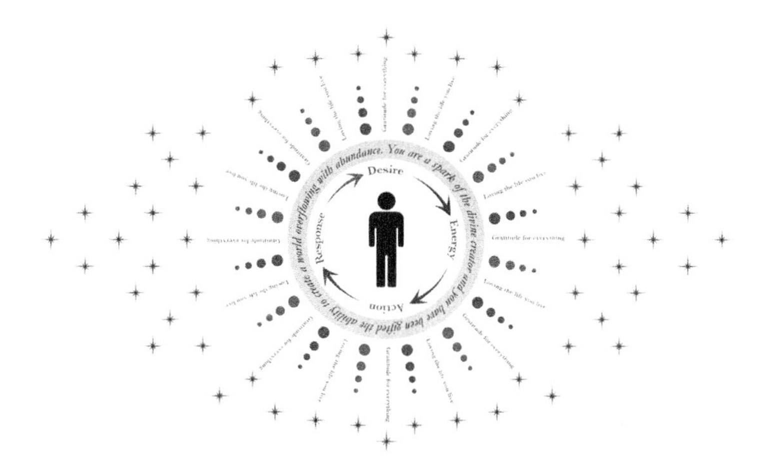

"It's a man's own mind, not his enemy or foe, that lures him to evil ways."

~ BUDDHA

Money is the *hardest* thing you'll ever consciously create, and money is the *easiest* thing you'll ever consciously create.

Why?

We start off with so many limiting beliefs and stumbling blocks around money that creating it will seem illusive and impossible—right up until we change the most limiting beliefs and kick each of those blocks out of the way. Once we create a clear path to the abundance we deserve, though, money will suddenly become the easiest thing we've ever created.

We've talked about beliefs (and I'm certain that you are well on your way to changing a lot of them) so now, let's start kicking those blocks!

Here is a question that causes many to stumble:

WHO CREATES "OUR" ABUNDANCE?

Many times, people in relationships where there is sharing of funds and/or resources—like marriage partners, significant others, business partners, family members, or others with combined finances—ask themselves, "Who is creating our joint finances?"

The confusion sounds something like this:

If only my husband would recognize that his worry is creating lack, we could be a lot better off.

I'm a stay-at-home mom. Does that mean my husband creates my income and I am powerless to impact his salary?

When I told my wife I was creating her raises, she told me I was crazy.

If my business partner would stop being so fearful, we could make some money in this company.

You create your reality. Period. No matter what anyone does around you, says around you, or thinks around you, *you* create your own reality. You are creating your abundance (including but not limited to money) no matter where that abundance comes from.

Your thoughts, feelings, and beliefs matter. They impact your finances, and everything else in your world as well.

But what about my partner's thoughts, feelings, and beliefs?

Maybe you didn't read what I just wrote.

You create your reality.
Period.
No matter what anyone does around you, says around you, or thinks around you, *you create your reality.*

But won't my partner's thoughts, feelings, and beliefs help (or hurt) our abundance?

Yes, *if* you let them. But you are still the one creating your reality. Don't get caught up in codependent thinking that says "I have to change this person so my world can change."

I know this is a hard concept. So, think of it this way.

You have many possible future selves, right? Well, so does your partner. Do you want to align with the future partner who is abundant, or the one who is impoverished?

I thought I couldn't control another person!

You can't. But you can create your world. Imagining your partner as abundant, successful, and happy can only help you both.

Okay, but if I do all that work, who gets the credit for creating the abundance?

That's your negative self talking. This isn't about being better than your partner, or about who gets credit. You both get credit, because if you both receive it, you both created it.

However, if your partner is the one bringing home the bacon …

Let Your Partner Know You're Grateful

Wait, what? You just said I was the one creating my abundance?

Yes, and you have created a reality where your partner brings that abundance to you. Be *grateful* for that.

Here's how it works in this kind of scenario. Your partner creates the money—but you create your partner who shares his or her abundance. So feel the gratitude for your partner, and for every other source of abundance. It will only bring you more abundance.

But I want credit from my partner for my part in the creating.

I suggest you have a talk with your child self, your adolescent self and/or your negative self. *They* are the ones who feel invalidated. Your adult self can understand that a quiet power comes with owning the fact that you create your own reality. And that self doesn't need to boast about it.

My partner thinks I'm a slacker. I want him/her to realize that I'm contributing too.

If your partner is open to that conversation, great! Go for it. But many aren't, and that's okay, too. You don't have to broadcast that you're creating your reality.

The more telling comment is, "My partner thinks I'm a slacker." This tells me that there is something in you that feels "less than" for not bringing in more money. That part of you needs to be healed in order to open the door for more abundance.

Check to see if you have beliefs such as:

- UNLESS I BRING IN MONEY, I AM NOT CONTRIBUTING.
- I AM NOT AS VALUABLE AS MY PARTNER BECAUSE S/HE BRINGS HOME A PAYCHECK.
- THE BREADWINNER IS THE MOST VALUABLE MEMBER OF A PARTNERSHIP.
- EQUALITY IN A PARTNERSHIP IS BASED ON A SIMILAR FINANCIAL CONTRIBUTION.
- I DON'T CREATE MY PARTNER'S INCOME.
- IF I DIDN'T HAVE MY PARTNER'S INCOME I WOULD BE DESTITUTE.

Once you've changed such beliefs, and spent some time with your other "selves," you should be clear that *you create it all,* whether or not another in your life is technically contributing.

The more you detach yourself from any expectation about how your partner does or does not contribute (as well as from expectations about how abundance comes to you), and simply take ownership of your financial abundance, the freer you'll be to create positive changes in your finances.

Your Partner Doesn't Need to Understand This

Most people have no clue about how the universe works. And yet, they're creating their worlds 100 percent of the time, without even knowing it.

And, because money is fraught with so much weight, making money doesn't come easily to most. The lion's share of people in this world live with a constant, underlying fear that the source of their money will disappear. This terror tends to worsen with age, changes in the economy, and technological evolution.

Many people stay in jobs, locations, or partnerships they dislike, or even hate, for the "security." Chained to situations that they feel could only get worse, they resign themselves to "dealing with it," and give up dreams of ever really prospering, doing what they love, or being free.

These choices may have been good choices at one time. Without knowing there are other options, it's rational and conscientious to do what's needed to ensure that money will continue to be available.

However, once you realize you can create money and other forms of abundance consciously, and you learn to truly *trust* that ability and power, your world will be forever changed.

And, once you've shifted your essence (and thus your reality) around money, you can focus your attention and energy on creating the things you love and long for. Eventually, you can create a different world.

Even after you break out of the mental trap of "security" and unhelpful beliefs and begin growing this new, abundant "you," you may be concerned about …

THE NEGATIVE IMPACT OF THOSE AROUND YOU

When you're a newbie creator, your energy will be a bit wobbly—but even seasoned creators can be affected by the negativity of others. Their concerns often sound like this:

> *My husband doesn't believe in the Law of Attraction. He rolls his eyes when I tell him about my "signs," and all my excitement goes out the window.*
>
> *I would be more successful in my creations if it weren't for my co-worker. All he does is complain, and he brings me down with him.*
>
> *I live with my mother, and she is a walking "doom-and-gloomer"! How can I stay positive with all that negativity around me?*
>
> *I love my best friend, but she's invested in believing she is a victim, even though she knows as well as I do that complaining all the time doesn't create what she wants. I want to spend time with her, but then again, I don't.*
>
> *The media is one big hate-fest. How can we stay optimistic with constant reminders of devastation, greed and cruelty all around us?*

Our hearts break when we see those we love steeped in pessimism we know will hurt them. We want to lash out at others who insensitively pull us into their personal pit of hell as we struggle valiantly to crawl out of our own. When overpowering negativity surrounds us in our jobs, our homes, or our world, we feel imprisoned and unable to escape.

This "negativity trap" is not only tiresome, it's boring and futile. Negativity hurts realities—which is why it upsets you so much when it happens. And it will hurt your reality too, but *only if you let it.*

You don't have to let it.

You can take your power back from the negativity in your life, and set yourself free to create all the joy, wonder, and abundance you desire without interference.

Here's how.

Stop Blaming

Yes, you feel challenged, and perhaps rightfully so. But it takes two to tango. No one can take your power unless you allow them to take it. *Ever.*

If you're not sure how to stop feeling victimized by the negativity around you, you need to add some tools to your toolkit to help you keep your positivity intact. With each little victory, you'll feel stronger and more capable.

Stop Trying to Change Other People

Everyone has his or her own path to enlightenment. Trust your loved ones' souls and higher selves to help them arrive in their own perfect timing. For all you know, the most negative person in your life could be the most enlightened being on the planet just playing the part of a negative person until you "get it."

The best way to support your loved ones is to pay attention to your own path and allow them to choose theirs. Compassionate detachment will free you both to soar as high as you can. When you do this, your loved ones may surprise you; when you let go and allow them to grow at a pace that is right for them, they may "get it" surprisingly quickly.

Set Boundaries

Boundaries are a way to love yourself—and, interestingly enough, to love others as well. Know what your boundaries are, and love yourself enough to implement them *all of the time.*

What do your healthy boundaries look like? Only you can choose—but here are some of mine.

No Abuse

Emotional, physical, or verbal abuse is never tolerated in my world.

A woman I know mentioned that her mother will often make comments such as, "Your hair looks like something the cat dragged in."

I know, she's her mother. But in my book, abuse is not okay. My response would be, "Sorry Mom, not only is that not loving, it's hurtful. Please speak to me with more respect."

After that, I'd give her one more chance. If she couldn't honor my request, I wouldn't see her.

Well, yeah, but she isn't your mother.

No, she's not. But I do understand the guilt and yearning to be with one's family. I was faced with a similar circumstance when my father was diagnosed with end-stage lung cancer and given only a few months to live.

As his illness progressed, my father became increasingly difficult and mean to his wife, my stepmom. I'm sure that facing your own imminent death isn't the easiest thing in the world, but in my book, treating others with respect is non-negotiable.

I called my dad one day and, sure enough, he started in on me, saying several mean and cutting things. I decided on the spot that, if this was the way he wanted to treat me in his last days, I was *not* about to go along for the ride. I hung up the phone with the resolve that his abuse was not okay with me.

"If I don't see him again," I thought, "at least I'll be left with loving memories."

Lo and behold, from that moment on, he changed. He was never again abusive to me. I traveled to Florida to visit him, and we had a beautiful week together. He was still mean to others around him, but not to me.

Why? Because I made the choice to be treated well. I never said a word to him about my choice—and yet, somehow he knew.

Your boundaries will be felt whether you verbalize them or not, and if you're clear about them, people will respect them.

No Complicit Agreement

I always respond to something I know to be untrue.

Oftentimes, when I'm around people who have no idea they're responsible for creating their reality, they will say things like, "Boy, if something can go wrong, it will."

No matter who says it, no matter their level of metaphysical or spiritual understanding, I must not agree by remaining silent. I don't want that complicit agreement going into my subconscious, and my opposing viewpoint may actually help them, if only in a subtle way.

In these situations, I disagree without judgment. I gently but firmly say something like, "In my experience, if something can go right, it does." Or even something like, "Not always." And then, I smile, and leave it at that.

No Motivating From "Shoulds"

One of my personal mottos is, "Never be nice. Always be kind."

Too often, we hear voices from our past chiding us to be nice to certain people, or that nice people do this or don't do that. That's when the "shoulds" begin.

I *should* call my mother because that's what a loving daughter would do. I *should* be a "good" friend and listen to my BFF bellyache yet again about her ex. I *should* be a congenial co-worker and join in with the boss-bashing.

Once you're in Shouldland, it's a very small step to letting others' negativity impact you; from there, it's onto Victimville. As you know, this journey doesn't end well.

But if you only do things you truly want to do, you never step onto that slippery slope.

This doesn't mean you'll never be around another negative person. But if your actions are motivated out of love and kindness and not "shoulds," your power will stay firmly where it belongs: with you.

No Selling Yourself Out

I try to stay in touch with my needs and respond accordingly.

For instance, I might say yes to an event where I know I'll be around negative people, because I want to support someone I love and am close to. However, if I feel particularly vulnerable, I'll cancel. There are some days when it's just not self-loving for me to be in a room full of negative energy!

What makes me feel vulnerable? Maybe I'm in the middle of some deep spiritual work. Maybe I'm not feeling at the top of my game physically. Or maybe I just feel that the situation will do me harm, emotionally or mentally. I don't need to have a "good" reason to change my plans—I just need to know that it's the right thing to do in order for me to take care of myself.

It does take a while to establish strong boundaries in a loving way. Boundaries will sometimes change a bit with circumstances, but knowing what yours are will serve you well when you do interact with others. Ultimately, sticking to your boundaries will result in you attracting people who are more positive, respectful, and loving.

Another way to insulate yourself from the negativity of others is to ...

Use Protection

Two people of different resonances can't be together for long without one or the other shifting—and if you're hanging out with someone of lower resonance, you don't want to be the person who shifts.

It takes practice to get good at dealing with negative people—and by the time you're good at it, you're creating a world populated by mostly positive people anyway. But even after you're good at setting boundaries and dealing with negativity, you'll come across people who just want to stay where they are—which is miserable. And sometimes, they desperately want you to be there, too.

Whatever the situation, energetic protection can help immensely. Here's a handy technique I use regularly:

Imagine yourself surrounded in a bubble of mirrors. The mirrors completely surround your body, and they are all facing outward, away from you. The mirrors will reflect any negative energy back to the sender—not to hurt them, but to show them the impact their negativity is having.

While you're imagining the bubble of mirrors, fill the inside (where you are) with beautiful white, sparkling light, and draw strength from that positivity.

But sometimes we forget to be proactive. If you find yourself impacted by someone else's negativity, it's time to ...

Reset Your Resonance

It happens. As much as you try to avoid it, sometimes your resonance will drop as a result of being around a negative person. If this happens, don't worry (worrying only makes it worse). Simply stock your toolkit with resonance boosters ready to activate!

Here are some ideas:

- ***Take a break.*** Somehow, get away to a place where you can be alone—even if that means hiding out in a bathroom stall for a few minutes. While you're there, remember your choices: to stay positive no matter what, to unconditionally love others, to feel compassionate detachment, and to hold your boundaries.

- ***Read or listen to something empowering.*** There are lots of resonance boosters in music, books, and audio recordings. Have a few of your favorites handy at all times. These days, your smart phone can be a literal library of positivity, right at your fingertips!

- ***Remember that you are powerful.*** It's easy for us to think of ourselves as impotent when others seem strong, but it's not true. Remember, you are the one in charge of your reality. Replay your successes in your mind, and make a choice to stay in your power.

- ***Ask for help.*** Your unseen friends are always available to help you hold a resonance of positivity. Call on them whenever you need them. You could say something like: "Higher self, this person has always been a challenge for me. Help me stay positive, powerful, and self-loving no matter what s/he says or does."

See Others As Healed

If the person who is challenging you is someone you care about, you can help by holding a picture in your mind of that person as happy, healthy, whole, and successful. Don't get caught up in wanting someone to do it the way you've done it; again, each of us has our own path and timing. Just see the result, and feel the way you'll feel when that person is healed.

Then, once you've imagined it, let it go—and expect the person to be different. You don't know when or how it will happen, but open your mind and allow him or her to show up in a brand new way.

Ask for Help

Of course you know that you can ask for help from your own higher self. But you can also ask for help from another person's higher self on his/her behalf.

Here is a technique I do for those I love. It is based upon a similar one I learned from Lazaris many years ago:

> Prepare your space for meditation. Lower the lights, close the door, play some soft music. Gently close your eyes and relax.
>
> Imagine yourself in a beautiful place in nature. Open your senses to the sounds, images, feelings, scents, and even tastes of this beautiful place. Know you are safe.
>
> Allow your higher self to join you. As you sit together in nature, ask for the higher self of your loved one to join you as well.
>
> You will see a person coming toward you, perhaps from behind a tree, or along a path. You know that this is your loved one's higher self. This higher self will likely be the same sex as the person's physical self; s/he may look like a more healed version of your loved one, or s/he may look totally different than anything you expected. The higher self of your loved one greets you and your own higher self, and the three of you sit together in a circle.
>
> You say to your loved one's higher self, "I would like to give you energy, love, and light to use for (your loved one's name). I would like you to use this for his/her highest good, in the way that will bring the greatest benefit."
>
> The person's higher self nods. You flow energy, love, and light into this being, this higher self of the one you love. Take as long as you like to flow this energy. Realize that you do not—cannot—know what type of healing will be the most beneficial for your loved one; instead, trust their higher self to use your love and support in the most beneficial way possible.
>
> When you are done, thank your higher self, and your loved one's higher self. Then, gently open your eyes.

This is a powerful meditation for many reasons, not least because it keeps you from trying to control the outcome.

Negative people will probably always be around, but you have a choice as to whether or not they impact you.

However, even when the people around you are positive, there's a subtle, sabotaging energy that you may not even be aware that you engage in …

COMPARISON AND COMPETITION

From the time we're little, we are taught to compare ourselves with others and to compete to be the best. As children, we compete in sports, in school, within our families, in our peer groups, and anywhere else we possibly can.

As adults, we compare ourselves to our coworkers, our family, our friends, our professional peers, and our neighbors. We're taught that we should "know our competition" in business and strive to make our company "better" than others in our chosen field.

Is it any wonder, then, that we compare our money and abundance as well?

And yet …

Comparison Hurts Our Creations

The minute you begin to compare your money, success, or any other type of abundance with someone else's, you start siphoning off energy from your own success.

I get it. I struggle with this, too. And there is a paradox, because we *do* want (and sometimes need) to know what others in our field are doing. We *do* desire to know what our family and friends are up to—but not at the expense of our own happiness and abundance.

How do we tell when we've crossed the line?

By the way we *feel.*

If hearing about someone who is doing "better than" you feels uplifting, inspiring, and motivating, you're thinking about his/her win in a constructive and uplifting way. Ultimately, their win can affect your success positively. (Remember when, in Chapter Twelve, we talked about signs, and how someone in your world succeeding at what you want can be a sign? That's how this works!)

If, however, hearing about someone else's win leaves you feeling disempowered, less-than, uninspired, or like a failure, the way you're holding this (mentally) will have a negative impact on your reality.

Funny, isn't it? The same exact thing can happen to two different people, and one will use it as fuel to explode their life and/or business into more happiness and success, while the other will use it as fuel to self-destruct.

How you approach your life with your thoughts, emotions, attitudes, and beliefs doesn't simply make you a fun (or not-so-fun) person to hang with—it creates an entirely different reality for you to hang within.

These aren't platitudes, my friend. They're facts. So get your act together and take this seriously if you want to accomplish what you came to do in this lifetime.

Exaggeration? No: truth. The ball is in your court.

Comparison: Close to Home

A few years back, I enjoyed my best year ever in my marketing company. I was having a great time creating success on my terms. Things were going so well that I actually had to stop marketing my company to slow down the sales to manageable levels!

I had just moved to a new home that, just a few years prior, would have been beyond my wildest dreams. It was nestled in the mountainside six miles up Sunshine Canyon, and was more than twice the size of my previous home. There was an abandoned gold mine on the property, and the location was absolutely, blissfully private.

I could barely believe I was creating this. I was beside myself with joy. I moved in, and had barely begun decorating it when I met the man who would soon become my second husband.

I hadn't been in my new home for even a year when I found myself packing to move again—this time, into a home that literally dwarfed my previous concept of "huge and beautiful." My new mate's home was double again the size of my canyon hideaway, with two additional homes on the property, ponds, horses, a swimming pool, a tennis court, and even a river.

At that point, my self-image was in culture shock. I had made my first million. I considered myself successful. But my husband's lifestyle made mine pale in comparison.

And compare I did, even though I knew better. I began to devalue the success I had created. When I did that, guess what happened to my business? You got it. The skyrocketing company that had just celebrated its best year ever began to lose momentum. Gradually, it declined more and more.

There were other reasons for that decline, which I'll share with you in a later chapter, but it all began with my comparisons.

The saddest effect of my comparing, though, was the loss of my joy. I had loved my work, my company, and the success, but viewing it as inconsequential compared to my mate's sucked the juice right out of it for me.

However …

Others' Successes *Should* Impact You

When someone has a success that you value, celebrate it! When others in your world have what you want, the universe is showing you that you can have it too (if you want it). You would not create others having success if success weren't a possibility for you as well.

You can have what they have, and so much more. From now on, see them and think, "They are in my life to show me what is possible. I accept this possibility, and even more!"

The key is to feel it. Feel grateful that they are showing you this sign. Feel excited. Feel as if you are on the brink of creating what they have created, and the fact that they are in your world is showing you that!

If this is hard for you to do, change these beliefs:

- I CAN'T CREATE THE SUCCESS THAT OTHERS CREATE IN THIS BUSINESS.
- I'M NOT AS GOOD AT BUSINESS AS OTHERS ARE.
- I'M NOT AS GOOD A __________ AS OTHERS ARE.

(Note: Even if your adult self believes you are just as good as others, your child self may not!)

It's time to start re-training your brain to respond to others' success in ways that makes you feel happy and excited for your own life. Otherwise, whenever you compare and feel disappointed in what you have, you will tell the universe, "Please create a reality for me where I am not enough and I do not measure up, thank you."

But wait, that's not all. If you keep going with this work, it's inevitable ...

OMG, IT'S HAPPENING! (AKA FEAR OF SUCCESS)

Me? Afraid of having lots of money? Frightened of success? I don't think so.

Well, maybe ... and maybe not. I didn't think I was afraid either—until it started impacting my creations.

Fear of success is far more prevalent than most of us acknowledge. Our lives may not be glamorous, exciting, or even beautiful, but they're ours. We know them, and we feel safe there.

My life was glamorous, exciting—and yes, even beautiful—and I was still petrified of success.

Wait a minute; haven't you created fabulous wealth, successful companies, great health, and beautiful relationships? What do you mean, you were "petrified of success"?

Interesting, huh? Humans are complex beings, and oftentimes we hold beliefs that oppose each other. This can result in some very curious realities.

Not too long ago, I had it wired that I could create success only so long as I could pawn the success off on someone or something else. As long as I could name my husband or my marketing company as the reason for my success, I was good. But the minute that I had to take ownership of my success for myself and become visible, I shut it down.

Fear of success is often the true reason behind our failures. We know failure intimately. If we fail, nothing changes. It's *success* that brings chaos and shifts in our world—and we're afraid of what those shifts will mean in our lives. We wonder what we'll have to sacrifice, or what we will need to do to keep up with the demands that true success entails. We even wonder if we'll be disappointed by our success. How funny is that?

Fear of success often shows up subconsciously, without us even knowing. We convince ourselves we really want success, and that we're ready for it, yet we sabotage it the minute so much as a hint of it shows up.

The underlying reason for this fear of success could be issues of deservability, which I've already covered. But it could also stem from a fear of what success means (to you) and a fear of what might happen once you are successful. Underlying both possibilities, of course, are beliefs.

To get to the bottom of your fear, ask yourself …

What Does It Mean to Be (Super) Successful?

Do any of your answers sound like this?

"If you're super successful …"

- You had to take others down on your way up.
- You have to have done something illegal.
- You have to have done something immoral.
- You're not a very nice person.
- You're cold-hearted.
- You'll do anything to grab and hold onto success.
- You give up your integrity, character, and values.
- You no longer care about "the little guy."
- You give up your freedom.

- You no longer belong.
- You are alone.
- Success owns you.

And while you are answering the above question, answer this one too …

What Will Happen After You Are (Really) Successful?

- People will badger me.
- I'll lose the money I make.
- I won't know how to handle success.
- I won't know how to invest the money.
- I'll end up like all those stupid lottery winners.
- Success will demand too much of me.
- I'll lose my family and friends.
- I'll lose my privacy.
- Someone will take my money and success away.
- If I'm really successful, it will go to my head.
- I'll be so vulnerable I'll get hurt, or worse.

If these are some of your answers, you are afraid of success.

If you have a few (or many) negative beliefs about successful people and the ramifications of success, don't worry: beliefs can be changed. See Appendix C for what beliefs might be underlying the answers above, as well as the corresponding positive beliefs. And don't forget to test for and change your beliefs!

I Didn't Realize I Was Afraid of Success

The way my fear of success showed up was that I was only able to be "just so" successful. Because I had been successful in other endeavors, I didn't realize this fear was holding me back—but when I personified success, I was shocked at what I truly believed.

When you "personify" success in meditation, you see success as a person. You can then dialogue with Success and learn a lot about your beliefs, fears, and expectations. Meditation puts us in an altered state that allows us to get to places we can't reach with our conscious minds.

In my meditation, as I called forth Success, I was amazed to see a hooded figure approach. This figure was dressed in a long, black robe, and carrying a sickle. My Success was *death itself*!

Similar to our night dreams, meditations often speak to us in metaphors. Success was showing me that I held a belief that if I was truly successful a part of me would die. I'd have to give up a piece of myself that I truly valued—in my case, my sacred solitude and my innocence.

I was in a circle of protection, but still, Success scared me. It looked so dark and menacing.

"I hate you," it sputtered.

Success hates me? I thought, shocked. (Although I can't say I felt very warm and fuzzy about *it*, either.)

It then said, sounding strangely like the Wicked Witch of the West, "I'm going to get you, my little pretty!"

It was then that the person guiding me through this meditation suggested, "Ask Success to forgive you for maligning it. Flood it with love. Success didn't want to be this way; you made it this way."

Wow. I had made Success my enemy.

I believed it would hurt me, so it had to show up that way. I felt such compassion for Success at that moment.

I imagined love coming from my heart and flowing into Success. I said I was sorry. I asked for forgiveness. And then, the strangest thing happened.

Success melted! Just like the Wicked Witch. Nothing was left but its black robe and sickle. My old version of Success was dead. I heard singing in my head, *Ding, dong, Success is dead ...*

And then I saw her—my new version of Success. Oh, my goodness, it was Glinda the Good Witch!

Now, Glinda probably wouldn't show up as your version of success personified, but to me she symbolized that Success loved me, truly cared about me, and would protect me through it all, no matter how successful I became.

I embraced Glinda. I was overjoyed. And my child self and adolescent self, who both loved Glinda, suddenly were no longer afraid of success either.

I continue to work with Glinda as my success personified. She counsels me and guides me. Success is now one of my cherished unseen friends.

You might wish to personify success in your own meditations to more fully understand your relationship with it. If so, here's how:

Personifying Success

Ready yourself and your environment to meditate. Lower the lights, light candles, and perhaps play some soft music. Find a comfortable position, either sitting or lying down.

Allow your body to relax. With every inhale, breathe in relaxation. With every exhale, let go of worry, tension, and the thoughts of the day. Feel relaxation softening your body, your muscles, your bones, as you allow yourself to sink deeper and deeper into the floor (or bed, or chair).

Allow your consciousness to drift as you relax. Feel as if you are floating.

At some point, feel yourself stabilize, and realize you're now sitting or lying in another place—a beautiful place in nature. Open your meditative senses to this beautiful place. Smell it. Feel it. Then, open your meditative eyes and look around at this beautiful place. Listen to the sounds of nature, and touch the grass, trees, and flowers. Taste the beauty. Know you are safe. Know you are protected in this place.

Your higher self joins you, and together you take a walk. As you walk, tell your higher self you want to meet success personified. Talk to your higher self of the struggles you've had with success. Talk of the disappointments, dashed hopes, and tattered dreams.

Before you know it, you are on one of the most beautiful beaches you've ever seen. Wide and flat, with gorgeous grasses and palm trees at the edge—this beach is magnificent.

Your higher self picks up a long, sturdy stick, and draws a circle around you. The circle is about twenty-five feet in diameter. You know, intuitively, that this circle is one of protection. As you have that thought, your higher self raises the stick and before your eyes manifests a clear dome. It looks to be made of plexiglass or something similar, but you know in your heart it is much, much stronger. In fact, it is impenetrable. You feel safe and secure in this bubble of protection.

Your higher self asks, "Are you ready?" You nod.

Success comes. It may appear out of the distance, out of the ocean mist, from behind the trees. It might slip out from behind a boulder. Success comes closer and closer to you. You shrink back in fear. Success comes right to the edge of your bubble, and tells you exactly what it thinks of you.

You listen. And you feel ashamed. You've given Success a bad rap. You look into Success's eyes, and apologize for treating it so poorly. You beg its forgiveness. And, perhaps reluctantly, it agrees.

Before your very eyes, Success transforms. Perhaps it dies and is born again. Perhaps it dematerializes and re-materializes. Perhaps it simply shape-shifts into a healthy, healed, loving, and supportive fan of yours.

The bubble of protection melts away, and you move to embrace Success, feeling deep in your core that life, as you know it, will never be the same.

What Do You Need to Do to Be Successful?

You need to do the work. Just that.

Do. The. Work.

Essence can be changed. And when essence changes, *voila!* Realities change.

But *you have to do the work.*

And the minute you begin to whine, "But I aaaaaammm doing the work … and it's just not haaaaaappening," please know, *you are not doing the work.*

- Doing the work includes not whining.
- Doing the work includes not feeling victimized.
- Doing the work includes not feeling like a martyr.

- Doing the work includes feeling grateful for every single drop of abundance in your life.
- Doing the work includes monitoring your feelings all day, every day.
- Doing the work includes making changing beliefs your new favorite pastime.
- Doing the work includes seeing less of friends who want to do nothing but complain, and who try to keep you as tiny as possible so they don't feel so worthless.
- Doing the work includes owning your divinity, and claiming your God and Goddess-given right to abundance in all areas.

Now. Choose again. And make that choice deeply this time.

Repeat after me:

I choose to claim my divine right to be abundant. I ask my higher self and all of my other unseen friends to accompany me on this journey of further growth and empowerment and to help me along the way. I ask that you gently point out where I get stuck, kindly show me the beliefs I need to change, and help me to change them. Assist me please, to the greatest extent possible—and I thank you in advance for your support and love, your guidance and grace.

You need nothing more than that choice, this book, and a commitment to do the work. And then, you, too, can create magnificent, fulfilling, unending abundance.

Are you ready?

A TRUE STORY OF CONSCIOUSLY CREATING ABUNDANCE

I worked closely with The Map *during the last quarter of 2014. I wrote in my journal what I wanted to see happen in 2015.*

This was my list:

- *Travel to The Seychelles on vacation.*
- *Move to a new, bigger apartment in a neighborhood that we love.*
- *Work with my body to prepare for the birth of our second child.*

In December we decided to go to The Seychelles the following January. Just a week before the trip, I began to talk about flying first class. I really wondered what it would be like to travel like that.

Obviously we did not buy first class tickets, because they were so expensive. But all I did was talk about it. Talking about it made me feel like I was about to open a Christmas gift. I just let the feeling stay with me, as if I had already traveled first class.

On the day of our departure, we were excited about our trip. At the check-in counter, we talked to an extremely nice man, and while we were talking I asked how much it would cost to upgrade to first class. It was far too expensive.

We left check-in to go to the gate. As we approached the gate, I heard our names being called to the counter—but it made no sense to us because we weren't late.

As the stewardess entered the information from our tickets, suddenly a red alert sign came up on the screen, and I got a bit confused, wondering what was going on.

She looked at me and said with a big smile, "You have been upgraded to first class." Holy Moses! Are you kidding me? Whee!

Let's just say that made us very happy and comfortable. The entire trip was beautiful—and to top it all off, my boyfriend got on his knees and proposed to me on a beautiful beach on Coco island.

I'm now a believer.

- Lilly U.

ABUNDANCE-ALTERING TAKEAWAYS

- *You* are the one creating your reality. Don't get caught up in codependent thinking that says you have to change another in order for your world to change.

- When it comes to sharing finances, you can't control another person, but you *can* create your world. Imagining another as abundant, successful, and happy can only help you both.

- If you want credit from your partner for your part in creating your joint finances, go have a talk with your child self, your adolescent self, and your negative self. They are the ones feeling invalidated. Your adult self can understand that a quiet power comes with owning the fact that you create your own reality. And that self doesn't need to boast about it.

- The more you can detach yourself from any expectation about how your partner does or does not contribute, and simply take ownership of your financial abundance, the freer you will be to create positive changes in that abundance.

- People you care about may be habitually negative, and negativity hurts realities, which is why it upsets you. Their negativity can hurt your reality too, if you let it—but you don't have to let it.

- You can support your loved ones by paying attention to your own path and allowing them to choose theirs. Compassionate detachment will free you both to soar as high as you can. When you do this, they may surprise you; when you let go and allow them to grow at a pace that is right for them, they may just "get it" instantly.

- Your boundaries will be felt whether you verbalize them or not, and people will respect them if you are clear about them.

- If you motivate out of love and not "shoulds," your power can stay firmly where it belongs: with you.

- The minute you begin to compare your money, success, or any other type of abundance with someone else's, you are siphoning off energy from your own success.

- When someone has a success that you value, celebrate it! Others having what you want shows you that *you can have it too.* You could not create others having success if it weren't a possibility for you, as well.

- Fear of success is often the true reason behind our failures. We know failure intimately. If we fail, nothing changes. No, it's success that brings chaos and shifts in our world.

- If you have any negative beliefs about successful people and the ramifications of success, don't worry. Beliefs can be changed.

- What do you need to do to be successful? You need to *do the work.* Just that.

YOUR NEXT STEPS

- Do you share money or resources with another? Have you been unclear about who creates that wealth? Write about the way you've held it in the past, and how you intend to think of it in the future.

- Make a list of the people in your life that you've allowed to impact you in a negative way. Write out how you'll handle the situation for each person the next time you're tempted to lower your resonance.

- Who do you compare yourself to? Can you shift your thinking and become excited that you could have what they have? If not, why? Do some detective work and change those beliefs!

- Have you created glimmers of success, or true success that has disappeared? Are you afraid of success? Make a list of your fears (and the related beliefs) around success, and change them.

- Do the Personifying Success Meditation. Write about your experience.

- Use the applied kinesiology techniques in Appendix B to test for the constricting beliefs in this chapter. Document the beliefs that need to be changed, and change them using a technique in Appendix D.

CHAPTER SIXTEEN

Keeping the Abundance You Create

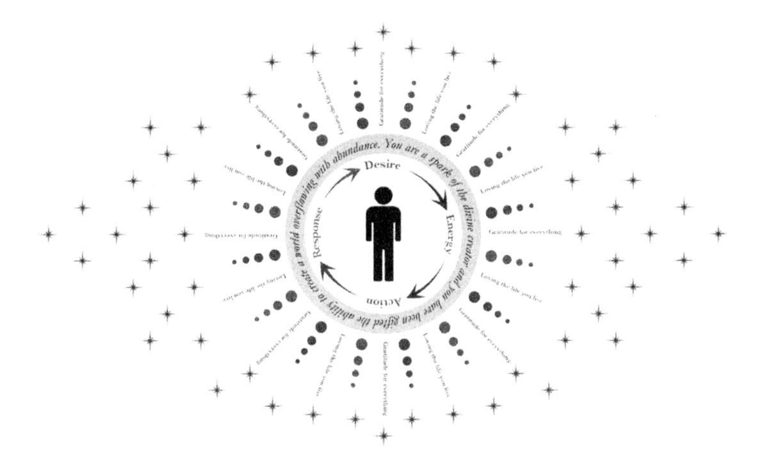

"If you see yourself as prosperous, you will be. If you see yourself as continually hard up, that is exactly what you will be."

~ ROBERT COLLIER

Everyone thinks they'd have absolutely no problem becoming rich. "Just try me," they say. But the fact is, no matter how much you think you've prepared for it, wealth is an adjustment—and the greater the wealth, the greater the adjustment.

What does this have to do with consciously creating abundance? *Everything.*

If you don't adjust to wealth—to having it, to accepting it as a way of life, to seeing yourself as wealthy, you will un-create that wealth.

Case In Point: Lottery Winners

Remember when we talked about the lottery trap in Chapter Four? Well, here's that statistic again: 70 percent of lottery winners end up broke again, no matter how many millions they win.[1] These stories are fascinating to read. One woman won the lottery two years in a row—a total of a whopping $5.4 million—but she lost it all, and as of this writing is living in a trailer.

It's not only the lottery. It happens to winners of mega-lawsuits, musicians, professional sports players, and actors who suddenly make it big.

Oh, but it wouldn't happen to me.

Don't bet on it. I can tell you firsthand that an influx of money brings up a lot of issues.

THE MONEY CHALLENGE

When I started my marketing company (yeah, the one I started for $50 and grew to a company with $5 million in annual sales), I was living in a rented condo. I moved to a home of my own a couple of years later.

It wasn't the first home I'd owned, but it *was* a special one. It was the first home I'd bought 100 percent for me. There was a special thrill to that. It was on a pretty little lake (a rare commodity in semi-arid Colorado), and it was the perfect house for me.

I loved that place. In fact, I loved it so much, I was afraid I'd lose it. It wasn't a big home, just 1,800 square feet, but I made

(1) "Twelve Things Not To Do If You Win The Lottery," www.USAToday.com, August 25, 2013.

it mine. I fixed it up, finished the basement, planted a moon garden, decorated it to my tastes—and all the while, I could barely believe my good fortune.

I remember driving home from work, suddenly panicked, thinking, "What if my house burned down today?"

I seriously thought that. Not just once, but day after day.

I didn't want my imaginative negativity to have an actual negative impact on my reality, so I quickly thought, "*Cancel*! Cancel that!" And I imagined the house surrounded in a bubble of sparkling white light, protecting it from all possible harm.

And, each day, I would turn the corner onto my street, and watch my house come into view. Seeing my pretty little home still standing, as wonderful as ever, I would exhale a breath I hadn't even known I was holding, and a huge flood of relief would sweep over me.

Why did that happen?

Because we see ourselves in a certain way around money. When we slip out of that comfort zone, we feel awkward and unfamiliar, as if we don't quite belong there.

This shows up for many as a peculiar need to spend any extra money that does come in. As one person put it, "I don't understand why I do it, but whenever I receive some extra cash and finally can allow myself to feel abundant, I have this compulsion to get rid of the money. I spend it as quickly as I can, almost unconsciously."

When our reality shifts to a new reality, our self-image must shift also, or our reality will snap back to the old one. That's why lottery winners lose their millions. It's why many people can't sustain good fortune of any type. It's why some create misfortune after every win. And it's why we find ourselves slipping back into old patterns, time and time again.

IF WE DON'T LOSE IT, WE MAY CREATE PROBLEMS WITH IT

I worked on improving my financial image, and settled into the little house of my dreams. The next big step for me was another lifelong dream: a new convertible.

My nineteen-year-old son was coming to live with me while he attended college, and I gave him my old car as a graduation gift. This meant that I was going to finally buy a car I loved—a car that wasn't used, and that wasn't a "mom car."

I settled on an Audi TT convertible, navy blue and as cute as could be. I proudly drove it home and, as I pulled into the driveway, my neighbor came running out of his house.

"Tell me that's yours!" he shouted.

My wide grin told him everything. I loved that car.

But my image got in my way. In the first six months, the car was in the body shop three times! First, I sideswiped a pole backing out of a parking space. Then, someone backed into me. And then, a short time later, I slid into a parked car.

"What is going on?" I thought.

It didn't take me long to figure it out. My self-image was of a person who struggled and who didn't have new, expensive things. My reality followed my energy, and "messed it up" a bit. After I worked on my image, the car issues ceased.

Don't Do It the Way I Did

Ideally, image work isn't done retroactively, after the reality has manifested. Instead, it should be done before the reality manifests. That way, the shifts you make in your image will not only make it easier to sustain your new dreams once they've manifested, but will help to create the dreams themselves.

You see, image is beyond using your imagination, thoughts, and emotions to create something.

Image is how you think of yourself.

You can create just about anything by putting forth great flows of emotional energy. As long as you believe it is possible, you can manifest it.

But in order to keep it in your reality, you need to continue to think of yourself as someone who has and deserves that reality. The minute fear, doubt, unworthiness, and other forms of not "living up to" a reality start to enter, they threaten the very reality you worked so hard to create.

HOW TO SHIFT YOUR IMAGE

First, it is important to note that the "image" step needs to come after you change your beliefs. Your beliefs have to support what you desire to create, or the image work won't hold.

As you work on your image, you may notice that more beliefs come to your attention and need to be changed. That's okay; it's to be expected.

Here is the process for shifting your self-image.

Look at the image you currently have around money.

First, take a hard look at the image you currently have around yourself and money. Write a paragraph about money in your life. It might look something like this:

> *There is simply never enough money. No matter how much comes in, the same amount goes out. I always seem*

to be able to pay for what I really need, but I never get ahead. I yearn for things I can't have. I want to travel. I want more freedom. I want more ease. But I never get exactly what I want when it comes to money. I suck at creating abundance.

Think about the image you would prefer to have around money.

Next, write a paragraph about money in your life with your new image. It might look something like this:

I am abundant. Money flows to me with ease and elegance. There is always more than enough money and it seems to find me in the most magical and synchronistic ways. The universe supports me in every way including sending me lots of money. I can always find ways to do whatever I dream of doing. I feel loved and protected by the universe, and money is my friend. I am rich in every meaning of the word.

Do a meditation to change the image you now have to the image you desire.

Find a comfortable space where you will not be disturbed. Lie down or sit comfortably. Perhaps play some soft music or light a candle. Close your eyes and relax. Feel your body slipping into deeper and deeper levels of relaxation.

Begin to imagine yourself in a beautiful place in nature. Open your senses, and see the beautiful vista around you. It may be morning, or night, or anytime in between. Touch the grass, the trees, the flowers. Smell the delicate fragrance of this beautiful place. Allow yourself to taste the beauty.

You know you're loved here; you're safe here as well. Before you know it, your higher self will join you and greet you in the way s/he does—with a look, a smile, a touch, or an embrace.

Tell your higher self that you desire to permanently shift your image around money and abundance. Of course, that's what your higher self wants for you too. S/he gently takes your hand, and together you walk.

And as you walk, you talk to your higher self. You disclose your current image around money. You explain how difficult it has been. You talk of the struggle you've experienced, the pain of scarcity, and the fear of never having enough.

Before you know it, your higher self leads you to another beautiful place—a charming little grotto. The trees and the land seem to shield this place. It's private, protected, and filled with magic.

Your higher self picks up a stick and draws a circle of protection around you. Then, s/he places both hands upon your shoulders, looks deeply into your eyes, and asks, "Are you ready to step out of your old image now?"

You nod. As your higher self's hands lift away from your body, a gray covering lifts from you as well. It forms a bubble around you—a dirty, gray bubble—and you know that this is your current image around money. Layer after layer of gray energy lifts from your body and darkens the bubble around you.

You watch as your higher self takes the bubble and rips an opening big enough for you to walk through. You step out of the bubble and feel a sense of relief. Your higher self gathers the bubble, wads it up into a gray ball, and throws it into the air, where it disappears in a sparkle of light.

Your higher self turns to you and asks, "What image would you like for yourself around money?"

You explain that you want money to be your friend. You want to feel abundant all the time—to feel financially secure, and trust that your needs will be met no matter what. You want to feel that money flows to you with ease and elegance, and in magical and synchronistic ways.

Your higher self's hands rise up, and a bubble of white, sparkling light forms before your very eyes. "If you don't mind," your higher self says, "I would like to offer my own additions to your image."

"Yes, please!" you reply with a smile. And as her/his hands begin to wave, the bubble begins to glow and sparkle with specks of gold, silver, pink, and baby blue. It looks magnificent.

Your higher self gently parts the bubble as if drawing back a curtain of light, and motions you to enter. You step through—and as you do, you suddenly feel magically and wonderfully abundant.

The bubble slowly settles down around you, as if you were being vacuum-packed inside abundance itself. You grin from ear to ear, and thank your higher self for this assistance.

You imagine your new life with this new image solidly within you. You feel the security of knowing your every need will be met. You feel the safety inherent in being 100 percent certain that the universe has your back. You feel what it would feel like if you had a money machine. And as you have that thought, you notice your higher self is handing you … a money machine.

"It creates $100 bills," your higher self says. You look at it and know that you will never have to worry about money again.

> Hang out here in your bubble. Play with the reality, and with your new money machine. What will you buy? What will you do? How will your life be different? Then, when you're ready, open your eyes.

Repeat this meditation as often as you'd like. Remember, as you go about your day, that your new self-image is one of abundance.

SUSTAINING THE ENERGY

When I was a little girl, money was extremely tight. Our family always had enough, but we seldom had extra. I remember gathering empty soda cans to take to the store for the bottle deposit refund so we could scrape together enough money for "dinner out"—aka hot dogs at the neighborhood fast food joint.

I remember repeating that same scenario as a young mother—not to splurge on fast food, but to put gas in the car. Not much changed in the years between my childhood and young adulthood—at least, not financially. I did have bigger dreams, though, and it wasn't long before my husband and I managed to purchase an old three-bedroom, two-bathroom Cape Cod home with a beautiful lot. That house qualified as a mansion in my family's eyes.

It was in that home that I discovered the concept of conscious creation for the first time. I remember walking up and down the narrow, dark staircase between the first and second floors, looking straight into the tiny wall that claustrophobically enclosed that staircase, but seeing in my mind's eye a huge picture window opening onto a breathtaking view.

I would travel up and down those stairs a dozen or more times a day. Every single time, I imagined a phenomenal view.

Yes, I had a great imagination. And it paid off.

Our next home was in Golden, Colorado, and it felt like a mansion to me. It was double the size of the Cape, and when I walked down the staircase I gazed directly out a huge three-story window at an amazing view of the Colorado foothills. It was exactly as I'd imagined.

Yes, my dreams were coming true—on the outside, anyway. On the one hand, we had more things than I had ever had, growing up. But on the other hand, we struggled as much as ever did.

Within a few years, I was back in a home the size of the Cape. A few years after that, even *that* home was in foreclosure—and these two homes were created after I began to create consciously!

Obviously, I was still mis-creating.

The thing I love most about the way our universe works is that it never screws up. Never. *Ever*. Not in a billion years.

I was learning how to create, all right, but I wasn't very good at sustaining the energy of my creations. I got scared—and when the fear started creeping in, things fell apart.

Circumstances changed in my life. My husband and I decided to separate, and then divorce, and I didn't think I could afford the first house. (See the belief and sustainment issues there?) With the next house, I just couldn't stop myself from thinking about everything that was wrong.

Instead of focusing on all of the possibilities that lay before me, I focused on the problems, like the fact that my income was non-existent apart from child support and alimony, and even those were soon to end. My teenage sons were acting out, my "career" in multi-level marketing wasn't taking off, and I couldn't seem to make any money teaching conscious creation. (Gee, I wonder why?)

I'm not the only one this has happened to. All conscious creators, at one point or another, face …

Sustainment Challenges

Sustaining energy is one of the biggest challenges for everyone who is learning to consciously create. I'm sure you've been there too—or you will be, if you're new at this.

Why is it such a challenge?

Well, there are a number of reasons.

We forget

There are so many things to remember! We have to remember to monitor our thoughts and our feelings, look at our beliefs, flow energy, take action, look for signs. If you're not at the point where these things come naturally, it's exhausting—and it's easy to forget one or more of these crucial elements for days or even weeks at a time.

But the real tragedy is that we forget that our universe is miraculous. We forget that we create it all, with no exceptions, no exemptions, and no excuses. I don't know about you, but I *still* have to keep letting that in, allowing it to hit me like a wave and wash over me, over and over and over again. I need to let the enormity of that truth really sink in.

We. Create. It. All.

Wow. Just stop for a moment and imagine the kind of world you could create with that kind of power! Not just for yourself, but for humanity. It's awe-inspiring.

And yet, we forget about this power *all the time*.

We go unconscious

We watch TV. We surf the web. We go to work and listen to our coworkers, family, and friends talk about their lives (most of whom are creating unconsciously), and we join them in their unconsciousness. We nod our heads in commiseration when they tell us their troubles. We join in their tirades about which politicians are "responsible" for the state of our nation. We sadly shake our heads at the thought of global warming.

When we go unconscious, we are no longer part of the solution. In fact, we are adding to the problem. We don't do this because we are bad or wrong; we are actually trying to be good people. But when we are unconscious, we know not what we do.

We disbelieve

We get excited when we learn that we create it all. We hop on the bandwagon, write out our intentions, and try to stay positive long enough for them to manifest.

But since we haven't done it for long enough to get good at it, the results are less than stellar, and we secretly wonder if we are grasping at rainbows. After the rah-rah has worn off, we sometimes wish we'd never heard of the stupid Law of Attraction. Life was less disappointing before we got our hopes up.

We let other aspects of us run the show. We allow our negative selves to talk in our heads, and assure us that we'll never attain the dreams we desperately desire.

We ignore our child selves, and then wonder why we feel so powerless, ineffectual, and scared.

We ignore our adolescent selves, and then wonder why we feel so impatient and panicked about our future.

We ignore our young adult selves, and then wonder why our past failures keep haunting us.

We become reactive

We look at our life, and notice that it's not anywhere near what we intend for our dream life. Extra bills come in, we have a fight with our partner, or our bodies feel worse than ever.

Then, we get scared: scared that it's all a crock; scared that we aren't able to pull it off; scared that we'll never, ever realize our dreams.

In our darkest hours, we are petrified that what we see is all there is.

We aren't proactive

We stop flowing energy. We stop asking for help. We stop taking inventory of our beliefs. We stop looking for signs that what we want is manifesting in our world.

And then, we wonder (since, after all, we read the books, took the seminars, and learned quite a bit about the Law of Attraction), "Why isn't this working?"

I did *all* of those things in my darkest hours.

It's easy to go there, believe me, I know: I went there. And when I did, my reality went from bad to worse.

It's important to remember though, that negativity is far less powerful than positivity. It takes a *lot* of negative emotion and beliefs to tip the scale toward lack and scarcity. That's why so many people who appear to be beacons of gloom actually do okay for themselves.

But, more importantly, remember it doesn't take much to tip the scales back to even, and then to tip them further into real success and abundance.

HOW TO SUSTAIN THE ESSENCE OF ABUNDANCE

There are definitely things you can do to help sustain the essence of abundance (or anything else you desire to create). It's important to remember, too, that this does get easier the more you do it.

On the other hand, no matter how good you get at conscious creation, or for how many years you do it, you will *never* have the luxury of being able to go unconscious. Those days are over—and good riddance, I say! Being unconscious results in crappy realities. No one needs those.

So how can we can stay conscious, sustain the essence of abundance, and reap the abundant rewards? Here are just a few ways I do it. You can work with any that feel good to you:

Four Steps to Sustaining the Essence of Abundance

1. ***Make time for conscious creating every single day.*** The average American spends nearly three hours a day watching TV, twenty-five minutes a day playing computer games, forty-one minutes a day socializing, and about thirty minutes a day reading. Certainly some of that time could be apportioned to your conscious creating? What on Earth could be more important? Even ten or fifteen minutes a day will make a *huge* difference in your life.

2. ***Make it your top priority—and I mean* top *priority.*** Think of it as more important than brushing your teeth, more important than showering, more

important than earning a living, more important than *anything*. Your consciousness is creating everything in your world, so by definition it is more important than anything. And if you start thinking of this work as the most important thing you do each day, then item #1 will become much easier to accomplish.

3. ***Check in regularly.*** Tie a ribbon around your wrist (guys, maybe a piece of jute twine?) to remind you to check in with yourself. Have you been focusing on abundance, or lack? Have you felt emotionally great, or lousy? Your emotions are creating whether you are aware of them or not—so begin to become aware of them. When you don't like what you've been feeling, figure out why. Change your thoughts, change your beliefs, or change your dream.

4. ***Stop thinking about it.*** I know, it seems contradictory to say, "Be sure to focus on it regularly," and then say, "Stop thinking about it"—but this letting go is essential.

Yes, you do have to flow energy toward what you want, make sure you pay attention to that creation, and look closely at all the elements necessary to manifest it in your world.

But once you've done that, you need to let it go. Stop thinking about it. Because any thinking you do after you've done your daily work of consciously creating your dream probably won't be about your excitement. Instead, it will probably be about fear that your dream won't manifest.

Ideally, let it go, and enjoy, enjoy, *enjoy* your life!

But how can I enjoy my life if my dreams haven't manifested yet?

It's your *life*. There is a lot to enjoy. You have been keeping track of what you're grateful for on a daily basis, right? And honestly, if you don't master enjoying your life, you'll never become really adept at conscious creating.

YOU *CAN* GET GOOD AT THIS

I did it, and you can too. There are lots of baby steps you can take to make it easier to sustain the resonance of abundance—so take them, and watch your world change.

Honestly, once you really start doing the work, it won't take all that much time for your world to respond. The more changes you start seeing in your world, the easier it will get to hold the resonance—and the better you get at holding it, the quicker your world will respond the next time around, until, before you know it, you are abundant.

A TRUE STORY OF CONSCIOUSLY CREATING ABUNDANCE

I never thought I'd be writing and sharing a success story.

For two years now, I've wanted to have a space to offer, share, and teach yoga. I have three yoga certifications and it's been a beautiful healing journey in my life.

I became a little weary because I couldn't find a home to share these gifts—that was, until I found The Map.

I began using the tools and techniques about a month ago. Yesterday, I met with a kind and beautiful pastor at a Lutheran church to see if the yoga I offered would be a good match for their church. It was a perfect match!

The reality I created was more than I could've asked for. The church is on one of the busiest streets in my town. Even more wonderful, the church is going through renovations and will be adding a marquee sign in the near future that will let everyone driving by know that the church now offers yoga and meditation!

Thank you! Thank you! Thank you Boni, God, Goddess, Angels, and all of my unseen friends. I feel eternally grateful for your love and assistance!

- Victoria D.

ABUNDANCE-ALTERING TAKEAWAYS

- If you don't adjust to wealth—to having it, to accepting it as a way of life, to seeing yourself as wealthy—you *will* un-create that very wealth.

- Because we see ourselves in a certain way around money (or any other subject, for that matter), when we slip out of that comfort zone, we feel awkward, unfamiliar, as if we don't quite belong there.

- When our reality shifts to a new reality, our image must shift also, or our reality will snap back to the old one.

- Ideally, image work isn't done retroactively, after the reality has manifested. Instead, it's done before the reality manifests. That way, the shifts you make in your image not only make it easier to sustain your new dreams once they've manifested, but your new self-image will also help to create the dreams!

- Sustaining the energy is one of the biggest challenges for everyone who is learning to consciously create.

- There are things you can do to help sustain the essence of abundance (or anything else you desire to create).

- You *can* get good at this. I did it, and you can, too. There are lots of baby steps you can take to make it easier to sustain the resonance of abundance.

YOUR NEXT STEPS

- Write out your old image and your new image, and do the "Image Changing Technique."

- Make a list of the "Four Steps to Sustaining the Essence of Abundance" and post it where you'll see it often. Make a commitment to yourself to do all four.

CHAPTER SEVENTEEN

The Most Important Thing to Remember

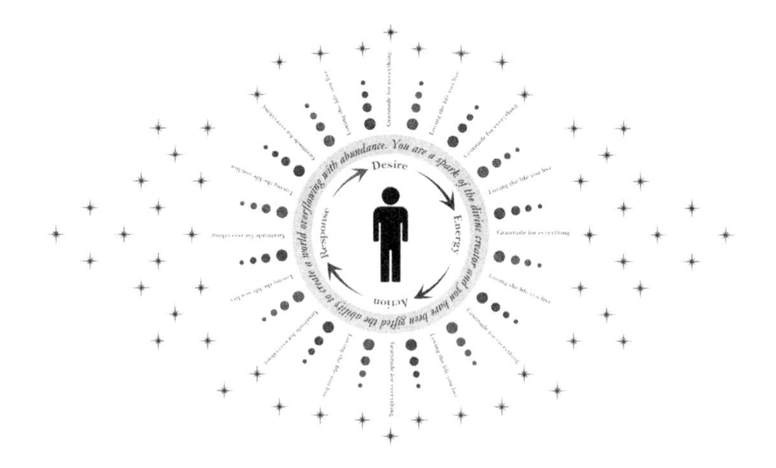

"Those who have not found their true wealth, which is the radiant joy of Being and the deep, unshakable peace that comes with it, are beggars, even if they have great material wealth. They are looking outside for scraps of pleasure or fulfillment, for validation, security, or love, while they have a treasure within that not only includes all those things but is infinitely greater than anything the world can offer."

~ ECKHART TOLLE

You may be wondering why the most important thing to remember about consciously creating abundance is at the end of this book, and not the beginning.

It's at the end because, while it is the most important thing, unless you've handled all of the other possible issues that could stop your abundance, this most important thing won't work for you.

THE MOST IMPORTANT THING TO REMEMBER

If you come away knowing one concept from this book, I hope it's this: The easiest way to create abundance (once you believe it's possible) is to forget about making money and focus on living a spectacular life.

I know some will be disappointed by this advice. And please know that by asking you to forget about making money, I'm not saying that you won't create it. Just don't focus on it. Instead, focus on the joy of your life.

If you are living your life with great joy, abandon, excitement, and passion, who the heck cares if it takes a while to be fully and totally abundant? You're having fun! Fun is the point. Joy is the point. Excitement is the point.

Money is not the point.

Money is a side effect of feeling joyously, passionately, beautifully, abundantly in love with your life.

And you can feel that way now.

Did you hear that?

You can feel that way *now*.

How Does It Feel?

An old friend and I caught up over dinner recently. At one point, she looked at me wistfully, and said, "How does it feel to always have more than enough money?"

I told her it was great, and we quickly changed the subject. But in hindsight, I wished I had said, "Dear friend, you should know how it feels to have more than enough money. You should be feeling that way nearly 100 percent of the time. Feeling as though you have more than enough of *everything* should be your intention and goal for every single day of your life!"

If money isn't showing up for you, the advice in the rest of this book will help, but living joyfully and gratefully every single day should be your main focus; if it is, the money will follow (as long as you believe it will).

MY FIRST MAJOR ABUNDANCE

As I was reading through old journals and writings to prepare for this book, I came across a list I wrote after hitting rock bottom and creating my way to my first major success.

I wrote this the year my marketing company reached its pinnacle: $5 million in sales. I wrote it because I wanted to remember how I created it so I could use that "map" to create in other areas of my life as well.

How I Created My Business & Prosperity

1. ***I created one good day.*** Then, I built upon that, day by day by day. I focused solely on having fun and expanding my positive feelings.

2. ***I didn't allow any room for worry.*** I never doubted where I was going, and I never second-guessed my choices.

3. ***I always knew that my successes might not be forever,*** but I also held that whatever came after would be even more spectacular.

4. ***I practiced feeling what the "next step" of abundance would feel like*** on a regular basis.

5. ***I welcomed, allowed, and expected miracles***—and there were miracles around every corner.

6. ***I regularly consulted with my team of guides*** (aka my unseen friends) regarding my business and finances.

7. ***I asked for help.***

8. ***I learned what I could in the physical world*** to strengthen and grow my business and finances.

9. ***No matter what happened, I didn't take it too seriously***, nor did I take it personally. (Remember, this world and everything in it is all an illusion!)

10. ***If I made a mistake or suffered a loss, I always held that something grander, better, and more fitting would replace it.***

11. ***I had fun.***

12. ***I was grateful.***

13. ***I knew that I was building and maintaining momentum toward exactly the reality I desired***, even if nothing positive seemed to be happening physically in my business or finances.

14. ***I trusted my intuition about what to do when.*** It had to feel safe and right before I made the next move. Sometimes, I would make a little move to test the waters; then, I would listen again to feel for the "rightness."

15. ***I wasn't in a hurry to create.*** I was having fun, feeling joy, and absolutely enjoying my business, my life, and the process of creation!

Rereading this list, I was happy to see that I still feel the same way about what it takes to create abundance as I did a dozen years ago. And, it must be working, because my abundance has grown exponentially since then! Yours will too—if you follow *The Map*.

It's all laid out for you. All you have to do is to follow *The Map* and do the work ...

...UNLESS YOUR SOUL HAS ANOTHER IDEA

You consciously create it all. No exceptions. But "you" are a multi-faceted being.

After the recession of 2008, my marketing company struggled, as did many other companies. But external events—even global events—are never an excuse to give up your power around your creations. You can't blame your lack of abundance on the economy, or anything else. You create it all—as do I.

At the time, though, I was *so* frustrated that I couldn't turn my company around.

I did every technique under the sun, and nothing worked.

I began to feel less and less joy in running that company. I thought it was because it wasn't doing as well financially—and that should have been my sign.

Anytime passion wanes, something needs adjusting. In my case, my soul stepped in to keep the company from growing so that I'd move on to write *The Map*. In hindsight, I wish I hadn't waited as long as I did. The minute I started writing and planning my new business, I got my passion and excitement back.

I thought I knew what I wanted, but my soul knew better—and so does yours.

When Your Soul Steps In ...

It's critical to understand that your soul *wants* you to be abundant. S/he wants you to be happy, have fun, be prosperous, feel loved, and be vitally healthy. Your soul wants you to enjoy every positive attribute you can think of.

The only time any of your unseen friends step in without your explicit invitation is to give you something even better than your energy is currently creating. This something is called a *miracle*.

Yes, miracles *do* happen. You can't control them or create them, but you can align yourself with them.

How?

- ***Believe in them.*** Do you have any beliefs like these?
  - MIRACLES ARE IMPOSSIBLE.
  - LIFE CAN ONLY GET SO GOOD.
  - MIRACLES CAN'T HAPPEN TO ME.

- WHEN LIFE IS GOING GREAT, THE OTHER SHOE WILL DROP.
- YOU HAVE TO BE DESPERATE TO BE GIVEN A MIRACLE.

If you do have these beliefs, change them. You are in complete and total charge of allowing good things into your life. Life itself is a miracle. Creating your own reality is pretty miraculous—but victimhood and miracle-making are, quite simply, two opposing energies.

- ***Ask for them.*** Your unseen friends can't wait to help you. But don't ask out of desperation, and don't ask from a place of hopelessness and helplessness. Ask as an empowered, conscious creator!

- ***Recognize them.*** Know what energy you are putting out. Keep track of your successes. But also know when something far better than you've ever dreamt drops into your reality. Don't call everything good a miracle—but when it happens, own that you let it in.

- ***Be grateful for them.*** When you receive a miracle, or even witness one, give thanks. Your unseen friends are the real miracle makers.

Miracles can be encouraged, and even expected. It's a beautiful, transcendent experience to allow divine grace to kiss your life. The more you can recognize miracles when they occur and be truly, deeply, grateful for them, the more miracles you will allow in your reality.

A TRUE STORY OF CONSCIOUSLY CREATING ABUNDANCE

Yesterday my husband and I took our son Chase and our pup Makena to the local dog park in Boulder. It is one of our favorite places to visit as a family. There is a huge tree in the center of the field on the west end, and we always stop to climb on it and take a picture or two. It is a special tree for us; our dogs have had fun climbing around on it for years, and now our young son climbs it, too.

My husband and I were throwing the tennis ball for Makena while our son Chase climbed the ginormous tree. All of a sudden, Chase came running over.

"Mom," he gushed. "I found this coin in the tree!"

I looked at it, expecting a penny—but it was a gold dollar coin! I told him that he must have discovered a magical money tree!

The look on his face was pure amazement. He went running back to look for more—and, unbelievably, found another *gold dollar coin sitting on a huge piece of bark, right at his eye level.*

Yes, he found $2 in a tree!

After we left the site of the treasure, I told Chase, "You are magical. You created that money being delivered to you! Do you believe it?"

He smiled at me and said, "Yeah, Mom. I am totally *magical."*

It was a huge moment for me.

I love that I am helping my little guy realize his magic so early on, and opening his consciousness to the amazing life he is so capable of creating for himself.

- Gwen B.

ABUNDANCE-ALTERING TAKEAWAYS

- If you come away knowing one concept from this book, I hope it is this: The easiest way to create abundance (once you believe it's possible) is to forget about making money and focus on living a spectacular life.

- If you are living your life with great joy, abandon, excitement, and passion, who the heck cares if it takes a while to be fully and totally abundant? You are having fun! Fun is the point. Joy is the point. Excitement is the point. Money is *not* the point.

- Money is a side effect of feeling joyously, passionately, beautifully, abundantly in love with your life. And *you can feel that way now.*

- Anytime passion wanes, *something* needs adjusting.

- Miracles can be encouraged, and even expected. It's a beautiful, transcendent experience to allow divine grace to kiss your life. The more you can recognize those miracles and be truly, deeply, grateful for them, the more miracles you will allow in your reality.

YOUR NEXT STEPS

- Imagine what your life will be like with unlimited abundance—both money and every other type of abundance. Write about that.

- Imagine what your life will look like when you are living a life you love and every day is filled with ease, elegance, love, joy, peace, excitement, passion, creativity, and fun. Write about that.

- Look at what you've written based on the questions above. How can you live that life now? Where can you add more joy? Excitement? Passion? Creativity? Gratitude? Fun? Love? Write about that.

- What do you think your soul and higher self want for you? Do you know that there is something you should be doing for your highest good, and that is in alignment with your destiny? Write about that.

CHAPTER EIGHTEEN

Your Plan for Creating Abundance

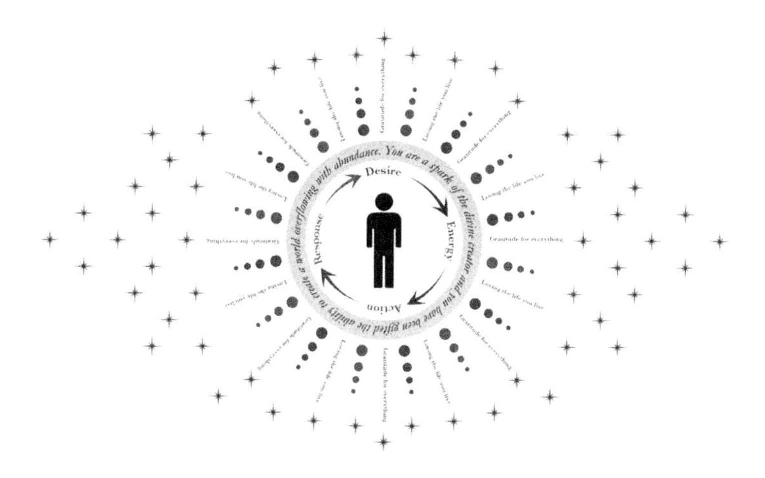

"Every great teacher who has ever walked the planet has told you that life was meant to be abundant."

~ JAMES RAY

Abundance is your birthright.

As a divine being on this planet, you not only deserve abundance, it's built in to your very being. You only need look at nature to recognize that fact.

However, because you are so powerful, you can also create lack, struggle, and hardship. It really *is* up to you. If you are committed to creating abundance, and you honestly do the work, you *will* succeed.

You can work *The Map to Abundance* fast or slow, with a friend or alone, according to the steps outlined or in an order that works more perfectly for you. This book is filled with truths, directions, and suggestions as to how to approach this work, but you should always follow your own heart and mind as to what to do, and when.

As always, the question to ask when evaluating any approach is: "Does this work for me?"

If my approach works for you, great. If another approach works for you, or if you want to tailor my approach to suit your temperament, that's great too. Trust yourself.

Regardless of the path you choose, I do suggest setting a regular schedule to work on expanding your abundance. When there are thousands of possible directions your mind can be pulled in each day, it's too easy to let this work fall by the wayside. Honor and love yourself enough to make this work a priority in your life.

BEFORE YOU BEGIN:

- Read this book at least once in its entirety and (ideally) complete the Your Next Steps actions at the end of each chapter.
- Reread any chapters or sections that felt particularly powerful to you.
- Write your intentions (at least your financial intentions, but ideally all of them) and date them. Each time you update your intentions, save a new copy with the current date.

SUGGESTED ABUNDANCE SESSIONS

Session One

Find a quiet place to be alone. Turn off your phone and Internet. If you like, light a candle and play some soft music. Find your center, and relax.

Call upon your unseen friends to guide and assist you during this session. Say something like:

> *Higher self, soul, counselors, angels, and other beings of love and light, help me to create an abundant life. Assist me in recognizing the beliefs, patterns, thoughts, and feelings that limit my abundance, and help me to change what stands in my way. Thank you.*

Pretend that you have stepped five or ten years into the future. Read your abundance intentions, *feeling* and *knowing* that every single one of them has come true. Think about how much your life has changed since you wrote them. Feel grateful.

If you have any beliefs from previous chapters that you tested for (or otherwise know are yours) that you haven't changed, change up to ten beliefs now.

Do the One-Minute Manifestor Technique from Chapter Ten for one of your intentions of abundance.

Revisit Chapter Six. Of the Abundance Stoppers listed in that chapter (fear, doubt, victimhood, self-pity, entitlement, envy, and guilt) which presents the biggest challenge for you? Write about your pattern of allowing this Abundance Stopper, and how you will handle it the next time it rears its ugly head.

Find support in your newly-created, abundant reality. Who can you turn to with questions, ideas, excitement for all of the new abundances manifesting and any challenges that may come up along the way? If you don't have people in your life right now to support you, find them elsewhere.[1]

Thank your unseen friends for the assistance they've given you throughout this session, and for the ongoing assistance they will provide. Say something like:

> *Higher self, soul, counselors, angels, and other beings of love and light, thank you for helping me to create an abundant life. Please continue to assist me in recognizing the beliefs, patterns, thoughts, and feelings that limit my abundance, and continue to help me to change what stands in my way. Thank you.*

Session Two

Find a quiet place to be alone. Turn off your phone and Internet. If you like, light a candle and play some soft music. Find your center, and relax.

Call upon your unseen friends to guide and assist you during this session. Say something like:

> *Higher self, soul, counselors, angels, and other beings of love and light, help me to create an abundant life. Assist me in recognizing the beliefs, patterns, thoughts, and feelings that limit my abundance, and help me to change what stands in my way. Thank you.*

Read your Commitment to Abundance (from Chapter Three). Recommit yourself to your abundance and the work you will do to create it.

(1) Consider the fellow creators who have signed up at www.LiveALifeYouLove.com/support.

Visit your child and adolescent selves in meditation. (Ask your higher self to take you to the child self or adolescent self that is most appropriate.) Allow your child and adolescent to fully express their fear, disappointment, guilt, and/or any other emotion around money. Give your child and adolescent selves a money machine (even if you have given them one before). Ask them what they plan to use the money for. Encourage them to spend the money freely, because there is always more where that came from.

Make a note to visit them in meditation again the following day to see how they spent the money. Be excited for them, and for yourself! The more easily money flows for your child and adolescent selves, the more easily money will flow for you.

If you have any beliefs from previous chapters that you tested for (or otherwise know are yours) that you haven't changed, change up to ten beliefs now.

Do the One-Minute Manifestor Technique. (Yes, this will be in every Abundance Session. Come on, it only takes one minute!)

Make note of any signs of abundance you have received. If you can't remember or haven't noticed, revisit Chapter Twelve to remind yourself how a sign might show up. Then set a reminder every day to think about the signs you may have received, and record them.

Thank your unseen friends for the assistance they've given you throughout this session, and for the ongoing assistance they will provide. Say something like:

> *Higher self, soul, counselors, angels, and other beings of love and light, thank you for helping me to create an abundant life. Please continue to assist me in recognizing the beliefs, patterns, thoughts, and feelings that limit my abundance, and continue to help me to change what stands in my way. Thank you.*

Session Three

Find a quiet place to be alone. Turn off your phone and Internet. If you like, light a candle and play some soft music. Find your center, and relax.

Call upon your unseen friends to guide and assist you during this session. Say something like:

> *Higher self, soul, counselors, angels, and other beings of love and light, help me to create an abundant life. Assist me in recognizing the beliefs, patterns, thoughts, and feelings that limit my abundance, and help me to change what stands in my way. Thank you.*

Do the One-Minute Manifestor Technique.

If you have any beliefs from previous chapters that you tested for (or otherwise know are yours) that you haven't changed, change up to ten beliefs now.

Talk to your negative self about your dreams of manifesting money and other forms of abundance. What does it say in response? Write that down, and determine if there are any underlying beliefs associated with your negative self's statements. If so, change them.

Make a list of twenty-five ways your life is already abundant, but which have nothing to do with money. Now choose to let the abundance you already have spread into your financial life.

Do the Abundant Future Self Technique from Chapter Ten.

Thank your unseen friends for the assistance they've given you throughout this session, and for the ongoing assistance they will provide. Say something like:

> *Higher self, soul, counselors, angels, and other beings of love and light, thank you for helping me to create an abundant*

life. Please continue to assist me in recognizing the beliefs, patterns, thoughts, and feelings that limit my abundance, and continue to help me to change what stands in my way. Thank you.

Session Four

Find a quiet place to be alone. Turn off your phone and Internet. If you like, light a candle and play some soft music. Find your center, and relax.

Call upon your unseen friends to guide and assist you during this session. Say something like:

Higher self, soul, counselors, angels, and other beings of love and light, help me to create an abundant life. Assist me in recognizing the beliefs, patterns, thoughts, and feelings that limit my abundance, and help me to change what stands in my way. Thank you.

If you have any beliefs from previous chapters that you tested for (or otherwise know are yours) that you haven't changed, change up to ten beliefs now.

Do the One-Minute Manifestor Technique.

Make note of any signs of abundance you have received.

When you think about who you are in relation to abundance and money, what do you come up with? Do you automatically think, "I am truly abundant. Money comes to me easily and elegantly. I will never have an issue with money again," or something like that? If not, do the image work outlined in Chapter Sixteen.

Thought Police: What thoughts do you continually have (especially around money)? There's no need to catch every thought; simply take your emotional temperature every hour, on the hour, for the next 24 hours. Anytime you don't feel fabulous, ask yourself why. Trace the feelings back to your thoughts. Investigate the underlying beliefs, then change them.

Thank your unseen friends for the assistance they've given you throughout this session, and for the ongoing assistance they will provide. Say something like:

> *Higher self, soul, counselors, angels, and other beings of love and light, thank you for helping me to create an abundant life. Please continue to assist me in recognizing the beliefs, patterns, thoughts, and feelings that limit my abundance, and continue to help me to change what stands in my way. Thank you.*

Session Five

Find a quiet place to be alone. Turn off your phone and Internet. If you like, light a candle and play some soft music. Find your center, and relax.

Call upon your unseen friends to guide and assist you during this session. Say something like:

> *Higher self, soul, counselors, angels, and other beings of love and light, help me to create an abundant life. Assist me in recognizing the beliefs, patterns, thoughts, and feelings that limit my abundance, and help me to change what stands in my way. Thank you.*

If you have any beliefs from previous chapters that you tested for (or otherwise know are yours) that you haven't changed, change up to ten beliefs now.

Do the One-Minute Manifestor Technique.

Revisit chapter Eight and make a list of the Dad and authority figures you had as a child/adolescent. Visit with each of them in meditation and tell them how you felt—the good and the bad. Allow that expression of emotion to heal them, and any issues with abundance.

Make note of any signs of abundance you have received.

Do you love your life? What can you do right now to love it even more? Spend 30-60 minutes doing something you absolutely adore, or schedule the time to do that within the next 72 hours.

Reality Check: How are you doing with the Four Steps to Sustaining the Essence of Abundance?

Thank your unseen friends for the assistance they've given you throughout this session, and for the ongoing assistance they will provide. Say something like:

> *Higher self, soul, counselors, angels, and other beings of love and light, thank you for helping me to create an abundant life. Please continue to assist me in recognizing the beliefs, patterns, thoughts, and feelings that limit my abundance, and continue to help me to change what stands in my way. Thank you.*

Session Six

Find a quiet place to be alone. Turn off your phone and Internet. If you like, light a candle and play some soft music. Find your center, and relax.

Call upon your unseen friends to guide and assist you during this session. Say something like:

> *Higher self, soul, counselors, angels, and other beings of love and light, help me to create an abundant life. Assist me in recognizing the beliefs, patterns, thoughts, and feelings that limit my abundance, and help me to change what stands in my way. Thank you.*

If you have any beliefs from previous chapters that you tested for (or otherwise know are yours) that you haven't changed, change up to ten beliefs now.

Do the One-Minute Manifestor Technique.

Write about what your life will be like when money is no longer an issue. What will you do differently? What choices will you make?

In meditation, visit the younger adult selves who had the most challenges regarding money and abundance. Assuming you worked with them at the end of Chapter Seven, go back and find out how their lives have changed since you gave them a reality where all their dreams came true. (If you haven't done that work, do it now. Then, revisit your younger adult selves in a day or so.)

On a scale of 1 to 10, how happy do you stay throughout your days? If less than a ten out of ten, how could you be happier? If you're not sure, you may want to revisit Chapter Thirteen.

Thank your unseen friends for the assistance they've given you throughout this session, and for the ongoing assistance they will provide. Say something like:

> *Higher self, soul, counselors, angels, and other beings of love and light, thank you for helping me to create an abundant life. Please continue to assist me in recognizing the beliefs, patterns, thoughts, and feelings that limit my abundance, and continue to help me to change what stands in my way. Thank you.*

Session Seven

Find a quiet place to be alone. Turn off your phone and Internet. If you like, light a candle and play some soft music. Find your center, and relax.

Call upon your unseen friends to guide and assist you during this session. Say something like:

> *Higher self, soul, counselors, angels, and other beings of love and light, help me to create an abundant life. Assist me in recognizing the beliefs, patterns, thoughts, and feelings that limit my abundance, and help me to change what stands in my way. Thank you.*

If you have any beliefs from previous chapters that you tested for (or otherwise know are yours) that you haven't changed, change up to ten beliefs now.

Do the One-Minute Manifestor Technique.

Go shopping (in a store or online). While you shop, do the I Can Afford Everything Here Technique.

Meditate with your future self—the one who is most abundant and happy. Ask for his or her advice in maintaining an abundant resonance.

How grateful are you? Do you count your blessings hourly? Daily? Weekly? Less often? Take some time right now to make a list of twenty-five things you are grateful for (including monetary items).

Thank your unseen friends for the assistance they've given you throughout this session, and for the ongoing assistance they will provide. Say something like:

> *Higher self, soul, counselors, angels, and other beings of love and light, thank you for helping me to create an abundant life. Please continue to assist me in recognizing the beliefs, patterns, thoughts, and feelings that limit my abundance, and continue to help me to change what stands in my way. Thank you.*

Obviously, these sessions are only suggestions to get you started on your own abundance practices. Do what feels good to you, but don't ignore the basic seven steps to *The Map*:

1. Know you are divine, and thereby have been gifted with the ability to create your reality.
2. Get clear on your desires.
3. Flow energy toward what you want, and stop flowing energy toward what you don't want.
4. Take action in the world.
5. Look for signs that these changes in your energy are showing up in your reality.
6. Stay in gratitude and joy as much as humanly possible.
7. Ask for help from your unseen friends.

WHAT TO DO NEXT

Keep doing the work, my friend, keep doing the work. There are people out there who want to be the exception to "we create it all"—but there are no exceptions. It always works, and there is *always* a reason for every creation. You may need help finding those answers, but the answers are there.

So, what do you do next? Have fun with your life! Have as much fun as you can, every day, while you are creating your dream.

And, before this book ends, I want you to know …

I'M GRATEFUL FOR YOU

It is my greatest joy to teach others about conscious creation, and get the word out about how this whole creation thing actually works. I know how exciting it is to watch your life change right before your eyes, as if by magic—and the next most exciting thing is watching others' lives change as they work the same magic.

Thank you for reading, my fellow creator. I wish you all the abundance in the world. It's there, just waiting for you to allow it in.

With all my love,

PS: Sharing your successes not only improves your ability to create (because by sharing it you make it more real), it inspires others and fills them with hope to create their own successes. Share your creations at www.LiveALifeYouLove.com/inspire.

AFTERWORD

A Note from Boni

It is my passion and joy to teach others how to consciously create a joyful, abundant life.

If you enjoyed this book or it proves useful to you, I'd be most grateful if you would let me know.

I'd truly appreciate it if you'd review this book on Amazon, Barnes & Noble, or wherever you purchased it. Reviews do matter to an author—I read them all!—and to readers. It would be a great honor for me to receive a review from you.

If you'd like to reach me personally, e-mail me at BoniLonnsburry@LiveALifeYouLove.com.

Thank you for reading!

APPENDIX A

In Case of Financial Emergency—Read This!

"If you are experiencing an ebb, with more money going out than coming in, don't panic. Do not lose confidence in yourself or think that somehow you have failed. The challenge of an ebb state is to believe in your future prosperity."

~ SANAYA ROMAN

There is nothing scarier than being afraid you won't survive. The next scariest thing to facing death itself is being afraid you won't survive *financially*—being petrified you will lose everything you own, and end up homeless, jobless, moneyless, and hopeless.

I have felt this kind of panic, desperation, and despair. It's not fun. In fact, it's quite painful. And the true tragedy is, that those very feelings of sadness, hopelessness, fear, and panic will draw more negative realities to you—which, of course, is exactly what you don't want.

I also know it's possible to turn around even the direst financial circumstances. If you look to our societal icons you'll see many millionaires and billionaires who have lost it all, only to turn around and create it again. There's no reason you can't do exactly the same thing.

But before I go into exactly how to begin to turn your finances around, I want to issue this ...

WARNING

If you are reading this, you are likely in a very bad place.

When you're in a bad place—a place of desperation, despair, hopelessness, and panic—you will be tempted to hop from one thing, to another, to yet another in a blind attempt to dig yourself out of your current mire. You want someone to offer you a magic pill, or fix it for you, or in some way take responsibility for your financial mess. (Yeah, I've been there!)

But, here's the thing: you won't change anything if you keep acting, thinking, and feeling the way you have always acted, thought, and felt.

Do you hear me? *You. Won't. Change. Anything.*

So don't just blow through this. If you want your finances to change, you need to actually do the work, and change the way you act, think, and feel about money. (End of sermon.)

Okay, now that that's over with, let's get those changes happening!

First, as in any emergency, you need to …

Stop the Bleeding

I'm not talking about the financial bleeding (although stopping that might not be a bad idea). No, I'm talking about the *emotional* bleeding. You are likely caught in a mental loop of, "Oh my God, my life is falling apart. I'm in trouble. I am out of money. There is nothing I can do about this."

And you need to *stop* feeling that way.

How? First, remember something that the channeled entity Galexis told me many years ago, "You are guaranteed survival." They went on to explain that no one dies before they're ready.

So if you are on Earth, you are guaranteed to survive until you're ready to depart this planet.

When I was the most panicked financially, remembering this truth took a huge weight from my shoulders. I began to relax.

Once you let that in—that you are guaranteed to survive—I suggest doing a technique to bring yourself back to center emotionally:

1. Find a place to sit quietly, alone.
2. Breathe slowly, in through your nose and out through your mouth, ten times.
3. While you are exhaling, imagine breathing out all of your negative emotions. Breathe out fear, scarcity, lack, struggle, and powerlessness.
4. While you are inhaling, imagine breathing in white, sparkling, cleansing light. Imagine this light entering your body and cleaning every single cell, filling them with choice, love, healing, and hope.

At the end of the ten breaths, you will feel lighter, cleaner, and free to make a different choice.

Then ...

Forgive Yourself

You didn't get here by accident. You created this reality—unconsciously, maybe, but still, you created it. Forgive yourself by saying these words:

"I forgive myself for creating this financial situation."

Yes. It can be that easy.

Next ...

Have a Little Talk With the Powerless Parts of You

You think you are an emotional basket case right now, but the fact is, you are more secure and empowered than you know. However, I'll bet anything there are parts of you who are scared to death—and those parts of you are making you feel much less in control of your destiny than you really are.

What are these "parts"? They are your child self and your adolescent self.

You see, they really don't have a clue. They can't create themselves out of this mess. They don't have the power, skills, or ability to create on their own. I mean, they're just kids! And yet, you unknowingly turn your problems over to them, time and time again.

This is not just an exercise, my friend.

Repeat. *This is not just an exercise.*

These aspects of you are *real*, and they have real impact on your world. These parts of you are terrified. And if you keep asking these terrified aspects of yourself to change your world, guess what you are going to get?

That's right—more terror.

So sit with them. Talk with them. Listen to them. Let them tell you how scared they are about what is happening in your world. Let them cry, scream, rant, and rave. And when they're spent, take them into your arms, and love them.

What? That's it? Love them?

Yeah. That's all they really want. That's all they've ever wanted. Oh, and keep them safe, too. You may want to give them a money tree, or a money machine to help them feel financially secure.

What? How will making them financially secure help me?

Because if the most powerless aspects of you feel safe, you will feel safer. Then, the adult you—who is not nearly as powerless—can step up and take control. What have you possibly got to lose?

And next …

Have a Talk With Your Inner Saboteur (aka Your Negative Self)

There is a part of you that is still beating yourself up over this reality, and that part of you does not have your best interest at heart. That part is what I call your negative self. It lies. It cheats. And it wants your life handed to it on a silver platter. Don't give it what it wants.

How do you stop your negative self?

Just listen. That's it. Just listen to it rant and rave. Your conversation may sound something like this:

You: "I have gotten myself into quite a financial pickle."

NS: "Yeah, I see that, Einstein."

You: "I'm not sure what to do, but I think I can turn this around."

NS: "Seriously? What kind of weed have you been smoking?"

You: "No, I think I can. I have come to realize we create our own reality."

NS: "Dude, you are sicker than I thought. Not only are you totally hopeless at creating money, you actually believe that crap!"

You: "Well, a lot of people have been creating amazing things."

NS: "Yeah, and I have a bridge in Brooklyn I wanna sell ya. Face it kid, you're washed up. You gave success a shot, but now it's time to face up to what you are, what you always have been, and what you always will be: a failure."

You: "Are you finished?"

NS: "No, not really. Since you brought this up, I wanna tell you that you'd better stop this airy-fairy dreaming stuff. Life is hard work, and then more hard work. Get used to it."

You: "Is that all?"

NS: No, God damn it! You need to wake up here, kid. Face the facts. All this head-in-the-clouds stuff has gotten you nowhere. No-where! So stop this crap, and face it: you're a loser."

You: "Are you done yet?"

NS: "Stop pushing me kid. There is *no* hope for you. Got it? *None.*"

You: "Now are you done?"

NS: "No. You should also know that those jeans look stupid on you. "

You: "Is that it?"

NS: "Yeah … for now."

And that is when you call upon your unseen friends to come and escort your negative self away for healing.

After that, breathe a sigh of relief. A huge burden has been lifted from you. Now, you're free to …

Get Real

Now that you have a little bit of emotional balance back, you can also gain some perspective. Remind yourself that:

1. You are in a tough spot short term.
2. Everything will change.
3. You can have total impact over what that change is.
4. You are unconditionally loved and supported.
5. What really matters isn't money.
6. If you have to let go of everything you have today and start tomorrow with a clean slate, you could create an amazingly abundant, love-filled, and beautiful life—if you choose to do so.
7. Letting go, at least energetically—as opposed to hanging on to where you are—may be the shortest path to creating that amazing life.

Now, take a few more deep breaths, because it's time to …

Take Your Power Back

If you've done what I've outlined above, you are already in a different place than you were before you started this "emergency" work. Like other "emergency response" work, this is meant to stabilize you, and get you back to the starting line, not guide you through your recovery.

In other words, you still have to do the real work of creating your reality:

1. Know you are divine, and thereby have been gifted with the ability to create your reality.
2. Get clear on your desires.
3. Flow energy toward what you want, and stop flowing energy toward what you don't want.
4. Take action in the world.
5. Look for signs that these changes in your energy are showing up in your reality.
6. Stay in gratitude and joy as much as humanly possible.
7. Ask for help from your unseen friends.

The Map for that has already been made—and it's right here in this book! Good luck my friend (not that you need it, insanely powerful divine creator that you are)!

APPENDIX B

How to Test for Beliefs

"Our bodies can talk. And they don't lie."
~ UWE ALBRECHT

For most people, the most challenging aspect of changing beliefs is determining which beliefs need changing. Of course, one way to determine your beliefs is to observe your reality and work backwards, asking: "What would someone have to believe in order to have created this reality?"

But even then, it's great to be able to determine that you actually hold the belief you think you hold, and then to test again, after you've changed the belief, to make certain it is indeed different.

I really like applied kinesiology, as a way to determine the beliefs you hold in your subconscious mind.

WHAT IS APPLIED KINESIOLOGY?

Applied kinesiology is sometimes called "muscle testing." It allows the body to indicate a true or false response when presented with a statement.

(Note: This does not indicate whether something is true or false for others or in the world—only whether it is predominantly true or false in your subconscious mind.)

The reason that applied kinesiology works is that the body is essentially an electrical circuit. Energy is always flowing within that circuitry.

When your energy is flowing smoothly, your body works the way it is supposed to. When something blocks the energy from flowing, your body doesn't work as well.

What causes the blockage? Anything that is untrue for you will cause an energy blockage. This is how we can use applied kinesiology to indicate whether we believe something or not.

This method works very well if you are centered and calm and believe it will work.

If you suspect you might not let this work, before anything, change these beliefs:

- APPLIED KINESIOLOGY WILL NOT WORK FOR ME TO DETERMINE MY BELIEFS.
- IT IS NOT SAFE TO USE APPLIED KINESIOLOGY TO DETERMINE MY BELIEFS.

When you've changed those beliefs, you're ready to learn …

THE SWAY TEST

The Sway Test is an easy way to test for beliefs, and unlike other forms of applied kinesiology, you don't need another person to assist you in the testing.

It may take some practice to become comfortable with this method, but once you do, it's fun and can be amazingly accurate.

How to Use The Sway Test to Determine Your Beliefs

1. Find a quiet place where you won't be disturbed.

2. Remove your shoes.

3. Stand up straight, with your feet shoulder width apart.

4. Become calm and centered. Take a few deep breaths to increase your centeredness.

5. Clear your energy field[(1)] by tapping on your breastbone 10 or so times (with medium pressure). Then tap on your thyroid gland (use the right hand to tap on the left side, your left hand to tap on the right side), 10 or so times (with medium pressure). And then tap on your forehead 10 or so times (with medium pressure).

6. Relax your body. Unlock your knees.

7. Imagine yourself lifting outside of your body, as if you were separate from your body—an observer rather than a participant. Imagine looking down at yourself through the eyes of your higher self.

8. Before you test for beliefs, practice how the true/untrue answers show themselves in your body. Close your eyes and say, "My name is (and say your name)." Notice that your body remains solid and strong. It will not be difficult to stand without swaying.

   Next, with your eyes still closed, say, "My name is (and make up a name or say someone else's name)." You will notice you will lose your balance. Your body will either fall slightly back, or slightly forward, or otherwise become

(1) This energy field clearing technique is from The Team, channeled by Jackie Salvitti. For more information, go to www.ETHealing.com.

wobbly. It does this because the "untruth" of saying your name is a name that isn't yours interferes with the energy flow of your body, causing your body to sway.

9. Repeat this "name game" a few times until you feel good about telling the difference between true and untrue in your body. You can also simply say "yes" or "no" and should have similar results.

10. Now say the belief you suspect you hold, such as "I do not create my entire reality."

11. If you do hold that belief, your body will hold strong and solid. If you do not hold the belief, your body will falter. Basically: strong = yes, wobbly = no.

12. Test for your beliefs. Be sure to always test the negative belief and not the positive one, because often times you hold both beliefs in your subconscious mind. However the positive beliefs are serving you, so no need to change those. Only test ten or so beliefs at one time, taking short breaks between the sets.

13. When you are complete, you have a list of negative beliefs to change into positive beliefs. Use the techniques in Appendix D to do so.

THE ARM LENGTH TEST

An alternative method to easily test for beliefs is the Arm Length Test. This test works similarly to the Sway Test in that if your body shows "yes," which indicates smoothly flowing circuitry, when you bring your arms together in front of you, they will be the same length. If your body shows "no," your arms will appear to be a different length.

How to Use The Arm Length Test to Determine Your Beliefs

1. Find a quiet place where you won't be disturbed.

2. Remove your shoes.

3. Stand up straight, with your feet shoulder width apart.

4. Become calm and centered. Take a few deep breaths to increase your centeredness.

5. Clear your energy field by tapping on your breastbone ten or so times (with medium pressure). Then tap on your thyroid gland (use the right hand to tap on the left side, your left hand to tap on the right side), ten or so times (with medium pressure). And then tap on your forehead ten or so times (with medium pressure).

6. Relax your body—unlock your knees.

7. Imagine yourself pulling back from your body, as if you were separate from your body—an observer rather than participant.

8. With your arms resting loosely at your sides, say "yes," and bring your arms together in front of you. Your thumbs should come together in your middle and be very close, if not exactly, the same length. Bring your arms back to the sides of your body.

"Yes" Arms

9. With your arms resting loosely at your sides, say "no," and bring your arms together in front of you. Your thumbs will no longer be matching, and your arms will appear to be different lengths. Bring your arms back to the sides of your body.

"No" Arms

10. Practice "yes" and "no" a few times.

11. Next practice using the "name game." Say, "My name is (and say your name)." Bring your arms out loosely in front of you. Notice they appear to be the same length. Next, say, "My name is (and make up a name or say someone else's name)." Bring your arms out loosely in front of you. Notice they appear to be different lengths.

12. Repeat this "name game" a few times until you feel good about telling the difference between true and untrue in your body. You can also simply say "yes" or "no" and should have similar results.

13. Now say the belief you suspect you hold, such as "I do not create my entire reality," and bring your arms together loosely in front of you. If you do hold that belief, arms will appear the same length. If you do not hold that belief your arms will appear to be different lengths. Basically: equal length = yes, different length = no.

14. Test for your beliefs. Be sure to always test the negative belief and not the positive one, because often times you hold both beliefs in your subconscious mind. However the positive beliefs are serving you, so no need to change those. Only test ten or so beliefs at one time, taking short breaks between the sets.

When you're complete, you will have a list of negative beliefs to change into positive beliefs. Use the techniques in Appendix D to do so.

MORE WAYS TO DETERMINE BELIEFS

I suggest using these applied kinesiology methods along with the other methods of determining beliefs:

1. Asking yourself if your reality reflects the belief.
2. Asking yourself whether the belief feels accurate to you in your gut.
3. Asking your child, adolescent, and young adult selves about their beliefs.

While there's no harm in changing a belief you don't really hold, there's also no benefit to it. You only have so many hours in a day, and you may as well use them effectively.

This test may not work for everyone. Why? Because some people really want to control and don't feel safe letting their body take over for a bit. That your safety can be threatened is of course a belief, and as always, beliefs can be changed. The more you practice these methods, the better they'll work for you.

If you don't prefer this type of testing (after you've changed the beliefs about applied kinesiology in Chapter Fifteen), use the other methods of determining your beliefs, covered in more detail in *The Map—To Our Responsive Universe, Where Dreams Really Do Come True!*

APPENDIX C

Beliefs: Positive & Negative

"Most beings in your physical world are not seeking. Most have adopted beliefs that were present around them on the day that they were born upon this earth. And most physical beings have done no real searching or thinking on their own. And so, as they do not search, it is not surprising that they do not find."

~ ABRAHAM

There are many negative beliefs stated throughout this book. In this Appendix, I have included one possible positive belief for each.

Please remember these beliefs are merely suggestions. If the positive (or negative) belief doesn't resonate with you, feel free to change the wording so that it's accurate for you. Also, these beliefs are not all-inclusive. Use them as a springboard to find your exact beliefs.

BELIEFS FROM CHAPTER ONE

- ~~MONEY MAKES THE WORLD GO ROUND.~~
  ENERGY MAKES THE WORLD GO ROUND.

- ~~MONEY IS DIFFICULT TO COME BY.~~
  MONEY IS EASY TO COME BY.

- ~~MONEY IS IN LIMITED SUPPLY.~~
  MONEY IS IN UNLIMITED SUPPLY.

- ~~A VERY SMALL PERCENTAGE OF PEOPLE HAVE MORE THAN ENOUGH MONEY.~~
  A VERY SMALL PERCENTAGE OF PEOPLE HAVE THE ABILITY TO CREATE MONEY.

- ~~THE RICH GET RICHER AND THE POOR GET POORER.~~
  THE CONSCIOUS CREATORS GET RICHER AND THE UNCONSCIOUS CREATORS GET POORER.

- ~~MONEY IS NECESSARY TO SURVIVE.~~
  WILL IS NECESSARY TO SURVIVE.

- ~~I CREATE MY OWN REALITY, BUT MONEY IS THE EXCEPTION.~~
  I CREATE MY OWN REALITY, AND MONEY IS THE PROOF.

BELIEFS FROM CHAPTER FOUR

- ~~I DON'T KNOW WHAT MY MEANINGFUL WORK WOULD BE.~~
  I WILL DISCOVER WHAT MY MEANINGFUL WORK WILL BE.

- ~~I DON'T HAVE A GENIUS TO BE EXPRESSED.~~
  EVERYONE HAS A GENIUS TO BE EXPRESSED.

- ~~I CAN'T FIND MY GIFTS, TALENTS, AND STRENGTHS.~~
  I CAN DISCOVER MY GIFTS, TALENTS, AND STRENGTHS.

- ~~I CAN'T MAKE ENOUGH MONEY DOING WHAT I TRULY LOVE.~~
  I CAN MAKE ENOUGH MONEY DOING WHAT I TRULY LOVE.

- ~~I CAN'T CREATE WORK THAT IS IN ALIGNMENT WITH MY TEMPERAMENT.~~
  I CAN CREATE WORK THAT IS IN ALIGNMENT WITH MY TEMPERAMENT.

- ~~I CAN'T CREATE WORKING WITH PEOPLE I LOVE.~~
  I CAN CREATE WORKING WITH PEOPLE I LOVE.

- ~~I CAN'T CREATE MY WORK BEING MY DREAM.~~
  I CAN CREATE MY WORK BEING MY DREAM.

- ~~IT'S A DOG-EAT-DOG WORLD OUT THERE.~~
  IT'S A LOVING AND BENEVOLENT WORLD OUT THERE.

- ~~MOST ENTREPRENEURS FAIL, THEREFORE THE ODDS ARE STACKED AGAINST ME.~~
  MOST ENTREPRENEURS DON'T KNOW HOW TO CREATE, THEREFORE THE ODDS ARE STACKED IN MY FAVOR.

- ~~SUCCESS IS DIFFICULT.~~
  SUCCESS IS EASY.

- ~~IN ORDER TO HAVE THE WORK I DESIRE I HAVE TO GIVE UP SOME THINGS I VALUE.~~
  IN ORDER TO HAVE THE WORK I DESIRE I HAVE TO GIVE UP MY POWERLESSNESS.

- ~~WORK IS HARD, BORING, AND THANKLESS.~~
  WORK IS FUN, EXCITING, AND PROFITABLE.

- ~~I DON'T HAVE THE MONEY TO START MY OWN BUSINESS.~~
  I CAN CREATE THE MONEY TO START MY OWN BUSINESS.

- ~~I AM RESPONSIBLE FOR [NAME] IN EVERY WAY.~~
  I AM RESPONSIBLE FOR MY REALITY IN EVERY WAY.

- ~~IF [NAME] CHOOSES TO SUFFER, I MUST SUFFER ALONG WITH THEM.~~
  IF [NAME] CHOOSES TO SUFFER, I WILL INSPIRE BY MY CREATIONS.

- ~~[NAME] CANNOT SURVIVE UNLESS I TAKE RESPONSIBILITY FOR THEM.~~
  [NAME] CAN THRIVE BY TAKING RESPONSIBILITY FOR HIM/HERSELF.

- ~~[NAME] IS YOUNG, INNOCENT, AND VULNERABLE.~~
  [NAME] IS ADULT, CAPABLE, AND POWERFUL.

- ~~[NAME] IS UNABLE TO BE SUCCESSFUL IN THE WORLD WITHOUT HELP.~~
  [NAME] IS FULLY ABLE TO BE SUCCESSFUL IN THE WORLD BY HIM/HERSELF.

- ~~[NAME] HAS DEBILITATING ISSUES THAT PREVENT THEIR SUCCESS.~~
  [NAME] HAS INTERESTING CHALLENGES THAT THEY CAN OVERCOME.

- ~~I CAN'T LOVE [NAME] WITHOUT BEING PULLED INTO NEGATIVE EMOTIONS SUCH AS GUILT, SHAME, AND FAILURE.~~
  I CAN LOVE [NAME] WITHOUT BEING PULLED INTO NEGATIVE EMOTIONS SUCH AS GUILT, SHAME, AND FAILURE.

- ~~IF I DON'T GIVE [NAME] WHAT THEY WANT, THEN I OWE THEM.~~
  IF I DON'T GIVE [NAME] WHAT THEY WANT, THEY'LL CREATE IT THEMSELVES.

- ~~IF I DON'T HELP [NAME], THEY WON'T LOVE ME ANYMORE.~~
  IF I DON'T ENABLE [NAME], THEY WILL LEARN TO LOVE THEMSELVES.

- ~~IT IS EMPOWERING TO THOSE I LOVE TO FIX THEIR PROBLEMS.~~
  IT IS ENABLING TO THOSE I LOVE TO FIX THEIR PROBLEMS.

- ~~BY FIXING OTHERS' PROBLEMS, I PROVE MY OWN WORTH.~~
  BY ALLOWING OTHERS TO SOLVE THEIR OWN PROBLEMS, I SHOW THEM MY LOVE.

- ~~I LIVE IN A UNIVERSE WITH A LIMITED AMOUNT OF ABUNDANCE.~~
  I LIVE IN A UNIVERSE WITH AN UNLIMITED AMOUNT OF ABUNDANCE.

- ~~THERE IS A LIMITED AMOUNT OF MONEY ON THIS PLANET.~~
  THERE IS AN UNLIMITED AMOUNT OF MONEY ON THIS PLANET.

- ~~THERE ISN'T ENOUGH MONEY TO GO AROUND.~~
  THERE IS MORE THAN ENOUGH MONEY TO GO AROUND.

- ~~IF I TAKE MORE THAN JUST ENOUGH MONEY, OTHERS WILL SUFFER.~~
  IF I CREATE AN ABUNDANCE OF MONEY, OTHERS WILL BENEFIT.

- ~~IT IS GREEDY TO WANT AN ABUNDANCE OF MONEY.~~
  IT IS HEALTHY TO WANT AN ABUNDANCE OF MONEY.

- ~~IT IS UNSPIRITUAL TO WANT AN ABUNDANCE OF MONEY.~~
  IT IS SPIRITUAL TO UNDERSTAND MONEY IS ENERGY.

- ~~A GOOD PERSON GIVES AWAY HIS/HER MONEY.~~
  A WISE PERSON DOES WHAT FEELS RIGHT WITH HIS/HER MONEY.

- ~~IT IS SELFISH TO WANT LOTS OF MONEY FOR MYSELF.~~
  IT IS SELF-LOVING TO WANT LOTS OF MONEY FOR MYSELF.

- ~~IF I DON'T HELP THE NEEDY, THEY WON'T BE HELPED.~~
  IF I DON'T HELP THE NEEDY, THEY CAN LEARN TO HELP THEMSELVES.

- ~~THE BEST WAY TO CREATE CHANGE IS THROUGH FINANCIAL SUPPORT.~~
  THE BEST WAY TO CREATE CHANGE IS DREAMING A NEW WORLD.

- ~~I AM POWERLESS TO CHANGE THE WORLD AROUND ME EXCEPT THROUGH MONEY.~~
  I AM POWERFUL ENOUGH TO CHANGE THE WORLD AROUND ME BY CREATING IT DIFFERENTLY.

- ~~THOSE I LOVE AND CARE ABOUT ARE POWERLESS TO CHANGE THEIR CIRCUMSTANCES WITHOUT ADDITIONAL RESOURCES.~~
  THOSE I LOVE AND CARE ABOUT ARE POWERFUL ENOUGH TO CHANGE THEIR CIRCUMSTANCES WITHOUT ADDITIONAL RESOURCES.

- ~~I DON'T DESERVE ABUNDANCE.~~
  I DO DESERVE ABUNDANCE.

- ~~I DON'T DESERVE A LIFE I LOVE.~~
  I DO DESERVE A LIFE I LOVE.

- ~~I AM NOT WORTHY OF UNLIMITED ABUNDANCE.~~
  I AM WORTHY OF UNLIMITED ABUNDANCE.

- ~~I AM NOT WORTHY OF A LIFE I LOVE.~~
  I AM WORTHY OF A LIFE I LOVE.

BELIEFS FROM CHAPTER FIVE

- ~~I DON'T DESERVE TO BE RICH.~~
  I DO DESERVE TO BE RICH.

- ~~I DON'T DESERVE TO BE ABUNDANT.~~
  I DO DESERVE TO BE ABUNDANT.

- ~~I AM NOT GOOD ENOUGH TO BE WEALTHY.~~
  I AM PLENTY GOOD ENOUGH TO BE WEALTHY.

- ~~MONEY IN THIS WORLD IS LIMITED.~~
  MONEY IN THIS WORLD IS UNLIMITED.

- ~~IF I CREATE MORE MONEY FOR MYSELF, SOMEONE WILL GO WITHOUT.~~
  IF I CREATE MORE MONEY FOR MYSELF, THERE WILL BE MORE MONEY IN THE WORLD.

- ~~IT IS WRONG TO DESIRE MONEY.~~
  IT IS HUMAN TO DESIRE MONEY.

- ~~MONEY IS BAD.~~
  MONEY IS ENERGY.

- ~~SPIRITUAL PEOPLE DO NOT DESIRE MONEY.~~
  SPIRITUAL PEOPLE DO DESIRE MONEY.

- ~~GOOD PEOPLE DO NOT SEEK TO BE WEALTHY.~~
  GOOD PEOPLE DO SEEK TO BE WEALTHY.

- ~~I CAN'T TRUST MYSELF TO CREATE MONEY WHEN I NEED OR WANT IT.~~
  I CAN TRUST MYSELF TO CREATE MONEY WHEN I NEED OR WANT IT.

- ~~I CAN'T TRUST MONEY TO COME IN EXACTLY WHEN I NEED OR WANT IT.~~
  I CAN TRUST MONEY TO COME IN EXACTLY WHEN I NEED OR WANT IT.

- I ~~HAVE TO BE UBER-PREPARED IN CASE OF EMERGENCY.~~
  I HAVE UNLIMITED INNER AND OUTER RESOURCES IN CASE OF EMERGENCY.

- ~~JUST WHEN SOME THINGS GO RIGHT, THE OTHER SHOE WILL DROP.~~
  JUST WHEN THINGS GO RIGHT, EVERYTHING ELSE WILL FALL INTO PLACE.

- ~~I MAY BE ABLE TO MANIFEST MONEY SOMETIMES, BUT NOT ALL THE TIME.~~
  I MAY NOT BE ABLE TO MANIFEST ALL THE TIME, BUT OFTEN ENOUGH TO CREATE ABUNDANCE.

- ~~I AM NOT WORTHY.~~
  I AM WORTHY.

- ~~MY WORTH IS BASED ON WHAT I HAVE, NOT WHO I AM.~~
  MY WORTH IS BASED ON WHO I AM, NOT WHAT I HAVE.

- ~~I AM NOT VALUABLE.~~
  I AM VALUABLE.

- ~~I AM A FAILURE.~~
  I AM A SUCCESS.

- ~~I AM A DISAPPOINTMENT.~~
  I AM AN INSPIRATION.

- ~~I NEED MONEY AND SUCCESS TO PROVE I AM WORTHY.~~
  I NEED TO KNOW I'M ALIVE TO KNOW I AM WORTHY.

- ~~I AM INHERENTLY FLAWED, AND THEREFORE UNABLE TO CREATE ABUNDANCE.~~
  I AM INHERENTLY DIVINE, AND THEREFORE FULLY ABLE TO CREATE ABUNDANCE.

- ~~I MUST BE SUCCESSFUL IN ORDER TO PROVE I AM AS GOOD AS [NAME].~~
  I MUST BE ALIVE IN ORDER TO KNOW I AM AS GOOD AS ANYONE.

- ~~I AM NOT GOOD ENOUGH.~~
  I AM GOOD ENOUGH.

- ~~THE UNIVERSE IS NOT ABUNDANT.~~
  THE UNIVERSE IS TOTALLY ABUNDANT.

- ~~MONEY CAN COME TO ME ONLY IN VERY LIMITED WAYS.~~
  MONEY WILL COME TO ME IN INFINITE AND UNLIMITED WAYS.

- ~~THE ONLY WAY I CAN BECOME EXTREMELY WEALTHY IS BY WINNING THE LOTTERY.~~
  THE ONLY WAY I CAN BECOME EXTREMELY WEALTHY IS BY CHANGING MY ESSENCE.

- ~~MONEY IS DIFFICULT TO CREATE.~~
  MONEY IS EASY TO CREATE.

- ~~I AM NOT CAPABLE OF CREATING MONEY OUT OF THIN AIR.~~
  I AM CAPABLE OF CREATING MONEY OUT OF THIN AIR.

- ~~I AM NOT SMART ENOUGH TO CREATE MONEY OTHER THAN BY WINNING IT.~~
  I AM SMART ENOUGH TO CREATE MONEY IN THOUSANDS OF WAYS.

- ~~YOU HAVE TO BE SMART OR LUCKY TO CREATE MONEY.~~
  YOU HAVE TO BE WILLING AND CONSCIOUS TO CREATE MONEY.

- ~~I NEED TO RECEIVE MONEY FROM SOMEONE OR SOMETHING OUTSIDE MYSELF, BECAUSE I CAN'T CREATE IT ON MY OWN.~~
  I CAN RECEIVE MONEY FROM ANYONE OR ANYTHING, BECAUSE THE POWER TO CREATE MONEY ISN'T OUTSIDE ME IT'S WITHIN ME.

- ~~MORE MONEY CAN ONLY COME TO ME BY __________ [GETTING A RAISE OR PROMOTION AT WORK, GETTING A NEW JOB, IF I MOVE AWAY, IF MY SPOUSE MAKES IT, BY AN INHERITANCE, FROM A COURT SETTLEMENT ETC.].~~
  MORE MONEY CAN COME TO ME IN UNLIMITED NUMBERS OF WAYS.

- ~~I'LL CREATE AN ABUNDANT LIFE WHEN I'M __________ [OLDER, WISER, LOSE WEIGHT, GET MARRIED, FINISH MY EDUCATION, MY PARENTS DON'T NEED ME AS MUCH, MY SPOUSE WHATEVER, MY KIDS GROW UP, ETC.]~~
  I'LL CREATE AN ABUNDANT LIFE WHEN I'M WILLING.

- ~~I CAN ONLY CREATE WEALTH THROUGH MY JOB.~~
  I CAN CREATE WEALTH THROUGH UNLIMITED AVENUES.

- ~~I CAN'T LOVE WHAT I DO AND BE WELL PAID AT THE SAME TIME.~~
  I CAN LOVE WHAT I DO AND BE WELL-PAID AT THE SAME TIME.

- ~~IT IS DIFFICULT TO FIND A JOB I ADORE.~~
  IT IS EASY TO FIND A JOB I ADORE.

- ~~I CAN'T LEAVE A PROFESSION IN WHICH I'VE INVESTED SO MUCH TIME AND/OR EDUCATION.~~
  I CAN LEAVE A PROFESSION IN WHICH I'VE INVESTED SO MUCH TIME AND/OR EDUCATION.

- ~~I DON'T KNOW WHAT MY PASSION IS.~~
  I CAN KNOW WHAT MY PASSION IS (AND I WILL).

- ~~I DON'T KNOW HOW TO CREATE A JOB I LOVE AND ABUNDANCE TOO.~~
  I DO KNOW HOW TO CREATE A JOB I LOVE AND ABUNDANCE TOO.

- ~~IF I'M GRATEFUL FOR SOMETHING I CLOSE THE DOOR TO RECEIVING MORE.~~
  IF I'M GRATEFUL FOR SOMETHING I OPEN THE DOOR TO RECEIVING MORE.

BELIEFS FROM CHAPTER SIX

- ~~THE CONCEPT OF REALITY CREATION IS A FANTASY.~~
  THE CONCEPT OF REALITY CREATION IS TRUTH.

- ~~I CAN'T CREATE MY OWN REALITY.~~
  I CAN CREATE MY OWN REALITY.

- ~~IF I MIS-CREATE SOMETHING IN MY REALITY, I CAN'T FIX IT.~~
  IF I MIS-CREATE SOMETHING IN MY REALITY, I CAN CREATE AGAIN.

- ~~I AM NOT POWERFUL ENOUGH TO CREATE A LIFE I LOVE.~~
  I AM POWERFUL ENOUGH TO CREATE A LIFE I LOVE.

- ~~I CAN'T HANDLE TAKING RESPONSIBILITY FOR MY ENTIRE LIFE.~~
  I CAN HANDLE TAKING RESPONSIBILITY FOR MY ENTIRE LIFE.

- ~~IF I CREATE ABUNDANCE I'LL JUST LOSE IT ALL.~~
  IF I CREATE ABUNDANCE I'LL CREATE MORE ABUNDANCE.

- ~~I AM ALWAYS IN DANGER.~~
  I AM ALWAYS CREATING SAFETY.

- ~~I CAN'T CONTROL UNWANTED THINGS FROM HAPPENING.~~
  I CAN CREATE THE DESIRED THINGS TO HAPPEN.

- ~~I DON'T FULLY CREATE MY OWN SAFETY AND SECURITY.~~
  I DO FULLY CREATE MY OWN SAFETY AND SECURITY.

- ~~MONEY IS NOT ABUNDANT IN MY LIFE~~.
  MONEY IS TOTALLY ABUNDANT IN MY LIFE.

- ~~MY NEEDS MIGHT NOT BE MET.~~
  MY NEEDS ARE ALWAYS MET.

- ~~I AM NOT FREE AND ABLE TO CREATE ANYTHING AND EVERYTHING I WANT.~~
  I AM FULLY FREE AND ABLE TO CREATE ANYTHING AND EVERYTHING I WANT.

- ~~I AM NOT IN CONTROL OF MY FINANCIAL FREEDOM.~~
  I AM IN CONTROL OF MY FINANCIAL FREEDOM.

- ~~I AM NOT ABLE TO CREATE MY OWN REALITY.~~
  I AM ABLE TO CREATE MY OWN REALITY.

- ~~MONEY IS HARD TO CREATE.~~
  MONEY IS EASY TO CREATE.

- ~~THERE IS ALWAYS A PRICE TO PAY FOR MONEY.~~
  THERE IS ALWAYS AN ENERGY TO GIVE FOR MONEY.

- ~~MY CHILDREN NEED MY SUPPORT TO SURVIVE (OR HEAL, OR BE SAFE, OR GROW).~~
  MY CHILDREN WILL CREATE WHAT THEY NEED TO SURVIVE (OR HEAL, OR BE SAFE, OR GROW).

- ~~I CANNOT CREATE ENOUGH MONEY FOR BOTH MY NEEDS AND MY CHILDREN'S NEEDS.~~
  I CAN CREATE ENOUGH MONEY FOR BOTH MY NEEDS AND MY CHILDREN'S NEEDS.

- ~~MY CHILDREN ARE KEEPING ME FROM ABUNDANCE.~~
  MY ENERGY IS CREATING A REALITY WITH ABUNDANCE.

- ~~IT IS ALWAYS UNLOVING TO SAY "NO" TO MY CHILD.~~
  IT IS SOMETIMES MOST LOVING TO SAY "NO" TO MY CHILD.

- ~~THERE IS A LIMITED AMOUNT OF MONEY AVAILABLE TO ME.~~
  THERE IS AN UNLIMITED AMOUNT OF MONEY AVAILABLE TO ME.

- ~~THERE IS NOT ENOUGH MONEY TO GO AROUND.~~
  THERE IS PLENTY OF MONEY TO GO AROUND.

- ~~THE LACK OF MONEY PREVENTS ME FROM HAVING THE BEST THINGS IN LIFE.~~
  REGARDLESS OF MY LEVEL OF INCOME, I CREATE HAVING THE BEST THINGS IN LIFE.

- ~~I NEVER HAVE ENOUGH MONEY.~~
  I ALWAYS HAVE ENOUGH MONEY.

- ~~I WILL NEVER HAVE ENOUGH MONEY.~~
  I WILL ALWAYS HAVE ENOUGH MONEY.

- ~~I NEVER HAVE MORE THAN ENOUGH MONEY.~~
  I ALWAYS HAVE MORE THAN ENOUGH MONEY.

- ~~THE UNIVERSE IS NOT ABUNDANT.~~
  THE UNIVERSE IS TOTALLY ABUNDANT.

- ~~I CAN'T CONTROL WHO SHARES IN MY ABUNDANCE.~~
  I CAN ALWAYS CONTROL WHO SHARES IN MY ABUNDANCE.

- ~~IF YOU HAVE MONEY YOU MUST SHARE IT.~~
  IF YOU HAVE MONEY YOU MUST ENJOY IT.

- ~~IT'S MOST LOVING TO SHARE YOUR ABUNDANCE WITH THOSE WHO NEED IT.~~
  IT'S MOST LOVING TO SHARE YOUR ABUNDANCE WITH ANYONE YOU WANT TO.

- ~~HAVING MONEY CREATES PROBLEMS.~~
  HAVING MONEY CREATES SOLUTIONS.

- ~~PEOPLE WILL DISLIKE ME IF I DON'T SHARE MY MONEY.~~
  PEOPLE WILL LIKE ME WHETHER OR NOT I SHARE MY MONEY.

- ~~I CAN'T BE RESPONSIBLE FOR GREAT SUMS OF MONEY.~~
  I CAN BE RESPONSIBLE FOR GREAT SUMS OF MONEY.

- ~~IF I CREATE A BEAUTIFUL, ABUNDANT LIFE, SOMEONE WILL TAKE IT AWAY.~~
  IF I CREATE A BEAUTIFUL, ABUNDANT LIFE, SOMEONE WILL GIVE ME MORE.

- ~~IF I AM VISIBLE, I'LL LOSE MY PRIVACY.~~
  IF I AM VISIBLE, I'LL KEEP MY PRIVACY.

- ~~IF I AM WEALTHY, PEOPLE WILL BE JEALOUS OF ME.~~
  IF I AM WEALTHY, PEOPLE WILL BE INSPIRED BY ME.

- ~~BEING WEALTHY PUTS ME AT RISK.~~
  BEING WEALTHY PROVIDES ME SECURITY.

- ~~IF I AM WEALTHY, I WILL NO LONGER BELONG.~~
  IF I AM WEALTHY, I WILL STILL BELONG.

- ~~I CANNOT CREATE MY REALITY.~~
  I CAN CREATE MY REALITY.

- ~~THE LAW OF ATTRACTION WORKS SOMETIMES FOR SOME PEOPLE.~~
  THE LAW OF ATTRACTION WORKS EVERY TIME FOR ALL PEOPLE.

- ~~I AM NOT POWERFUL ENOUGH TO CREATE REALLY BIG DREAMS.~~
  I AM POWERFUL ENOUGH TO CREATE REALLY BIG DREAMS.

- ~~THE LAW OF ATTRACTION IS A SILLY FANTASY.~~
  THE LAW OF ATTRACTION IS A PLAIN FACT.

- ~~IF WE REALLY DO CREATE OUR REALITIES, EVERYONE WOULD KNOW ABOUT IT.~~
  WE REALLY DO CREATE OUR REALITIES, EVEN IF EVERYONE DOESN'T KNOW IT.

- ~~YOU ONLY GET SO MUCH GOOD, AND IF YOU STILL WANT MORE YOU'RE BEING GREEDY.~~
  YOU GET AN UNLIMITED AMOUNT OF GOOD, AND THE MORE YOU DREAM THE MORE YOU GET.

- ~~IF LIFE GETS TOO GOOD, SOMEONE WILL TAKE IT AWAY.~~
  WHEN LIFE GETS REALLY GOOD, SOMETHING WILL MAKE IT BETTER.

- ~~I CREATE MY OWN REALITY, EXCEPT WHEN IT COMES TO ______.~~
  I CREATE MY OWN REALITY, ESPECIALLY WHEN IT COMES TO ________.

- ~~THE LAW OF ATTRACTION HAS EXCEPTIONS.~~
  THE LAW OF ATTRACTION APPLIES TO EVERYTHING.

- ~~I DON'T DESERVE TO HAVE EVERYTHING I WANT.~~
  I DO DESERVE TO HAVE EVERYTHING I WANT.

- ~~I MUST CONTROL MY WORLD IN ORDER TO BE SAFE.~~
  I MUST CREATE MY WORLD IN ORDER TO BE SAFE.

- ~~SUCCESS COMES WITH A PRICE.~~
  SUCCESS COMES WITH A REWARD.

- ~~I CAN CREATE THE SUCCESS ITSELF, BUT NOT THE RESULTS OF THAT SUCCESS.~~
  I CAN CREATE THE SUCCESS ITSELF, AS WELL AS THE RESULTS OF THAT SUCCESS.

- ~~I MIGHT LOSE WHAT I HAVE IF I DREAM BIGGER DREAMS.~~
  I COULD KEEP WHAT I HAVE WHEN I CREATE BIGGER DREAMS.

- ~~THE UNKNOWN IS DANGEROUS.~~
  THE UNKNOWN IS SAFE.

- ~~I AM POWERLESS TO CHANGE MY REALITY.~~
  I AM POWERFUL ENOUGH TO CHANGE MY REALITY.

- ~~NOTHING EVER WORKS FOR ME.~~
  EVERYTHING ALWAYS WORKS FOR ME.

- ~~I MESS UP EVERYTHING I TRY.~~
  I SUCCEED AT EVERYTHING I TRY.

- ~~SOMETHING IS WRONG WITH ME.~~
  SOMETHING IS DIVINE IN ME.

- ~~I CAN NEVER HAVE WHAT I WANT.~~
  I CAN ALWAYS HAVE WHAT I REALLY WANT.

- ~~IF SOMETHING CAN GO WRONG, IT WILL.~~
  IF SOMETHING CAN GO RIGHT, IT WILL

- ~~I CAN NEVER GET AHEAD.~~
  I CAN EASILY GET AHEAD.

- ~~I MUST EARN MY WEALTH.~~
  I MUST CREATE MY WEALTH.

- ~~IF YOU WORK AND STRUGGLE LONG ENOUGH YOU WILL RECEIVE ABUNDANCE.~~
  IF YOU FLOW UNOPPOSED ESSENCE LONG ENOUGH YOU WILL RECEIVE ABUNDANCE.

- ~~I AM UNAPPRECIATED.~~
  I AM APPRECIATED.

- ~~I AM UNLOVED.~~
  I AM LOVED.

- ~~MONEY IS HARD TO COME BY.~~
  MONEY IS EASY TO COME BY.

- ~~IF OTHERS I KNOW ARE ABUNDANT THEY SHOULD SHARE THEIR WEALTH WITH ME.~~
  IF OTHERS I KNOW ARE ABUNDANT IT IS SHOWING WEALTH IS COMING CLOSER TO ME.

- ~~IF OTHERS CREATE ABUNDANCE, I DON'T HAVE TO.~~
  IF OTHERS CREATE ABUNDANCE, I AM INSPIRED TO.

- ~~OTHERS CAN CREATE ABUNDANCE, BUT NOT ME.~~
  IF OTHERS CAN CREATE ABUNDANCE, SO CAN I.

- ~~I AM NOT POWERFUL ENOUGH (OR SMART ENOUGH) TO CREATE GREAT WEALTH.~~
  I AM POWERFUL ENOUGH (OR SMART ENOUGH) TO CREATE GREAT WEALTH.

- ~~THE ONLY WAY I'LL GET CLOSE TO GREAT ABUNDANCE IS TO HAVE [NAME] SHARE THEIRS WITH ME.~~
  THE ONLY WAY I'LL GET CLOSE TO GREAT ABUNDANCE IS TO CREATE IT FOR MYSELF.

- ~~I CAN'T HOLD ONTO THE SUCCESS I CREATE.~~
  I CAN HOLD ONTO THE SUCCESS I CREATE.

- ~~I ALWAYS GET SCREWED.~~
  I ALWAYS CREATE MIRACLES.

- ~~PEOPLE TAKE ADVANTAGE OF ME.~~
  PEOPLE SUPPORT AND NURTURE ME.

- ~~I ATTRACT DISHONEST PEOPLE.~~
  I ATTRACT HONEST PEOPLE.

- ~~IF SOMEONE OWES ME MONEY IT'S MY JOB TO GET HIM OR HER TO PAY.~~
  IF SOMEONE OWES ME MONEY IT WILL COME TO ME ONE WAY OR ANOTHER.

- ~~I DON'T DESERVE A SPECTACULAR LIFE.~~
  I DO DESERVE A SPECTACULAR LIFE.

- ~~OTHER PEOPLE CAN HAVE WONDERFUL THINGS, BUT I CAN'T.~~
  OTHER PEOPLE CAN HAVE WONDERFUL THINGS, AND I CAN TOO.

- ~~SOME THINGS ARE BEYOND MY ABILITY TO CREATE.~~
  EVERYTHING IS WITHIN MY ABILITY TO CREATE.

- ~~I DON'T HAVE WHAT IT TAKES TO CREATE __________.~~
  I DO HAVE WHAT IT TAKES TO CREATE __________.

- ~~I AM NOT LOVABLE.~~
  I AM TOTALLY LOVABLE.

- ~~I AM NOT WORTHY OF GREAT SUCCESS.~~
  I AM WORTHY OF GREAT SUCCESS.

- ~~THERE IS A LIMITED AMOUNT OF MONEY AVAILABLE.~~
  THERE IS AN UNLIMITED AMOUNT OF MONEY AVAILABLE.

- ~~I AM RESPONSIBLE FOR [NAME]'S ABUNDANCE.~~
  [NAME] IS RESPONSIBLE FOR [NAME]'S ABUNDANCE.

- ~~I MUST SHOW MY LOVE BY STAYING IN SCARCITY.~~
  I CAN SHOW MY LOVE BY STAYING IN ABUNDANCE.

- ~~[NAME] WON'T LOVE ME IF I AM RICH AND SUCCESSFUL.~~
  [NAME]WILL LOVE ME EVEN IF I AM RICH AND SUCCESSFUL.

- ~~[NAME]WON'T LOVE ME IF I DON'T TAKE CARE OF THEM FINANCIALLY.~~
  [NAME] WILL LOVE ME EVEN IF I ALLOW THEM TO CREATE THEIR ABUNDANCE THEMSELVES.

BELIEFS FROM CHAPTER SEVEN

- ~~I AM A FAILURE.~~
  I AM A SUCCESS.

- ~~I AM FLAWED.~~
  I AM DIVINE.

- ~~I AM POWERLESS.~~
  I AM POWERFUL.

- ~~MONEY CAN COME TO ME FROM ONLY ONE SOURCE.~~
  MONEY CAN COME TO ME FROM UNLIMITED SOURCES.

- ~~I AM NOT RECEIVING MONEY.~~
  I AM RECEIVING ABUNDANCE, AND MORE EVERY DAY.

- ~~I AM NOT IN CONTROL OF WHETHER OR NOT I AM ABUNDANT.~~
  I AM IN CONTROL OF WHETHER OR NOT I AM ABUNDANT.

- ~~[NAME, ENTITY, OR SITUATION] IS IN CONTROL OF WHETHER OR NOT I AM ABUNDANT.~~
  I AM IN CONTROL OF WHETHER OR NOT I AM ABUNDANT.

- ~~I AM NOT GOOD ENOUGH.~~
  I AM GOOD ENOUGH.

- ~~I NEVER SUCCEED.~~
  I ALWAYS SUCCEED.

- ~~I AM UNWORTHY OF SUCCESS.~~
  I AM WORTHY OF SUCCESS.

- ~~I CAN MANIFEST SIGNS, BUT I CAN'T SUSTAIN THE ENERGY.~~
  I CAN MANIFEST SIGNS, AND I CAN SUSTAIN THE ENERGY.

- ~~SOME THINGS REALLY ARE TOO GOOD TO BE TRUE.~~
  NOTHING IS EVER TOO GOOD TO BE TRUE.

BELIEFS FROM CHAPTER EIGHT

- ~~GOD DOESN'T WANT ME TO HAVE MONEY.~~
  GOD WANTS EVERYONE TO HAVE MONEY.

- ~~GOD WANTS US TO SUFFER.~~
  GOD WANTS US TO THRIVE.

- ~~GOD WANTS US TO STRUGGLE.~~
  GOD WANTS US TO HAVE EASE.

- ~~MONEY IS NOT SPIRITUAL.~~
  EVERYTHING IS SPIRITUAL.

- ~~MONEY IS A SIN.~~
  MONEY IS ENERGY.

- ~~MONEY IS EVIL.~~
  MONEY IS NEUTRAL.

- ~~RICH PEOPLE DON'T GO TO HEAVEN.~~
  EVERYONE REUNITES WITH GOD AND GODDESS.

- ~~YOU MUST SELL YOUR SOUL TO BECOME RICH.~~
  YOU MUST CHANGE YOUR ENERGY TO BECOME RICH.

- ~~IT'S NOT SAFE TO BE/SHOW MY TRUE, WHOLE SELF.~~
  IT'S SAFE TO BE/SHOW MY TRUE, WHOLE SELF.

- ~~IT'S NOT SAFE TO BE VISIBLE IN THE WORLD.~~
  IT'S SAFE TO BE VISIBLE IN THE WORLD.

- ~~IT'S UNMANLY TO HONOR/SHOW MY FEMININE SIDE.~~
  IT'S MANLY TO HONOR/SHOW MY FEMININE SIDE.

- ~~IT'S UNFEMININE TO HONOR/SHOW MY MASCULINE SIDE.~~
  IT'S FEMININE TO HONOR/SHOW MY MASCULINE SIDE.

BELIEFS FROM CHAPTER NINE

- ~~IT'S AN UNSAFE WORLD.~~
  IT'S A SAFE WORLD.

- ~~MONEY DOESN'T COME EASILY.~~
  MONEY DOES COME EASILY.

- ~~YOU MUST SACRIFICE IN ORDER TO HAVE MONEY.~~
  YOU MUST BE WILLING IN ORDER TO HAVE MONEY.

- ~~MAKING MONEY IS DANGEROUS WORK.~~
  MAKING MONEY IS FUN AND REWARDING WORK.

- ~~BAD THINGS HAPPEN THAT CAN TAKE AWAY EVERYTHING.~~
  GOOD THINGS HAPPEN THAT CAN MAKE EVERYTHING EVEN BETTER.

- ~~ONCE YOU DO GET AHEAD, SOMETHING AWFUL WILL HAPPEN.~~
  ONCE YOU DO GET AHEAD, YOU CAN RELAX AND ENJOY IT.

- ~~WANTING MONEY MAKES YOU UNHAPPY.~~
  WANTING MONEY MAKES YOU HUMAN.

- ~~THERE IS NOTHING MORE IMPORTANT THAN MONEY.~~
  THERE IS NOTHING MORE IMPORTANT THAN MY CONNECTION WITH THE DIVINE.

- ~~IT IS IMPOSSIBLE FOR EVEN THE MOST POWERFUL PEOPLE TO CONTROL MONEY.~~
  IT IS POSSIBLE FOR ANYONE TO BE IN CONTROL OF THEIR ABUNDANCE.

- ~~THERE IS NEVER, EVER ENOUGH MONEY.~~
  THERE IS ALWAYS MORE THAN ENOUGH MONEY.

- ~~THE DESIRE FOR MONEY MAKES YOU DO BAD THINGS.~~
  THE CREATION OF MONEY ALLOWS YOU TO DO GOOD THINGS.

- ~~MONEY IS RESPONSIBLE FOR RELATIONSHIP DIFFICULTIES.~~
  PEOPLE ARE RESPONSIBLE FOR RELATIONSHIP DIFFICULTIES.

- ~~LIFE IS UNFAIR.~~
  LIFE IS FAIR.

- ~~EVENTUALLY EVERYTHING GOOD GOES AWAY.~~
  EVENTUALLY EVERYTHING GOOD MULTIPLIES EXPONENTIALLY.

- ~~THERE IS NO REAL SECURITY.~~
  I CAN CREATE REAL SECURITY.

- ~~MONEY IS A STRUGGLE.~~
  MONEY IS A JOY.

- ~~YOU CAN'T TRUST ANYTHING.~~
  YOU CAN TRUST SOME THINGS.

Foundational Beliefs

It is not possible/easy:

- ~~WE DON'T REALLY CREATE OUR OWN REALITIES.~~
  WE DO REALLY CREATE OUR OWN REALITIES.

- ~~I CAN'T CREATE MY REALITY.~~
  I CAN CREATE MY REALITY.

- ~~I CAN'T CHANGE MY BELIEFS.~~
  I CAN CHANGE MY BELIEFS.

- ~~IT IS DIFFICULT TO CREATE MY REALITY.~~
  IT IS EASY TO CREATE MY REALITY.

- ~~IT IS HARD TO CHANGE BELIEFS.~~
  IT IS EASY TO CHANGE BELIEFS.

- ~~I CAN'T EASILY DISCOVER MY SUBCONSCIOUS BELIEFS.~~
  I CAN EASILY DISCOVER MY SUBCONSCIOUS BELIEFS.

- ~~I CAN'T CHANGE MY BELIEFS ABOUT _______ (MONEY, LOVE, MEN, WOMEN, HEALTH, WORK, OTHER PEOPLE, ETC.)~~
  I CAN CHANGE MY BELIEFS ABOUT _______ (MONEY, LOVE, MEN, WOMEN, HEALTH, WORK, OTHER PEOPLE, ETC.)

It works for everyone else but me:

- ~~EVEN IF I "CHANGE MY BELIEFS," MY WORLD WILL NOT CHANGE.~~
  AS SOON AS I CHANGE MY BELIEFS, MY WORLD WILL CHANGE.

- ~~NOTHING EVER WORKS FOR ME.~~
  EVERYTHING ALWAYS WORKS FOR ME.

- ~~I DON'T HAVE WHAT IT TAKES TO CHANGE MY BELIEFS, AND THUS MY LIFE.~~
  I DO HAVE WHAT IT TAKES TO CHANGE MY BELIEFS, AND THUS MY LIFE.

- ~~I DON'T HAVE THE POWER OR ABILITY TO CREATE MY WORLD.~~
  I DO HAVE THE POWER OR ABILITY TO CREATE MY WORLD.

- ~~IT IS HARD TO CREATE WHAT I WANT.~~
  IT IS EASY TO CREATE WHAT I WANT.

- ~~I AM NOT POWERFUL ENOUGH TO CHANGE MY BELIEFS.~~
  I AM POWERFUL ENOUGH TO CHANGE MY BELIEFS.

It is wrong/unspiritual to create my reality:

- ~~IT IS WRONG TO CHANGE MY BELIEFS.~~
  IT IS RIGHT (OR GOOD) TO CHANGE MY BELIEFS.

- ~~I'LL BE PUNISHED IF I CHANGE MY BELIEFS.~~
  I'LL BE REWARDED IF I CHANGE MY BELIEFS.

- ~~ONLY GOD CAN CHANGE MY BELIEFS.~~
  ONLY I CAN CHANGE MY BELIEFS.

- ~~IT IS UNSPIRITUAL TO CHANGE MY BELIEFS.~~
  IT IS SPIRITUAL TO CHANGE MY BELIEFS.

- ~~ONLY GOD CAN CREATE MY REALITY.~~
  ONLY I CAN CREATE MY REALITY.

- ~~IT IS BLASPHEMOUS TO BELIEVE I CAN CREATE MY OWN REALITY.~~
  IT IS LOVING TO BELIEVE I CAN CREATE MY OWN REALITY.

I'm not ready:

- ~~I'M NOT READY TO CHANGE MY BELIEFS ABOUT ___________ (MONEY, LOVE, MEN, HEALTH, WORK, OTHER PEOPLE, ETC.).~~
  I'M READY TO CHANGE MY BELIEFS ABOUT ___________ (MONEY, LOVE, MEN, HEALTH, WORK, OTHER PEOPLE, ETC.).

- ~~I'M NOT READY FOR THE SUCCESS THAT WILL HAPPEN WHEN I CHANGE MY BELIEFS.~~
  I'M READY FOR THE SUCCESS THAT WILL HAPPEN WHEN I CHANGE MY BELIEFS.

- ~~I CAN HAVE THE REALITIES I DESIRE ONLY AFTER I CLEAR OUT ALL MY BLOCKAGES.~~
  I CAN HAVE THE REALITIES I DESIRE AND CLEAR ANY BLOCKAGES AT THE SAME TIME.
  - OR-
  I CAN HAVE THE REALITIES I DESIRE ONCE I AM WILLING TO RECEIVE THEM.

- ~~I'M NOT HEALED ENOUGH TO CREATE MY REALITY.~~
  I'M HEALED ENOUGH TO CREATE MY REALITY.

- ~~IF I SUCCESSFULLY CREATE MY OWN REALITY, THE RESPONSIBILITY OF MAINTAINING IT WOULD BE TOO MUCH FOR ME TO HANDLE.~~
  WHEN I SUCCESSFULLY CREATE MY OWN REALITY, THE RESPONSIBILITY OF MAINTAINING IT WILL BE EASY FOR ME TO HANDLE.

- ~~I'M NOT (OLD, YOUNG, WISE, CAPABLE, SEASONED, EXPERIENCED, SMART, ETC.) ENOUGH TO CREATE MY OWN REALITY.~~
  I'M (OLD, YOUNG, WISE, CAPABLE, SEASONED, EXPERIENCED, SMART, ETC.) ENOUGH TO CREATE MY OWN REALITY.

It's not safe:

- ~~MY SUCCESS THAT HAPPENS AS A RESULT OF CHANGING MY BELIEFS WILL MAKE PEOPLE I CARE ABOUT FEEL BADLY ABOUT THEIR OWN LIVES.~~
  MY SUCCESS THAT HAPPENS AS A RESULT OF CHANGING MY BELIEFS WILL MAKE PEOPLE I CARE ABOUT BE INSPIRED TO CREATE THEIR OWN DREAMS.

- ~~IF I CHANGE MY BELIEFS ABOUT _________ (MONEY, LOVE, MEN, HEALTH, WORK, OTHER PEOPLE, ETC.) AND MY WORLD CHANGES, SOMEONE I CARE ABOUT WILL BE HURT.~~
  IF I CHANGE MY BELIEFS ABOUT _________ (MONEY, LOVE, MEN, HEALTH, WORK, OTHER PEOPLE, ETC.) AND MY WORLD CHANGES, SOMEONE I CARE ABOUT WILL BE HELPED.

- ~~SOMETHING BAD WILL HAPPEN IF I CHANGE MY BELIEFS.~~
  SOMETHING GREAT WILL HAPPEN WHEN I CHANGE MY BELIEFS.

- ~~IT'S NOT SAFE TO CREATE ALL THAT I WANT.~~
  IT'S TOTALLY SAFE TO CREATE ALL THAT I WANT.

- ~~IF I BELIEVE IN THIS INFORMATION OTHERS WILL RIDICULE ME.~~
  IF I BELIEVE IN THIS INFORMATION OTHERS WILL SUPPORT ME.

Beliefs About Money

Beliefs about the value of money:

- ~~MONEY IS THE ROOT OF ALL EVIL.~~
  MONEY IS SIMPLY ENERGY.

- ~~MONEY IS DIRTY.~~
  MONEY IS INNOCUOUS.

- ~~MONEY IS A CURSE.~~
  MONEY IS A BLESSING.

- ~~MONEY IS POWER.~~
  CONSCIOUS CREATION IS POWER.

- ~~MONEY IS FREEDOM.~~
  FREEDOM IS FREEDOM.

- ~~MONEY IS EVERYTHING.~~
  MONEY IS ENERGY.

- ~~MONEY MEASURES WORTH.~~
  MONEY MEASURES WILLINGNESS TO RECEIVE IT.

- ~~MONEY MAKES YOU DESIRABLE TO OTHERS.~~
  YOU MAKE YOURSELF DESIRABLE TO OTHERS.

- ~~MONEY MAKES YOU HAPPY.~~
  YOU MAKE YOURSELF HAPPY.

- ~~RICH PEOPLE ARE BETTER THAN POOR PEOPLE.~~
  POOR PEOPLE ARE AS VALUABLE AS RICH PEOPLE.

- ~~POOR PEOPLE ARE BETTER THAN RICH PEOPLE.~~
  RICH PEOPLE ARE AS VALUABLE AS POOR PEOPLE.

Beliefs about you and money:

- ~~I DON'T DESERVE A LOT OF MONEY.~~
  I DO DESERVE A LOT OF MONEY.

- ~~MY SPOUSE/PARTNER CREATES MONEY BUT I DON'T.~~
  I CREATE MONEY IN MY LIFE AND I'M GRATEFUL FOR MY SPOUSE/PARTNER FOR BEING ONE OF THE WAYS IT MANIFESTS.

- ~~I CAN'T HANDLE HAVING MONEY.~~
  I CAN HANDLE HAVING MONEY.

- ~~I CAN'T HAVE MONEY.~~
  I CAN HAVE MONEY.

- ~~I CAN'T SAVE MONEY.~~
  I CAN SAVE MONEY.

- ~~I AM ALWAYS IN DEBT.~~
  I AM ALWAYS IN ABUNDANCE.

- ~~I DON'T HAVE ENOUGH MONEY TO SHARE OR GIVE AWAY.~~
  I DO HAVE ENOUGH MONEY TO SHARE OR GIVE AWAY.

- ~~I AM SMART AND TALENTED, THEREFORE I SHOULD GET MORE MONEY.~~
  I AM SMART AND TALENTED, AND I CAN CREATE AS MUCH MONEY AS I WANT.

- ~~I WORK SUPER HARD, I DESERVE MORE MONEY.~~
  NO MATTER HOW MUCH I WORK, I DESERVE MORE MONEY.

- ~~I DON'T KNOW HOW TO MAKE MONEY.~~
  I DO KNOW HOW TO MAKE MONEY.

- ~~I DON'T KNOW HOW TO CREATE MONEY.~~
  I DO KNOW HOW TO CREATE MONEY.

- ~~I CAN NEVER GET AHEAD.~~
  I CAN EASILY AND ELEGANTLY GET AHEAD.

- ~~I HATE MONEY.~~
  I LOVE MONEY.

- ~~I AM A FAILURE WHEN IT COMES TO MONEY.~~
  I AM A SUCCESS WHEN IT COMES TO MONEY.

- ~~I WOULD FEEL GUILTY IF I HAD MORE MONEY THAN [NAME].~~
  I WOULD FEEL GRATEFUL IF I HAD MORE MONEY TO BE AN INSPIRATION TO [NAME] TO CREATE MORE.

- ~~OTHERS CAN CREATE MONEY BUT NOT ME.~~
  OTHERS CAN CREATE MONEY AND SO CAN I.

- ~~THE ECONOMY IS RESPONSIBLE FOR MY MONEY PROBLEMS.~~
  I AM RESPONSIBLE FOR MY MONEY PROBLEMS AND SUCCESSES.

- ~~[NAME, ENTITY, EVENT] IS RESPONSIBLE FOR MY MONEY PROBLEMS.~~
  I AM RESPONSIBLE FOR MY MONEY PROBLEMS AND SUCCESSES.

- ~~IF I DON'T WORRY ABOUT MONEY SOMETHING BAD WILL HAPPEN.~~
  IF I DON'T WORRY ABOUT MONEY SOMETHING GOOD WILL HAPPEN.

***Beliefs about the ease with which money comes to you*:**

- ~~YOU HAVE TO EARN THE MONEY YOU MAKE.~~
  YOU HAVE TO ALLOW THE MONEY YOU MAKE.

- ~~MONEY COMES WITH INCREDIBLE STRUGGLE.~~
  MONEY COMES WITH INCREDIBLE EASE.

- ~~MAKING MONEY TAKES A LOT OF HARD WORK.~~
  MAKING MONEY TAKES A BIT OF INNER WORK.

- ~~IT TAKES MONEY TO MAKE MONEY.~~
  IT TAKES MY CONSCIOUS CREATING TO MAKE MONEY.

- ~~THERE IS NEVER ENOUGH MONEY.~~
  THERE IS ALWAYS ENOUGH MONEY.

- ~~THERE IS ALWAYS JUST ENOUGH MONEY.~~
  THERE IS ALWAYS MORE THAN ENOUGH MONEY.

- ~~THERE IS NEVER MORE THAN ENOUGH MONEY.~~
  THERE IS ALWAYS MORE THAN ENOUGH MONEY.

- ~~MONEY IS HARD TO COME BY.~~
  MONEY IS EASY TO COME BY.

- ~~I NEED TO EARN MY MONEY.~~
  I NEED TO RECEIVE MY MONEY.

- ~~THERE IS NOT ENOUGH MONEY TO GO AROUND.~~
  THERE IS ALWAYS ENOUGH MONEY TO GO AROUND.

- ~~THE UNIVERSE IS LIMITED IN ITS ABUNDANCE.~~
  THE UNIVERSE IS UNLIMITED IN ITS ABUNDANCE.

- ~~MONEY ONLY COMES TO ME THROUGH MY JOB.~~
  MONEY COMES TO ME THROUGH MANY WAYS.

- ~~ONLY A SELECT FEW GET TO HAVE MONEY.~~
  ANYONE WILLING TO CREATE IT GETS TO HAVE MONEY.

- ~~IF A LOT OF MONEY COMES EASILY, IT MUST BE ILLEGAL.~~
  IF A LOT OF MONEY COMES EASILY, IT MUST BE I'M GETTING GOOD AT CONSCIOUS CREATING.

- ~~YOU NEED TO BE SUPER SMART TO MAKE A LOT OF MONEY.~~
  YOU NEED TO BE WILLING TO DO THE WORK TO CREATE A LOT OF MONEY.

Beliefs about what you have to give up to get money:

- ~~IF I AM FINANCIALLY ABUNDANT, I WILL HAVE TO SACRIFICE MY HAPPINESS.~~
  IF I AM FINANCIALLY ABUNDANT, I WILL HAVE TO SACRIFICE MY VICTIMHOOD.

- ~~IF I AM FINANCIALLY ABUNDANT, I WILL HAVE TO SACRIFICE MY FAMILY.~~
  IF I AM FINANCIALLY ABUNDANT, I WILL HAVE TO SACRIFICE MY MARTYRDOM.

- ~~IF I AM FINANCIALLY ABUNDANT, I WILL HAVE TO SACRIFICE MY FREEDOM.~~
  IF I AM FINANCIALLY ABUNDANT, I WILL INCREASE MY FREEDOM.

- ~~IF I AM FINANCIALLY ABUNDANT, I WILL HAVE TO SACRIFICE MY INTEGRITY.~~
  IF I AM FINANCIALLY ABUNDANT, I WILL HAVE TO SACRIFICE NOTHING OF VALUE.

- ~~IF I REALLY LIVE MY TRUTH, I'LL END UP BROKE.~~
  IF I REALLY LIVE MY TRUTH, I'LL END UP RICH.

- ~~IN ORDER TO BE RICH, YOU MUST SACRIFICE YOUR FREE TIME.~~
  IN ORDER TO BE RICH, YOU MUST SACRIFICE YOUR EXCUSES.

- ~~YOU CAN'T HAVE MONEY AND HAPPINESS.~~
  YOU CAN HAVE MONEY AND HAPPINESS.

- ~~I WILL HAVE TO DO WHAT I HATE IN ORDER TO HAVE MONEY.~~
  I WILL HAVE TO DO WHAT I LOVE IN ORDER TO HAVE MONEY.

- ~~MONEY WILL CHANGE ME FOR THE WORSE.~~
  MONEY WILL CHANGE ME FOR THE BETTER.

- ~~YOU HAVE TO DO LOTS OF THINGS YOU DON'T LIKE IN ORDER TO HAVE MONEY.~~
  YOU HAVE TO DO LOTS OF THINGS YOU LOVE IN ORDER TO HAVE MONEY.

- ~~MONEY ALWAYS COMES WITH STRINGS ATTACHED.~~
  MONEY ALWAYS COMES WITH NO STRINGS ATTACHED.

- ~~IT TAKES MONEY TO MAKE MONEY.~~
  IT TAKES WILLINGNESS TO MAKE MONEY.

Beliefs about what it means when you have (or don't have) money:

- ~~IF A LOT OF MONEY COMES EASILY, IT MUST BE ILLEGAL.~~
  IF A LOT OF MONEY COMES EASILY, IT MUST BE I'M GETTING GOOD AT CONSCIOUS CREATING.

- ~~BEING RICH IS A SIN.~~
  BEING RICH IS A DIVINE CHOICE.

- ~~HAVING MONEY IS GREEDY.~~
  HAVING MONEY IS SETTING THE EXAMPLE FOR OTHERS TO CREATE IT TOO.

- ~~WANTING MORE MONEY IS SELFISH.~~
  WANTING MORE MONEY IS SELF-LOVING.

- ~~MONEY SPOILS YOU.~~
  MONEY FREES YOU.

- ~~RICH PEOPLE ARE SNOBS.~~
  RICH PEOPLE ARE REGULAR PEOPLE.
  -OR-
  SOME RICH PEOPLE ARE REGULAR PEOPLE.

- ~~RICH PEOPLE ARE EGOTISTICAL.~~
  RICH PEOPLE ARE PEOPLE WHO HAVE ALLOWED MONEY.

- ~~RICH PEOPLE ARE SELFISH.~~
  RICH PEOPLE ARE GENEROUS.
  -OR-
  SOME RICH PEOPLE ARE GENEROUS.

- ~~RICH PEOPLE ARE EVIL.~~
  RICH PEOPLE ARE AS GOOD AS OTHER PEOPLE.
  -OR-
  SOME RICH PEOPLE ARE GOOD.

- ~~RICH PEOPLE ARE CORRUPT.~~
  RICH PEOPLE ARE HONEST.
  -OR-
  SOME RICH PEOPLE ARE HONEST.

- ~~RICH PEOPLE BECOME WEALTHY BY TAKING ADVANTAGE OF OTHERS.~~
  RICH PEOPLE BECOME WEALTHY BY DESIRE, BELIEF, ACTION, AND RECEIVING.

- ~~THERE IS NOBILITY IN BEING POOR.~~
  THERE IS FULFILLMENT IN CONSCIOUSLY CREATING ABUNDANCE.

- ~~MONEY EQUALS POWER AND POWER CORRUPTS.~~
  CONSCIOUS CREATION EQUALS POWER AND POWER INSPIRES.

- ~~IF YOU DON'T HAVE MONEY, YOU'RE POWERLESS.~~
  IF YOU DON'T HAVE THE BELIEF THAT YOU ARE POWERFUL, YOU'RE POWERLESS. I AM POWERFUL.

Beliefs about what you have to do to keep money:

- ~~I MUST BE SUPER CONSCIOUS OF EVERY SINGLE DOLLAR TO BE SURE I DON'T LOSE THE MONEY I CREATE~~.
  I CAN TRUST THAT I WILL KEEP THE MONEY THAT I CREATE AND THEN CREATE EVEN MORE.

- ~~I MUST SACRIFICE TO SAVE MY MONEY.~~
  I MUST BE CREATIVE TO SAVE MY MONEY.

- ~~IF I AM NOT HYPER-VIGILANT SOMEONE WILL TAKE MY MONEY.~~
  I AM TRUSTING AND RELAXED, KNOWING MY MONEY IS SAFE.

- ~~I MUST HIDE THE MONEY I CREATE.~~
  I MUST RESPECT THE MONEY I CREATE.

Beliefs about what happens when you get money:

- ~~ACCEPTING MONEY OBLIGATES ME.~~
  ACCEPTING MONEY FREES ME.

- ~~WHEN I AM RICH, I WON'T HAVE TIME FOR MY SPIRITUALITY.~~
  WHEN I AM RICH, I'LL STILL HAVE TIME FOR MY SPIRITUALITY.

- ~~WHEN I AM RICH, I WON'T HAVE TIME FOR MY FRIENDS.~~
  WHEN I AM RICH, I'LL STILL HAVE TIME FOR MY FRIENDS.

- ~~WHEN I AM RICH, I WON'T HAVE TIME FOR MY FAMILY.~~
  WHEN I AM RICH, I'LL STILL HAVE TIME FOR MY FAMILY.

- ~~WHEN I AM RICH, I'LL BE TIED TO OBLIGATIONS AND STRESSED OUT.~~
  WHEN I AM RICH, I'LL BE FREE TO CHOOSE HOW TO SPEND MY TIME AND RELAXED.

- ~~WHEN I AM RICH, I WON'T BE ABLE TO HANDLE THE RESPONSIBILITY.~~
  WHEN I AM RICH, I'LL EASILY BE ABLE TO HANDLE THE RESPONSIBILITY.

- ~~PEOPLE WILL LOVE ME ONLY FOR MY MONEY.~~
  PEOPLE WILL LOVE ME BECAUSE I'M LOVABLE.

- ~~PEOPLE WILL SCORN ME BECAUSE I HAVE MONEY.~~
  PEOPLE WILL LOVE ME WHETHER OR NOT I HAVE MONEY.

- ~~MONEY COMES WITH A LOT OF RESPONSIBILITY.~~
  MONEY COMES WITH A LOT OF FREEDOM.

- ~~PEOPLE ARE MEAN TO RICH PEOPLE.~~
  PEOPLE ARE KIND TO RICH PEOPLE.

- ~~IF I HAVE MONEY, I'LL JUST LOSE IT ANYWAY.~~
  IF I HAVE MONEY, I'LL JUST BUILD ON THAT WEALTH.

- ~~IF I HAVE MONEY, I'LL LOSE ALL MY FRIENDS.~~
  IF I HAVE MONEY, I'LL KEEP ALL MY FRIENDS.

- ~~IF I HAVE MONEY, PEOPLE WILL BE AFTER ME FOR MY MONEY.~~
  IF I HAVE MONEY, PEOPLE WON'T EVEN KNOW I HAVE MONEY.

- ~~IF I HAVE MONEY, PEOPLE WILL BE JEALOUS OF ME.~~
  IF I HAVE MONEY, PEOPLE WILL BE CONSIDERATE OF ME.

- ~~IF I HAVE MONEY, PEOPLE WILL JUST WANT ME FOR MY MONEY.~~
  IF I HAVE MONEY, PEOPLE WILL WANT ME FOR MY UNIQUE VALUE.

- ~~IF I HAVE MONEY, OTHERS WILL BE GOING WITHOUT.~~
  IF I HAVE MONEY, OTHERS WILL BE INSPIRED TO CREATE WEALTH.

- ~~IF I HAVE MONEY, I'LL BE MORE VISIBLE.~~
  IF I HAVE MONEY, I'LL BE MORE INSULATED.

- ~~IF I HAVE MONEY, I'LL BE HELD TO PUBLIC SCRUTINY.~~
  IF I HAVE MONEY, I'LL BE TREATED LIKE EVERYONE ELSE.

Beliefs About Success & Work

Beliefs about whether and how success comes to you:

- ~~I CAN'T HANDLE SUCCESS.~~
  I CAN HANDLE SUCCESS.

- ~~OTHERS ARE RESPONSIBLE FOR MY SUCCESS.~~
  I AM RESPONSIBLE FOR MY SUCCESS.

- ~~IF I AM SUCCESSFUL PEOPLE WILL HATE ME.~~
  IF I AM SUCCESSFUL PEOPLE WILL LIKE ME.

- ~~SUCCESS IS DIFFICULT.~~
  SUCCESS IS EASY.

- ~~I CAN'T BE SUCCESSFUL AND TRUE TO MYSELF AT THE SAME TIME.~~
  I CAN BE SUCCESSFUL AND TRUE TO MYSELF AT THE SAME TIME.

Beliefs about what happens when you're successful:

- ~~IF I'M TOO SUCCESSFUL, SOMEONE WILL TAKE IT AWAY.~~
  IF I'M VERY SUCCESSFUL, OTHERS WILL CELEBRATE MY SUCCESS.

- ~~IF I'M TOO VISIBLE, SOMEONE WILL MAKE ME PAY.~~
  I CAN BE VISIBLE, BECAUSE VISIBILITY IS MY CHOICE.

- ~~IF I'M SUCCESSFUL, PEOPLE WILL HATE ME.~~
  WHETHER OR NOT I'M SUCCESSFUL, PEOPLE WILL LIKE ME.

- ~~IF I'M SUCCESSFUL, I WON'T BE ABLE TO KEEP IT UP.~~
  ONCE I'M SUCCESSFUL, IT WILL BE EASY TO KEEP IT UP.

- ~~I CAN'T HANDLE SUCCESS.~~
  I CAN HANDLE SUCCESS.

Beliefs about work:

- ~~I CAN'T MAKE THE KIND OF MONEY I WANT DOING SOMETHING THAT FILLS ME WITH JOY.~~
  I CAN MAKE THE KIND OF MONEY I WANT DOING SOMETHING THAT FILLS ME WITH JOY.

- ~~I CAN'T MAKE ENOUGH MONEY DOING WHAT I TRULY LOVE.~~
  I CAN MAKE ENOUGH MONEY DOING WHAT I TRULY LOVE.

- ~~IT'S A DOG-EAT-DOG WORLD OUT THERE.~~
  IT'S A KIND AND LOVING WORLD OUT THERE.

- ~~MOST ENTREPRENEURS FAIL, THEREFORE THE ODDS ARE STACKED AGAINST ME.~~
  MOST ENTREPRENEURS AREN'T ME, AND THEY DON'T CONSCIOUSLY CREATE THEIR SUCCESS.

- ~~IN ORDER TO HAVE THE WORK I DESIRE, I HAVE TO GIVE UP SOME THINGS I VALUE.~~
  IN ORDER TO HAVE THE WORK I DESIRE, I HAVE TO FLOW ENERGY TOWARD THE OUTCOME I WANT.

- ~~I DON'T KNOW WHAT MY PASSION IS.~~
  I DO KNOW WHAT MY PASSION IS—MORE AND MORE EVERY DAY.

Core Beliefs

- ~~I AM NOT GOOD ENOUGH.~~
  I AM GOOD ENOUGH.

- ~~I AM FLAWED.~~
  I AM DIVINE.

- ~~I AM UNWORTHY.~~
  I AM WORTHY.

- ~~I AM NO GOOD.~~
  I AM DIVINELY GOOD.
  -OR-
  I AM GOOD.

- ~~I AM UNSUCCESSFUL.~~
  I AM SUCCESSFUL.

- ~~I AM NOT VALUABLE.~~
  I AM VALUABLE.

- ~~I AM INFERIOR.~~
  I AM WORTHWHILE.

- ~~I AM NOTHING.~~
  I AM WORTHWHILE.
  -OR-
  I AM DIVINE.

- ~~I AM INVISIBLE.~~
  I AM VISIBLE.

- ~~I AM INSIG~~NIFICANT.
  I AM SIGNIFICANT.

- ~~I AM UNLOVABLE.~~
  I AM LOVABLE.

- ~~I AM UNACCEPTABLE.~~
  I AM ACCEPTABLE.

- ~~I DON'T MATTER.~~
  I DO MATTER.

- ~~I AM UNIMPORTANT.~~
  I AM IMPORTANT.

- ~~I AM A MISTAKE.~~
  I AM DIVINE.

- ~~I DON'T BELONG.~~
  I DO BELONG.

- ~~I AM UNWANTED.~~
  I AM WANTED.

- ~~I AM UNWELCOME~~.
  I AM WELCOME.

- ~~I DON'T FIT IN ANYWHERE.~~
  I DO FIT IN EVERYWHERE.

- ~~I AM UNBALANCED.~~
  I AM BALANCED.

- ~~I AM A FAILURE.~~
  I AM A SUCCESS.

- ~~I DON'T DESERVE.~~
  I DO DESERVE.

- ~~I AM A LOSER.~~
  I AM A WINNER.

- ~~I AM INADEQUATE.~~
  I AM FULLY ADEQUATE.

BELIEFS FROM CHAPTER TWELVE

- ~~I CAN'T MAKE AS MUCH MONEY BEING AN ARTIST AS I CAN AT A "REAL JOB."~~
  I CAN MAKE AS MUCH MONEY BEING AN ARTIST AS I CAN AT ANY OTHER JOB.

- I ~~MUST BE FORCED TO QUIT MY JOB AND FOLLOW MY HEART BECAUSE JUST QUITTING IS TOO SCARY.~~
  I CAN AND WILL MOVE ON FROM MY JOB WHEN IT'S TIME. I WILL FOLLOW MY HEART WITH GREAT REWARDS.

BELIEFS FROM CHAPTER THIRTEEN

- ~~IF I ADMIT I RECEIVED SOMETHING GOOD, I WON'T RECEIVE ANY MORE GOOD.~~
  IF I ADMIT I RECEIVED SOMETHING GOOD, I WILL DOUBLE THAT GOOD OR MORE.

BELIEFS FROM CHAPTER FIFTEEN

Beliefs About Being Who Creates Abundance

- ~~UNLESS I BRING IN MONEY, I AM NOT CONTRIBUTING.~~
  WHETHER OR NOT I BRING IN MONEY, I AM CONTRIBUTING.

- ~~I AM NOT AS VALUABLE AS MY PARTNER BECAUSE S/HE BRINGS HOME A PAYCHECK.~~
  I AM JUST AS VALUABLE AS MY PARTNER WHETHER OR NOT I BRING HOME A PAYCHECK.

- ~~THE BREADWINNER IS THE MOST VALUABLE MEMBER OF A PARTNERSHIP.~~
  THERE IS NO SUCH THING AS THE MOST VALUABLE MEMBER OF A PARTNERSHIP.

- ~~EQUALITY IN A PARTNERSHIP IS BASED ON A SIMILAR FINANCIAL CONTRIBUTION.~~
  EQUALITY IN A PARTNERSHIP IS BASED ON BOTH PEOPLE BEING SOURCED FROM THE DIVINE.

- ~~I DON'T CREATE MY PARTNER'S INCOME.~~
  I DO CREATE MY OWN ABUNDANCE.

- ~~IF I DIDN'T HAVE MY PARTNER'S INCOME I WOULD BE DESTITUTE.~~
  IF I DIDN'T HAVE MY PARTNER'S INCOME I WOULD BE FINE.

Beliefs About Comparison & Competition

- ~~I CAN'T CREATE THE SUCCESS THAT OTHERS CREATE IN THIS BUSINESS.~~
  I CAN CREATE THE SUCCESS THAT OTHERS CREATE IN THIS BUSINESS.

- ~~I AM NOT AS GOOD AT BUSINESS AS OTHERS ARE.~~
  I AM AS GOOD AT BUSINESS AS OTHERS ARE.

- ~~I'M NOT AS GOOD A ____________ AS OTHERS ARE.~~
  I'M AS GOOD A ____________ AS OTHERS ARE.

Beliefs About Being Successful

- ~~TO BE SUCCESSFUL, YOU HAVE TO TAKE OTHERS DOWN ON THE WAY UP.~~
  TO BE SUCCESSFUL, YOU HAVE YOUR THOUGHTS, FEELINGS, BELIEFS, AND DREAMS IN ALIGNMENT.

- ~~TO BE SUCCESSFUL, YOU HAVE TO HAVE DONE SOMETHING ILLEGAL.~~
  TO BE SUCCESSFUL, YOU HAVE TO HAVE DONE SOMETHING INTERNALLY RIGHT.

- ~~TO BE SUCCESSFUL, YOU HAVE TO HAVE DONE SOMETHING IMMORAL.~~
  TO BE SUCCESSFUL, YOU HAVE YOUR PASSIONS, ACTIONS, ENERGY, AND DREAMS ALIGNED.

- ~~SUPER SUCCESSFUL PEOPLE ARE NOT VERY NICE PEOPLE.~~
  SUPER SUCCESSFUL PEOPLE CAN BE VERY NICE PEOPLE.

- ~~IN ORDER TO BE SUPER SUCCESSFUL, YOU MUST BE COLD-HEARTED.~~
  OFTEN, THOSE WHO ARE SUPER SUCCESSFUL ARE ALSO WARM-HEARTED.

- ~~IN ORDER TO BE SUPER SUCCESSFUL, YOU MUST DO ANYTHING TO GRAB AND HOLD ONTO SUCCESS.~~
  IN ORDER TO BE SUPER SUCCESSFUL, YOU MUST DO WHAT YOU LOVE, BELIEVE SUCCESS IS POSSIBLE, AND HAVE A BLAST EACH AND EVERY DAY.

- ~~IN ORDER TO BE SUPER SUCCESSFUL, YOU MUST GIVE UP YOUR INTEGRITY, CHARACTER, AND VALUES.~~
  IT'S EASY FOR SUPER SUCCESS TO INCLUDE PERSONAL INTEGRITY, CHARACTER, AND VALUES.

- ~~SUPER SUCCESSFUL PEOPLE HURT OTHERS ON THE WAY UP.~~
  SUPER SUCCESSFUL PEOPLE CARE ABOUT OTHERS AND TAKE EVERY OPPORTUNITY TO GIVE BACK.

- ~~IN ORDER TO BE SUPER SUCCESSFUL, YOU MUST GIVE UP YOUR FREEDOM.~~
  IN ORDER TO BE SUPER SUCCESSFUL, YOU MUST GIVE, CHERISH, AND PROTECT YOUR FREEDOM.

- ~~SUPER SUCCESSFUL PEOPLE NO LONGER BELONG.~~
  SUPER SUCCESSFUL PEOPLE, AFTER COMING INTO THEIR TRUE SELVES, FEEL THEY TRULY BELONG.

- ~~IN ORDER TO BE SUPER SUCCESSFUL YOU MUST BE ALONE.~~
  YOU CAN CREATE BEING SUPER SUCCESSFUL WHETHER ALONE OR NOT.

- ~~IF YOU'RE SUPER SUCCESSFUL, SUCCESS OWNS YOU.~~
  IF YOU'RE SUPER SUCCESSFUL, YOU OWN SUCCESS.

Beliefs About the Consequences of Success

- ~~WHEN I AM SUCCESSFUL, PEOPLE WILL BADGER ME.~~
  WHEN I AM SUCCESSFUL, PEOPLE WILL HONOR MY PRIVACY.

- ~~WHEN I AM SUCCESSFUL, I'LL LOSE THE MONEY I MAKE.~~
  WHEN I AM SUCCESSFUL, I'LL CREATE MORE WEALTH WITH THE MONEY I MAKE.

- ~~WHEN I AM SUCCESSFUL, I WON'T KNOW HOW TO HANDLE THE SUCCESS.~~
  WHEN I AM SUCCESSFUL, I WILL KNOW OR FIND OUT HOW TO HANDLE THE SUCCESS.

- ~~WHEN I AM SUCCESSFUL, I WON'T KNOW HOW TO INVEST MY MONEY.~~
  WHEN I AM SUCCESSFUL, I WILL KNOW OR FIND OUT HOW TO INVEST MY MONEY.

- ~~WHEN I AM SUCCESSFUL, I'LL END UP LIKE ALL THOSE STUPID LOTTERY WINNERS.~~
  WHEN I AM SUCCESSFUL, I'LL END UP EXACTLY AS I DREAM MYSELF TO BE—OR BETTER.

- ~~WHEN I AM SUCCESSFUL, SUCCESS WILL DEMAND TOO MUCH OF ME.~~
  WHEN I AM SUCCESSFUL, SUCCESS WILL DEMAND NOTHING OF ME.

- ~~WHEN I AM SUCCESSFUL, I'LL LOSE MY FAMILY AND FRIENDS.~~
  WHEN I AM SUCCESSFUL, I'LL BE HONORED BY MY FAMILY AND FRIENDS—AND I WILL HONOR THEM.

- ~~WHEN I AM SUCCESSFUL, I'LL LOSE MY PRIVACY.~~
  WHEN I AM SUCCESSFUL, I'LL HAVE AS MUCH PRIVACY AS I DESIRE.

- ~~WHEN I AM SUCCESSFUL, SOMEONE WILL TAKE MY MONEY AND SUCCESS AWAY.~~
  WHEN I AM SUCCESSFUL, ONLY I CAN SABOTAGE IT—AND EVEN THEN, I CAN SIMPLY RECREATE IT.

- ~~IF I'M REALLY SUCCESSFUL, IT WILL GO TO MY HEAD.~~
  EVEN WHEN I'M REALLY SUCCESSFUL, I'LL ALWAYS BE HUMBLE.

- ~~WHEN I AM SUCCESSFUL, I'LL BE SO VULNERABLE I'LL GET HURT, OR WORSE.~~
  IF I CAN CREATE SUCCESS, I CAN CREATE PROTECTION FROM ANYTHING AND ANYONE.

BELIEFS FROM CHAPTER SEVENTEEN

- ~~MIRACLES ARE IMPOSSIBLE.~~
  MIRACLES ARE POSSIBLE.

- ~~LIFE CAN ONLY GET SO GOOD.~~
  LIFE ALWAYS GETS BETTER.

- ~~MIRACLES CAN'T HAPPEN TO ME.~~
  MIRACLES CAN HAPPEN TO ME.

- ~~WHEN LIFE IS GOING GREAT, THE OTHER SHOE WILL DROP.~~
  WHEN LIFE IS GOING GREAT, THEN IT GETS EVEN BETTER.

- ~~YOU HAVE TO BE DESPERATE TO BE GIVEN A MIRACLE.~~
  YOU HAVE TO BE OPEN TO BE GIVEN A MIRACLE.

BELIEFS FROM APPENDIX B

- ~~APPLIED KINESIOLOGY WILL NOT WORK FOR ME TO DETERMINE MY BELIEFS.~~
  APPLIED KINESIOLOGY WILL WORK FOR ME TO DETERMINE MY BELIEFS.

- ~~IT IS NOT SAFE TO USE APPLIED KINESIOLOGY TO DETERMINE MY BELIEFS.~~
  IT IS SAFE TO USE APPLIED KINESIOLOGY TO DETERMINE MY BELIEFS.

APPENDIX D

How to Change Beliefs

"Physical reality springs from the imagination, which follows the path of your beliefs."
~ SETH

Most of the beliefs you will change in your lifetime—especially those relating to money—will be Level Two beliefs. However changing a Level Three (or core belief) will have the biggest impact on your life. For your convenience, I have included excerpts from *The Map—To Our Responsive Universe, Where Dreams Really Do Come True!*

CHANGING A LEVEL TWO BELIEF

Most of our beliefs (those beliefs that mess with our reality, anyway) are Level Two beliefs. These beliefs are far more impactful on our reality and far more ingrained in our subconscious than Level One beliefs, which are fairly innocuous beliefs that generally don't even require changing.

Level Two beliefs encompass all areas of life. These beliefs were given to us by our parents, our siblings, our grandparents, aunts, uncles, teachers, and other authority figures like religious leaders and scoutmasters. Even society and the media have helped to form our beliefs about the world.

How to Change a Level Two Belief

Write out or print the old and the new beliefs.

Get into a quiet space, and close your eyes. Have your list of old and new beliefs with you. Call upon your unseen friends (it doesn't matter if you don't know who they are) to assist you. You can say something like:

> *I call on my angels, higher self, guides, and others who desire to help me successfully change these beliefs. Gently guide, protect, and assist me please, with harm to none.*

Imagine yourself in a beautiful place in nature. This place is serene, quiet, and safe. Then imagine your unseen friends coming to be with you, surrounding you in a bubble of love and light. Take a few moments to close your mental eyes and feel the wonderful love and light. Feel the love, guidance, and protection of your unseen friends. When you open your mental eyes you are surrounded in mist. And before you is a grand marble staircase. You, and your unseen friends, begin to walk up this staircase … up, up, up, into the clouds.

At the very top of this staircase, you will be at the entrance to a city, which represents your subconscious mind. It could be modern or ancient. It could be a city in nature, with natural caves and carvings in the rocks. It could look like anything at all. It may change shape. Whatever it looks like it is perfect for you.

The king or queen of this city (your subconscious) will soon come to welcome you. Tell them you want to change your beliefs. They will look to your higher self for permission, and your higher self will nod its consent.

Follow the king or queen to the Building of Beliefs. Your higher self will join you. They will take you to the room in this building that holds your Level Two beliefs. You will enter a gigantic circular room, lined floor to ceiling with filing cabinets. There will be a ladder that slides around the room on a rail, to access the high drawers. You gaze around in amazement.

Tell them the first belief you want to change (it's okay to peek at your paper). They will go to a drawer, open it, and pull out the belief. It is written out on an 8½ x 11 piece of cardstock, plain as day.

You take the belief and bring it to a small table in the center of the room. On the table is a big, fat black marker. You take off the cap, and strike through the entire belief. You then rip it into tiny pieces, and place it into a silver bowl lying on the tabletop. Your higher self points a finger, and the belief bursts into flames, quickly extinguishing and leaving nothing, not even ashes, behind.

You take a clean, white piece of card stock from a shelf underneath the table, and with a smaller black marker, write your new belief. Feel your hand shape each letter and say each and every letter in your mind as you write.

You hand the new belief to the king/queen and they deftly replace the belief.

You repeat this process with every belief you want to change.

When you are finished, thank your higher self and the king or queen. They will appreciatively accept your thanks.

When you're ready, open your eyes.

CONSCIOUS MIND FOLLOW-UP: Write or type out only the new beliefs. Every day, for sixty days, read the new beliefs, with as much excitement and joy as you can muster. (If you skip a day, just add another day at the end.)

That's it! As you see, Level Two beliefs are a bit more work ... but you'll see a lot more change in your life as a result of changing this type of belief.

CHANGING A LEVEL THREE (CORE) BELIEF

Level Three beliefs are core beliefs. These are beliefs that speak to the very nature of who you are and the world you live in.

A Level Three belief might be something like:

- I DON'T DESERVE.
- I AM NOT GOOD ENOUGH.
- I DON'T MATTER.
- I AM NOT WORTHY.
- I AM FLAWED.
- I AM NOT ENOUGH.

If you try unsuccessfully to change a belief with a Level Two process, it's likely a Level Three belief. If you want to be extra sure a belief will change, use the Level Three approach. It can't hurt.

Level Three beliefs are the most important beliefs to change and you will be astounded at how many areas of your life are affected by them. When you change a Level Three belief, your entire reality will shift. That's the upside.

The downside is that it takes more work to change them. But if you follow this procedure with an open heart and mind, and fully feel your emotions along the way, you can change a Level Three belief ... believe it or not!

How to Change a Level Three Belief

Preparation

Be specific and really think about how this belief has affected you for your entire life. Write a few paragraphs about this.

If, for example, you were changing the belief, "I am not good enough," the answer may be something like this:

> *I wish to change the belief that I am not good enough because it keeps me stuck in mediocrity. I have always been afraid to try my best. I have a 'why bother' attitude about life and about dreaming bigger dreams. I can't imagine a person of the caliber I want to attract being interested in me.*
>
> *This belief has stopped my dreams from manifesting over and over, no matter how close I came to receiving them: Not getting the job at nineteen as the head of maintenance for the stadium; not being accepted to the college I really wanted; losing the internship after college to my best friend; being one of the last three candidates for that job in Los Angeles—my dream job—and losing it at the very last minute, etc.*
>
> *I purposely hold my dreams small and those I do go for never succeed to the extent they could if I truly believed I was good enough. It has kept me from speaking my truth (what right do I have?). I do not feel worthy of the life I have, let alone a life containing a bigger dream.*

I have passed this belief on to my children, whom I love more than anything. I have judged my friends and relationships as being less than—after all, if they were not losers what were they doing with me? I have stayed in relationships I should have ended. I have been defensive. The list goes on and on.

Now, write a paragraph about why you *don't* want to change this belief.

Yes, there is a part of you that doesn't want to change the belief. Think about this. What are you afraid of? What could go wrong?

Using the example from above, the answer might be:

I don't want to change this belief because I'm afraid it won't work. Then I may as well give up on life because I'll never ever stand a chance of being good enough. I am also a little afraid that it will work. Then I will have no more excuses for not making my life work. That is scary too.

Next, check in with your child, adolescent, and young adult selves. What do they need to be okay with you changing this belief? Talk to them, individually, and ask them to give you permission to change this belief. Explain to them why you want to change it. Ask them what it would take for them to give you the okay. And whatever it is, give it to them. (Return to Chapter Seven, if necessary, to review this technique.)

Next, write out how your life will change once you have adopted the new belief.

With the new belief "I am good enough," the answer might read something like this:

I will allow my joy and fun and abundance! I will allow more happiness. I will be more secure and kinder and more loving to myself and others. I will be more powerful. I will allow more success! I will be comfortable dreaming bigger dreams and allowing them to manifest. I will be able to make a bigger impact on my world. I will be at peace with speaking my truth.

Finally, consider how your self-concept will change with the new belief, and write a paragraph about this.

With a belief that says, "I am good enough," you might see your new self-concept as:

I am happy, peaceful, content, excited, joyous, and fulfilled. I am confident, loving, and sure of myself. I am bold in painting my life with joy and people and adventures and experiences. I am at peace, with who I am and who I am becoming.

Changing a Level Three Belief In Your Subconscious Mind

(Note: The first four steps are identical to those used to change a Level Two belief.)

Write out or print out the old and the new beliefs.

Get into a quiet space, and close your eyes. Have your list of old and new beliefs with you. Call upon your unseen friends (it doesn't matter if you don't know who they are) to assist you. You can say something like:

I call on my angels, higher self, guides, and others who desire to help me successfully change these beliefs. Gently guide, protect, and assist me please, with harm to none.

Imagine you are in a beautiful place in nature. This place is serene, quiet, and safe. Then imagine your unseen friends coming to be with you, surrounding you in a bubble of love and light. Take a few moments to close your mental eyes and feel the wonderful love and light. Feel the love, guidance, and protection of your unseen friends. When you open your mental eyes you are surrounded in mist. And before you is a grand marble staircase. You, and your unseen friends, begin to walk up this staircase … up, up, up into the clouds.

At the very top of this staircase, you will be at the entrance to a city, which represents your subconscious mind. It could be modern or ancient. It could be a city in nature, with natural caves and carvings in the rocks. It could look like anything at all. It may change shape. Whatever it looks like it is perfect for you.

The king or queen of this city (your subconscious) will soon come to welcome you. Tell them you want to change your beliefs. They will look to your higher self for permission, and your higher self will nod its consent. "Are you *sure?*" they will ask. Your higher self will look at you, and back at the king/queen and say, "Yes, it is time."

Follow the king or queen to the Building of Beliefs. Your higher self will join you. They will take you to the room that holds your Level Three beliefs. They press a secret button—you cannot tell exactly how—and an entire section of cabinets opens up to reveal a secret door.

The king/queen goes through the doorway and beckons you to follow. You and your higher self do follow, but you barely catch a glimpse of them as they head down a hallway, and then turn a corner. They twist through long passageways, this way and that. Finally they enter an elevator and you follow, barely making it in before the doors close. The elevator goes up, over, down, then down, over and up … over and over. You have entirely lost track of where you are. The doors open, and the king/queen leads you to a door marked, "Core Beliefs: Do Not Enter."

They unlock the door and allow you to enter. It is a small room. A table sits in the middle of it and on the table is a thin book marked, "My Core Beliefs."

"Now," the king/queen says, "Tell me the belief you want to change."

Tell them the belief you want to change. They will open the book to exactly that belief.

Picking up the thick black marker, you cross out the belief obliterating every word. You rip the page neatly out of the book and tear it into tiny shreds. Your higher self looks at you and asks, "Are you certain? This will change everything." You nod your head. And your higher self points its finger and the belief bursts into flames, leaving nothing behind.

You look down at a clean white page in the book, pick up a thin black marker and begin to write your new belief, saying each and every letter in your mind as you write.

You put down the marker and close the book.

Your higher self and your subconscious mind are grinning. You grin back, thanking them with your eyes. You say your goodbyes, close your mental eyes, and allow yourself to be back where you started ... but you are different.

Now, open your eyes.

CONSCIOUS MIND FOLLOW-UP: Write or type out the new belief. Every day, for ninety days, read the new belief twice a day, with as much excitement and joy as you can muster. (If you skip a day, just add another day at the end.)

ALL BELIEFS CAN BE CHANGED

Every belief can be changed. If your beliefs are not changing easily with the above techniques, I suggest revisiting whether you hold any foundational beliefs (Chapter Nine).

After that, look to whether you may be receiving some type of payoff that gives you a "reward" for holding onto a negative belief. Payoffs might be something like being a victim gets you attention, or living in martyrdom lets you feel "better than."

And sometimes we won't let ourselves change a belief until we have healed the root cause of the belief. So if your child or adolescent self need to release the emotion and heal some aspect of the past, you may hold onto a belief until that healing is complete.

So the message is, if a belief isn't changing there is always a reason. Do what you know you should do—intend to find the cause, ask for help in doing so, and work your butt off to make absolutely sure you've left no stone unturned.

Remember, my friend, it sometimes gets better than the energy we put out but it never gets worse. Whatever challenges you face, you have the keys within you to unlock them, forgive yourself, heal, and change.

INDEX

ACKNOWLEDGMENTS

I owe a huge debt of gratitude to Bryna René Haynes, editor, cover designer, and layout designer of this book. Bryna, you made this process so easy and enjoyable. Thank you from the bottom of my heart!

To Carla Johnson and Linda Hendrick: thank you for reading this book aloud to me so I could hear it through another voice. Your gift was incredibly helpful.

Thank you to Gwen Buehler for handling the day-to-day at Inner Art, and to Heidi Wattier for handling so many details of my personal life. The space you two created gave me precious time to write.

Thank you to the Team (channeled by Jackie Salvitti), for your belief in me and your continual encouragement to continue this work. I'm deeply grateful to Lazaris (channeled by Jach Pursel), for thirty years of love, wisdom, and healing.

To my unseen friends: thank you for always being there for me, for your guidance, love, and support.

To Brandon and Brett: I am so grateful for you in my life. I cherish my time with each of you and I'm so proud of the men you've become.

And to my readers: thank you for having the courage to look beyond what you've been told and seek what might be. If you do the work, your bravery *will* pay off.

ABOUT THE AUTHOR

Boni Lonnsburry

Boni Lonnsburry is the Chief Visionary Officer of Inner Art Inc., an expert on conscious creation, and the author of four books, including the best-selling book *The Map—To Our Responsive Universe, Where Dreams Really Do Come True!*

The Map has won eight book awards, including the prestigious Nautilus Award, and was named "Best Law of Attraction Book of 2013" by Law of Attraction Leaders.

By applying the Universal Law of Attraction, Boni transformed her life of poverty, loneliness, and despair to one of abundance, love, and joy. She now teaches others to do the same.

Learn more about Boni at www.LiveALifeYouLove.com and www.CreationSchool.com.

ALSO BY BONI LONNSBURRY

The Map—To Our Responsive Universe, Where Dreams Really Do Come True! (2013)

The Map Workbook (2015)

Messages from Your Unseen Friends – Volume I (2015)

Life on Planet Earth: A User's Guide (e-book)

RESOURCES

ON THE WEB

To purchase other books by Boni, guided meditations mentioned in this book, and Success and Creation Journals, visit www.LiveALifeYouLove.com/shop.

Learn more about Boni's eight-week training program and other courses at www.CreationSchool.com.

SOCIAL MEDIA

Facebook: www.Facebook.com/BoniLonnsburryAuthor

Twitter: @BoniLonnsburry

YouTube: www.YouTube.com/user/BoniLonnsburry

OTHER

To learn more about Lazaris, visit www.Lazaris.com

Printed in Great Britain
by Amazon